PETAL PUSHER

PETAL PUSHER

A ROCK AND ROLL CINDERELLA STORY

LAURIE LINDEEN

ATRIA BOOKS

NEW YORK   LONDON   TORONTO   SYDNEY

ATRIA BOOKS

1230 Avenue of the Americas
New York, NY 10020

Library of Congress Cataloging-in-Publication Data is available

ISBN-13: 978-0-7432-9232-0
ISBN-10:   0-7432-9232-4

First Atria Books hardcover edition June 2007

10 9 8 7 6 5 4 3 2 1

ATRIA BOOKS is a trademark of Simon & Schuster, Inc.

Manufactured in the United States of America

For information about special discounts for bulk purchases,
please contact Simon & Schuster Special Sales at
1-800-456-6798 or business@simonandschuster.com.

Contents

For Johnny for everything good in my life. For Paul for yesterday, tomorrow, and today. For my family for always letting me be whomever and whatever; for putting up with . . . For Co and Linda for the biggest damn blast and putting up with . . . I love you all.

The events in this book are true as far as my flawed, holey memory can tell. I wrote about the past in the present tense to prevent myself from judging the material. I didn't make up stuff to make my life seem better or worse than it was. Many of the names of incidental characters are changed or guessed at. I didn't change the names of most band members, musicians, boyfriends, close friends, and family—it would be too weird (sorry about that).

There are some things you can't cover up with lipstick and powder.

—ELVIS COSTELLO, "Girls Talk"

PART ONE

THE URGE FOR GOING

1 : Hitchin' a Ride

MY left thumb is out, my right hand is folded over on my hip; I'm hitchhiking. Don't worry, I'm on Martha's Vineyard—out here hitchhiking is the preferred mode of public transportation. The island setting enforces a sort of geographical honor system: When you're on a small island you can't be a perv or an ax murderer because you'd have to wait in a long line at a ferry to get off the island once you've committed your crime, which leaves plenty of time to get busted, unless, of course you have your own boat. I suppose there are a lot of nooks and crannies in which you could hide once you've chopped up some poor hitchhiker, but what a hassle. Eventually you'd have to show up at Cumberland Farms or the A&P for a pack of smokes or a Mountain Dew, and everyone would know it was you because they've all had an eye on you since you showed up on this island. I spend a lot of time thinking about these types of things.

It's a hot late morning in August of 1984 and my hairdresser friend from Boston, Naomi, is with me and we're hitchhiking from Vineyard Haven, where I live, to South Beach, which is two towns over with a right turn out of Edgartown. Because it's 1984, Naomi has a long eighties, naturally wavy girl-mullet in ash blonde. She wears a pull-on skirt and a T-shirt over her vintage forties one-piece swimming suit. I have clumpy waves of blonde and brown hair fashioned in a sort of inverse mullet, party in the front, short in back. I'm wearing a rayon vintage dress in a blue floral print over my tatty old swimming suit. We're probably both wearing Converse high-tops in shades of pink or baby blue and tiny round John Lennon sunglasses. Slightly hungover, a day at the beach, prone on a towel with the sound of the surf and the smells of salt and suntan lotion, will lull us into all-day naps. I have the day off from my job at an eighteen-stool diner; Naomi's my guest for a couple of days. We went to the University of Wisconsin together. She just graduated with a degree in art and went directly to New York to learn how to color hair she could fund her art habit. Smart girl. I was in college at the same time, sort of studying English; I've yet to graduate. We weren't superclose in college, but she's the closest person to me from that world, so I invited her out. It seems only fair since I regularly invite myself to crash at her apartment in Boston when there are rock shows that I want to attend.

A couple of cars whiz past us. "A lot of tourists out here in August; they don't get it," I say, hoping that Naomi won't be discouraged. Tourists don't know that this is how we, the carless, get around the island. Maybe we look too quirky, we are far cries from the usual Vineyard preppy. A royal blue Volvo station wagon pulls onto the grass at the side of the road. Thank God it's not a pickup truck full of summer house painters where we'd have to sit in the open-air flat bed and smile mutely while they smirked at us in our crazy get-ups. We run to hop in. As the veteran hitchhiker, I sit up front.

The driver is a beautifully tanned woman in her thirties with long wavy brown hair and full lips. She's superstar thin to our baby fat and beer-belly curves. Wait a minute. Holy shit. Could it be? Yes, it could. It's Miss Carly "We've got no secrets" Simon herself. I glance over my left shoulder at Naomi in the backseat; she is grinning and silently giggling into her hand with her shoulders lifted up to her ears.

"Thanks for stopping," I offer, deciding to be casual, deciding to make this an everyday occurrence. "We're headed to South Beach."

"I can take you as far as Edgartown," she says in a voice both smooth and quivery like you'd expect. "I have an errand in town."

"That would be great."

Uncomfortable silence.

More uncomfortable silence.

"Do you work on the island?" Miss Simon asks in an effort to be engaged and friendly.

"I work at Dock Street coffee shop on the Edgartown harbor," I report.

"I'm a hair colorist in Boston," Naomi offers, adding, "I just moved there from New York."

Now that we're all used to the arrangement, I'm feeling smart-assy and am tempted to ask Carly if she works on the island, but I don't.

More uncomfortable silence.

"Where are you from?" asks the chanteuse with the famous case of stage fright.

"Madison, Wisconsin," I recite.

"Princeton, New Jersey," says Naomi. We're all looking straight ahead, afraid to openly take in one another in a gawking fashion. I'm painfully aware that everyone I know has more interesting answers to the stock questions normally asked by strangers.

Again silence. Carly fumbles for a radio station, and because we're in the middle of nowhere, the center of an island with grassy pastures on both sides, nothing is tuning in, just white noise. She sighs and presses play on her cassette deck. And this is the part I hesitate to tell because I don't want Carly Simon's risk of being a nice, normal (yet extraordinary) person to backfire in her face, because I'm a fan of her music and her life. Because I feel honored that my friend and I look cool enough to be picked up hitchhiking by a pop star. But when the cassette begins playing, Carly Simon's voice comes out of the dashboard speakers. We are listening to the singing voice of the lady in the driver's seat. At this point I'm inwardly freaking out. Does she want us to say something like "Miss Simon, is this your latest effort?" or does she just want to stop the awkward silence? Maybe she assumes that the next thing that is coming is "Are you Carly

Simon?" and she wants to tell us without being asked. Or could she be so vain? Oh no, not her. Or maybe she thinks we haven't a clue as to who she is so she'll just listen to her demos until she can redeposit us on the roadside where we belong.

We're pulling onto upper Main Street in Edgartown, the quietest, most conservative town on the island. "We can get off here," I say. "Thanks a lot," we both recite while gently closing her car doors before she pulls out. Naomi and I lock oh-my-God eyes, drop our jaws, and laugh uproariously before sticking our thumbs out again on the side of the road that leads to the beach.

In the past, when I've embellished this story and taken liberties, I added a section: While sitting in Carly Simon's front seat I'm holding in my lap a copy of *Playboy* magazine. Carly notices but says nothing until I say, "I wanted to see those Madonna pictures to see what the big deal's all about." In my made-up story, Carly pulls over on the side of the road to drop us off, but first we all peruse the pictures together, all wondering what kind of sleazeball would sell these art photos from Madonna's past now that she's a superstar, and how they're not worthy of the hype. Exposed boobs and hairy armpits, big deal, we've all been through that phase. But that tall tale is just me wanting to connect as many themes in pop culture and women's lives as I can, wanting to create a scene where pop divas past, present, and future all converge in Carly Simon's blue Volvo. In case you're wondering, I like to think of myself as pop diva future, I like to think of my chance meeting with Carly Simon as her symbolically and unknowingly passing me the torch singer torch. I know I'm probably way out of line.

AFTER summer turns to late fall on Martha's Vineyard, I move back home to Madison to plot my next move. I'm a twenty-four-year-old college dropout. At the "UW", as it's called, I was more interested in the round booth at the Plaza Bar and tequila shots than I was in *Beowulf*. Dancing in dark nightclubs to "Mirror in the Bathroom" took precedence over Dante and Milton. Any jobs emerging from the college education I've half-assed worked toward for six years seems remote. I want excitement, a little glamour. The kids from New York and Chicago who flocked to the University of Wisconsin for a quaint and wholesome college experience made me painfully aware of the sophisticated world outside of Madison. I'm a damn townie. I know every bar, restaurant, and used clothing store in Madison and its surrounding counties. Everyone here knows everything about me. Ronald Reagan has been president all of my young adult life.

I think I might be an artist, either a writer or a singer. But so far I only write letters to friends in other cities, and I'm not singing anywhere except in cars and showers. I don't have a persona or personal mythology—something I know is vital when forging an artistic identity. The process of myth making requires a shift in perception, if not location—which is why I spent six months waitressing (yes, it is a verb) on Martha's Vineyard. From there it was easy to breeze into Boston or New York for a show or a concert. I spend most of my time listening to and thinking about music, everything from Devo to Dylan, or watching live music, rock 'n' roll, punk rock, new wave, whatever. This music hits me in my chest and in my brain and in my groin; it understands me. Now that I'm trapped back in Madison, a place they call Mad Town, har har, I have designed an independent study of sorts learning how to start, play, and live in a rock 'n' roll band. This is not for college credit; this is my life.

"Rock 'n' roll band" sounds too Bob Seger, so let me clarify; I want to start an all-women punk rock band. My definition of punk rock is do-it-yourself, who cares if it's sloppy or unprofessional. My definition of punk has little or nothing to do with politics or shaved heads and everything to do with what's new and not in the mainstream. It's about going on stage as you, full of rage, heartbreak, and laughs. It's about making the music you hear in your head and heart. When I was first into music as a kid, it only came out of California, New York, or London. The new movement of mid-1980s make-your-own-rules music, the sounds drawn from influences as diverse as Johnny Cash and Johnny Rotten, is coming from places like Athens, Georgia, and Minneapolis, Minnesota—places I can relate to. The people making this music seem to be a lot like my friends and me with their thrift shop wardrobes, messy hair, and penchants for nicotine. I want my band to be all women because I want us girls to be in charge, to call all the shots.

It's taken me this long to figure out that I could, and my friends could, start a band and make that exciting life of song and guitar feedback, travel and intrigue, carousing and cavorting our own. It's not like it's a job you land after an internship. It's not an encouraged career move. There are no courses to show you how (not yet, anyway). This band thing is nothing that will please our parents. All of the guys that I hung out with in college had bands in their rented basements. What else was there to do really? Become yuppies? In Madison winter lasts for at least half of the year; you really need an indoor hobby, especially if, like me, you hate the Green Bay Packers. I'm pretty sure I can pick up a guitar and figure something out, judging from my guy friends' hellish din that happens to sound like music to my ears. I've been slow to connect my interest and my longing to something I could do—rather than spend the rest of my life watching.

My nightly "field trips" are spent in bars watching live music. This all started long before I threw in the academic towel after flunking out of college a record-breaking four times. I'm sure there's a connection there. So far I've studied the small clubs in Madison, Chicago, Boston, and Martha's Vineyard. The bars are usually seedy and the bands are usually loud. If the music moves me and I'm feeling gregarious after a couple of drinks, I'll attempt to make conversation with the musicians to get a feel for their lifestyle (hard-drinking or pot-addicted), their background (Ivy League-educated or high school dropout), and their musical tastes (Kraftwerk or Hank Williams). I've learned that, like chasing a degree in literature, there are no definitive right answers; it's all about absorption and interpretation. Because ninety-five percent of these musicians are male, I may appear to be a groupie seeking a love connection. I am not. I consider these guys peers, equals. "How long have you been playing guitar?" I might ask a flannel-clad fella. Or, "How did you buy a van?" And he might answer me, "Huh? Oh . . . *mumble* . . . I ain't been home in months. Got a smoke? Buy you a beer?" Clearly it does not require a high IQ, so I've got that going for me.

I don't want to be with a guy in a band; I want to be in the band. Repeat: I want to be *in* the band. It's easy to confuse these two ideas, though. Those scruffy, skinny boy-men with their stick-outy hair and deep tobacco-tinged voices are awfully cute, and they're such a breath of fresh air after a decade of those heavily made-up new wave cross-dressers or spandex and permed "rockers." But when you emerge from a motel room assaulted by the morning sun, with razor stubble-burned lips and chin, with black bruises on your inner thighs because these guys are so ungodly skinny, you vow to take musical revenge by acquiring the same power he exercised over you rather than get mad at yourself for exercising poor judgment. The sex wasn't that great, he wasn't exactly focused on me per se. I know that we don't have a future together; I know he's not really going to write a song about a girl standing in a cornfield that's supposed to be me (though probably secretly in my heart of hearts, I sort of hope that he will). Maybe someday I'll write songs about him and about the fact that his live-in girlfriend hasn't a clue about how he conducts himself on the road because, again, that is preferable to chastising myself for my understandable lapse in common sense. Sometimes you can't help yourself; rock 'n' roll is sexy as hell. There is no right answer, no guilty party. Except I do feel guilty; he told me he had a girlfriend back home. How would *I* like it?

So yeah, I'm going to start a band with my girlfriends and we're all planning on a move to the current, or I should say closest, music capital of the world, Minneapolis, Minnesota. My Vineyard phase was an exclusively summer engagement; we're all Midwest-based. A lot of our college friends are from Minneapolis and have moved back home after graduation. It's a musical hotbed—the resident superstar is Prince. My favorite bands, the Replacements and Soul Asylum, are serving up an irresistible fusion of punk, classic rock, pop, country, and blues. The city is teeming with handsome boy-men with gravelly voices, profound street poetry, self-deprecating humor, and jangly guitars. All eyes in the music industry are resting on Minneapolis at the moment. Clearly there's something in the water, and I want a drink. It's the land of ten thousand lakes and ten thousand bands. Minneapolis is pretty and clean, all blue lakes and green trees. It looks easier to live in than the other midwestern city—steely gray Chicago with its mean-looking lake. I love the ocean and I love Martha's Vineyard; it's just that I sensed that I had to leave while I was still young or I'd never leave again. There wasn't a potent music scene out there, just a lot of heavenly scenery. Besides, Minneapolis has that appealing Mary Tyler Moore mythology, like maybe I could make it after all.

Oh, as for that small issue about not having spent our teen years locked in our bedrooms jacking off with guitars (but rather cheerleading and memorizing the choreography from numbers in *Grease*): no problem. First of all, we look the part: My friend Phyll has a wild mop of curly red hair, curvy hips, and a wardrobe that relies heavily upon cowboy boots and pencil skirts. Phyll vibrates with intensity; she's like Annie Oakley meets Patsy Cline had either of them hailed from Milwaukee. Co looks like Natalie Wood if she had traveled to India with the Beatles, sort of like a grooved-out late-1950s movie star. A former cheerleader gone off the arty deep end, Co is a mixture of the young Cher and Maureen O'Sullivan. I'm a poor man's Connie Stevens on a good day, a punk rock Joey Heatherton on a bad day. Phyll calls me the rock 'n' roll Ethel Kennedy whenever I wear a sleeveless shift. We're all smart and sassy, well-nourished and starving for experience, and very vulnerable (okay, ultranaïve). I can carry a tune and I know the three chords to "Wild Thing" on the guitar, so I'm almost there. Looking the part and thinking the part is more than halfway to living the part; it's called the Think System and I learned it as a little girl watching *The Music Man*.

We are going to keep our band project a secret until we acquire skills, equipment, and write some songs. No boys allowed. I want me and the girls to be coddled, protected, and admired like the guys I've been watching. These are the pictures I dream up of the life we're going to lead:

Hot guy: Do you need a place to stay tonight/a drink/a meal/
an orgasm?
Hot girl: You rock, I work at a vintage clothing store/record
store/bar/restaurant, come in and I'll set you up.
Club manager: We're so glad to have you here, anything you
need? Herbal tea/cocaine/a backrub?
Crowd watching us perform: appreciative frenzy of whoops
and cheers/mouthing the words to our songs like they're
prayers/hot guys at the lip of the stage wanting us bad.

Yes sir, we will rock you—and all we have to do is wake up at an ungodly hour, hang out, jam, fiddle with song ideas on a tape recorder, practice a couple of times a week, play a gig now and then, record an album a year, and tell wry, clever jokes. In exchange, we will have our choice of the cream of the opposite sex and the protection and admiration of our peers. Everyone will want us; everyone will want to buy us a drink. What a great job.

Keep in mind that my favorite song as a little girl was "Daydream Believer."

2: Magic Bus

I'M so bored I could spit; whenever the phone rings I'm positively giddy.

"Hellooooo?" I sing into the receiver, trying to sound like Lovie from *Gilligan's Island*. It's a hot afternoon in early July, the summer after the Vineyard, and I'm in my mom's kitchen soaking up her central air, something that wasn't installed until after I moved out to go to college.

"Hey, it's Phyll." She sounds all business, she must be working. "I've had it. Let's move to Minnie."

"Cool. I'm so there."

Tired of a thankless entry-level job in graphic design (aka typing) and an oppressive, hot summer in her circulationless apartment next to Chicago's el tracks, her apartment caked with grit and smelling like tar, Phyll is ready for our Minneapolis experiment. I've been waiting, laying low at my mom's house in Madison; taking a couple guitar lessons and biding my time working the graveyard shift as an operator at an answering service.

After our brief phone conversation, we make things happen quickly to prevent any overthinking about the gamble we're about to take. Phyll moves up to Minneapolis in less than a week after our tête-à-tête; she's renting a spare room in our friends' Dave and Rachel's apartment on the corner of Eleventh and Franklin. Dave, a cute blond stoner, is in the band Soul Asylum. Rachel, a friend from college, is quietly sexy, an excellent conversationalist, and Dave's longtime girlfriend. Eleventh and Franklin is a rough part of town filled with displaced Native Americans, some of whom suck on Lysol cans in Phyll's new backyard in order to get high. I supplied Phyll with a crappy used guitar from the Buy and Sell shop in Madison, and a tiny flowered slumber party suitcase filled with a Mel Bay beginning guitar book, sheet music, guitar strings, and picks. I'm trying to equip our future band with the necessary gear. In music, I'm hoping that accessories will make the outfit.

On a weekend visit I put down a deposit on a one-bedroom apartment above a rib joint on Hennepin Avenue in the Uptown neighborhood. The apartment's three windows are covered with black wrought-iron bars, and the orange shag carpeting is badly stained and matted with candle wax, but it will be my first apartment alone and I think it's fabulous. It has a kitchen, living room, bedroom, and bathroom—all separate—and a buzzer to get inside. Urban. Uptown is where you live if you are young and hungering for a scene, or at least wanting to be close to one. Uptown is less real-life than Phyll's neighborhood; it's full of hipsters and poseurs fresh out of college or art school or modeling school or technical college— we're all fresh out of something.

At midnight on August 1, 1985, my lease begins in Minneapolis. Wishing not to waste a minute, I move to Minneapolis an hour into my lease on a Greyhound bus at 1:20 A.M., not that I have another choice. My friends Anita and Bill see me off after whiling away the evening in the Willy Bear tavern—my going-away party is sparsely attended with half-interested friends or past acquaintances. Time to move on. Madison is a great place to grow up in (which I've yet to do), and an excellent place to leave. We've had enough of each other, Madison and me. Triumphant and tipsy, I load the cargo hold of the hissing, diesel-farting bus with five enormous boxes stuffed with my earthly possessions—clothes, journals, jackets, music, guitar, a few kitchen utensils and dishes. Shoes. It's polyester-dress-stuck-to-my-body hot.

The bus is nearly full with sleeping couples, crying babies with soiled diapers, and an odd collection of lone adults. Who are we who still get around on a Greyhound? Poor. Old-fashioned. Without cars. Working class, if that. I plop down next to a harmless-looking older gentleman of about sixty. His eyes are watery and he looks like Hank Williams might've had he lived to see sixty. He says "good evening" and offers me a flask filled with whiskey. As the whiskey burns down my throat, the man introduces himself.

"I just graduated from clown school at the Barnum and Bailey Circus University down in Florida," he says, his words sounding like well-rehearsed lines. "I decided to bring laughter to others after my wife and daughter were killed in a car crash." His testimonial has a sobering effect on me. "Let me introduce myself," he says with a wink and a nod. "I am the Clown Who Cried the Golden Tears."

"Pleased to meet you, sir," I stammer, wanting to say something like "I'm the Blonde Who Cries the Crocodile Tears," but it's rude, and it's late, and we're both buzzed. "I'm Laurie, and I'm moving to Minneapolis to become a musician."

He nods like it's an everyday occurrence.

Whoa. Okay. I'm now officially completely freaked-out and sad. I can't connect the dots—how does a huge personal loss lead one to the clown industry? Perhaps I'm taking liberties in assuming this man doesn't follow opera or Fellini films. I wonder why I've been chosen to hear this story on this particular night.

I'm sure everyone who's traveled by all-night Greyhound has a weird story to tell. Some might call the clown a messenger from God in the form of the aged Hank Williams. What should I make of this random freak-out? Am I supposed to conclude that I'm lucky, after all, because my family hasn't been erased in a tragedy? Maybe. Clowns have always given me the creeps, though. I stare out the window into a black Wisconsin night, a slight hangover headache pouring into my neck and temples.

WHEN I was a senior in high school, we had Christmas Eve dinner at my aunt Chris's (my mom's younger sister) house. We never had anything at Aunt Chris's, because she was too busy in graduate school and she had two kids and no husband. She wasn't destitute or anything; she lived on the west side in a modern house, in a great neighborhood—something we never managed to pull off. Her kids, my cousins, were sort of quiet and angry, but normal enough.

My family in 1979 consisted of two parents approaching forty: an adorable eight-year-old boy, my youngest sibling and only brother, Chris; a perfect-in-every-way ten-year-old, my sister Hillary; and an exceedingly kind and likable fourteen-year-old, my sister Megan. Being neither adorable, nor perfect, nor exceedingly kind, I was the aloof oldest girl who couldn't wait to shake my dorky family and get out into the world.

When the six of us came tramping into Aunt Chris's, her voice was shrill and fast because she was nervous. The younger kids shuffled down to the rec room in the basement to sit in beanbag chairs and play Atari. Being a senior, I remained upstairs with the adults. Aunt Chris had invited a male friend with a beard and a female friend who was flat-chested and braless and wearing a purple silk blouse that was vaguely buttoned. They were all loud, smoking, and in the psychology business. In no time, my dad was downstairs initiating a game of tape ball hockey. I remained upstairs, studying these new people who were in their early thirties. My mom was thirty-nine, but she was not single and not hanging out in the Fez Hotel downtown, nor did she wear her silk blouses braless. My mom and Aunt Chris were never that close.

Because we were in a room with a couple of strangers, I decided to ask my mom a question I'd been mulling over, thinking that our new audience might make her more likely to grant permission to an unlikely proposition.

"Mom, Dee [my summer friend from vacation who lived in Washington, D.C.] is going to be a debutante at the Plaza in New York on New Year's Eve . . ." I began.

My mom was helping Aunt Chris with a Caesar salad and

croissants, unusual Christmas Eve fare for our roast-eating household.

"Mmm-hmmm?" she answered without looking up.

"Can I go? Please?"

"Absolutely not." That was her stock answer for anything that might've been extra fun.

"But Mom," I moaned, trying not to be whiny, "it's the opportunity of a lifetime."

And not that Dee had even invited me; she only told me about it in a letter, and "debutante ball at the Plaza" sounded so fascinating and foreign that I would've figured out a way to gain entree after my mom granted permission. I had no tools for understanding that there was no way in hell that Dee would ever invite me, that I was probably her equally fascinating cracker friend, compelling in the tube top/Supertramp kind of way.

"You're just an ordinary girl from Madison, Wisconsin, and that's all you'll ever be," my mom snapped, abruptly ending any chance of further discussion.

My mom is not normally a buzz kill; I suppose she was trying to extinguish any further interaction in front of strangers, but I went black inside at the sound of the words "just an ordinary girl." Couldn't she say "middle-class" or "we can't afford it"— even "normal" would be (slightly) better. I mean, she was the one making sure I was set apart from my peers by taking me to extraordinary places that none of them had ever even heard of, then she turns around and insists that I'm just ordinary. That defeating phrase rang in my ears. I am *not* just an ordinary girl, I seethed inwardly. Someday, someway, I'll show her.

My mom was the person who took me to places like "summer on Martha's Vineyard" and "shopping in Chicago"? Was I to assume that I could visit these fabulous places, while at the same time, I was to "know my place"? What *was* my place? Some unacknowledged neverland between "used to have a little old money" and "no money." Reflections in the mirror may appear richer than they are. My Susie's Casuals outfits from the

East Towne Mall looked "trashy" and "cheap" to my mom. Maybe she was trying to protect me from the inevitable inferiority I'd feel in the Plaza ballroom wearing the wrong thing that I absolutely loved until I got there.

A s a seventeen-year-old freshman in college, sitting on the front steps of my dorm, Slichter Hall, I drunkenly babbled to passersby after a good time in a downtown bar. I recognized Co with an inner groan as she approached—she had been a cheerleader at a rival Madison high school and her school had a reputation for excessive peppiness. I went to the bong-hits-before-the-game high school.

"Greetings and salutations!" I may have bellowed, mimicking a drunk in an old movie I'd once seen.

Co found me amusing and said, "You crack me up," or something equally neutral, and we became instant friends.

Co (who's full name is Coleen, with one L, not two) was beautiful in a way that I could never be: both curvy and slender, pretty Irish face with an upturned nose, a sprinkling of freckles, emerald green eyes, clear skin, long sleek dark brown hair done up in ponytails and ribbons. Fortunately for me, underneath Co's untouchable exterior lurked a fellow freak ("freak" being a term of endearment). Co loved funk music. In her room she listened to everyone from Michael Jackson, Pat Benatar, and AC/DC to the Brothers Johnson. She experimented with pot in my dorm room, and being a newcomer to the drug, had highly entertaining meltdowns that sent her fleeing back to her room in fits of paranoia. Sometimes Co drank too many California Motherfuckers, a big yellow drink with a zillion shots in it served in a beer mug at the Kollege Klub, and her boyfriend, a University of Wisconsin hockey player, looked on with concern when her head dropped to the table, soon to throw up. I also threw up a lot after drinking; it was hard work building up a tolerance. One thing Co managed that was be-

yond me was maintaining a responsible student profile on the
outside. But she was a wild girl on the inside. Besides, how
could you not love someone who thought the chorus to
Michael Jackson's "Don't Stop 'Til You Get Enough" started
with the lyrics, "Kiss off, we're the Flintstones."

I met Phyll a few years later through a mutual friend. Phyll
was one year younger, and because I was a sophomore for a
couple of years, my peers kept getting younger and younger. I
don't think she had a surprising former identity like Co, and I
don't remember our first meeting. I just know that she was appealing and intense with that vague aura of an artist without an
art—a strong immediate bond was forged. We hung out constantly until she, too, graduated on time and moved to Chicago.

I WAS a high school overachiever, a cheerleader, a choir jock,
the features editor on the school newspaper, committees galore, a strong core of girlfriends, and an incredibly nice first
boyfriend. I had the curling-iron roll of dishwater blonde hair
down the side of my face and wore cowl-neck sweaters acces-
sorized with stickpins, painter's pants, and clogs. A dermatolo-
gist treated my acne (why I'm sharing this is beyond me, it does
nothing for my highly suspect street cred). Popularity was a
perk—but not guaranteed—for all of my heaping involvement.
I never felt popular personally, merely by association. There
were a few glitches: I got so crazily puke-and-pass-out drunk at
my first homecoming that the principal had to carry me out of
the gauzy rainbow-decorated building during "Color My
World." I told my mom I had the flu and she marched into
school the following Monday and made sure I wasn't kicked off
the cheerleading squad. The truth was obvious; I reeked of
blackberry brandy provided by someone's parents, and I liked
the little click inside brought on by drinking. I have no idea why
she didn't challenge my weak flu excuse except that it was easier to deal with. I lost my virginity before all of my friends. In-

tercourse did not compare to the hours of making out and mashing, and I scratched it from the roster for a couple of years.

An imposter jock, I longed for the art class stoner boys who wouldn't give me the time of day because I was a cheerleader. Lynyrd Skynyrd and REO Speedwagon serenaded us at keg parties in garages or basements (sometimes the parents were Up North hunting, sometimes they were partying with us). I loved Aerosmith with every fiber of my being. My senior year, I dated a stoner boy with blue eyes and a black white-boy Afro who turned me on to Queen and the Stones, and I fell too in love with him because of the music. I scared him off; he dumped me. That intensity thing.

Dreaming of going far away to college, to Vermont or Boston, my high school guidance counselors didn't know how to help me get there. Apparently no one ventured beyond the state of Wisconsin on my side of town, where I knew more than one kid who had a father with a lopped-off digit or two, compliments of his meat-cutting job at Oscar Mayer's.

My college girlfriends and I were teenagers in the late seventies when the chief goal in life was to be as wasted as possible at all times. The mothers in my neighborhood were screamers and yellers, silent fuming carpet-raking speed cleaners or detached unkempt anticleaners, all-day-luncheon martini drinkers, chain smokers prostrate on the couch with bookcases filled with accounts of JFK and Camelot. I grew up in a neighborhood inhabited by sulking makers of strange casseroles with inappropriate crunchy things sprinkled on top to divert our attention from the hamburger/cream of mushroom soup goulash that lurked underneath. My mother was famous for sticking her hand out of the half-bathroom, otherwise known as her phone booth, and snapping her fingers; it meant "Get me a light for my cigarette. Now!" Sucking on Tic Tacs to disguise our pot/cig/beer breath, we listened to our mothers' endless lectures about the fact that we had choices and opportunities that they never had coming up in the Eisenhower era.

All of our mothers had already borne children by the time they were our age. Co, Phyll, and I, all the eldest of four, feel like we already raised children—our siblings and all the neighborhood brats we babysat. Not only that, all three of us are children of divorce, each family story a dysfunctional work of art in varying degrees. Needless to say, "marriage and family" do not look promising.

"Fabulous exciting career" seems out of reach, none of us have exceeded entry level, and we're staring at our mid-twenties. We're the lost girls of Generation Why?. Why finish school on time (oh ya, both Phyll and Co did)? Why bother with serious relationships? Why push ourselves toward corporate careers—why would we want to work eight-plus hours a day at the same place for the rest of our lives? Why don't we feel like doing anything deemed productive? Why were so many moms unhappy? One thing we all agree on, none of us ever wants to say, "I wonder what would've happened if I had . . . ?"

I'VE been sitting on this bus wide awake all night, remembering, obsessing, and worrying. It's daybreak in Minneapolis when the Greyhound pulls in; the bus depot is a dark domed cave. I'm here. The Clown Who Cried the Golden Tears awakens from his catnap when the bus hisses to a stop.

"Good luck, young lady," he says, tipping his Barnum & Bailey baseball cap.

"Thanks. Good luck to you, too."

We're both gonna need it. I step off the bus, kick all of my boxes across the concrete onto the sidewalk, through a sliding door, and out to the curb, one at a time, figuring no one's interested in running off with a one-hundred-pound box at 6:00 A.M. on a Sunday. After an hour of trying to coerce passing taxis to stop, I divine that you can't hail a cab in Minneapolis; you must call for one.

3: Are You Lonesome Tonight?

MINNEAPOLIS here I am, wrap your lovin' arms around me! Nice thought, anyway, an important illusion to bolster my nerve to make this move. Our friends from Madison, now back in their native Minneapolis, seem ambivalent about our relocation. We've invaded their turf and it's a very insular protective turf. "Move up here," I was encouraged on the phone. "Oh, you're really here" is how Phyll and I are greeted through forced wary smiles. Our college friends, a group of artistic, resourceful, beautiful, independent, talented women, are reunited with their guy friends who all seem to be future rock stars. They all grew up together, many of them hailing from the Kenwood neighborhood, the prime urban Lake of the Isles real estate, a beautiful old lakeshore neighborhood filled with lofty old manors. Mary Tyler Moore's television apartment house, the one with Rhoda upstairs and Phyllis as a landlady, is in Kenwood. This whole scene is kind of intimidating. When a couple of jovial Madison party girls come bouncing in like they belong, it is only just tolerated.

Minneapolis is large and spread out, with giant chunks of the grid cut out and transplanted at random throughout its sprawling landscape; it's a veritable jigsaw puzzle of a city. Hennepin Avenue appears in three different unrelated places; uptown, downtown, and to the east, though none of these strands of the same street are connected; this happens with many of the main thoroughfares in Minneapolis. The Mississippi River slices through the middle separating Minneapolis from St. Paul, the American West from the East. There is no public transportation to speak of and you can't hail a cab. My first order of business is to buy a cheap car; there is no other way to get around, especially if you keep rock 'n' roll hours. I sacrifice four hundred dollars of my stockpiled money to buy a '69 Chevy Nova from a man who owns a lighting store on Interstate 94. "The car belongs to my elderly mother, she only drove it to church on Sundays." In this case, the Oldest Story in the Book is believable; it's a cherry of a car, baby blue and free of rust.

The people of Minneapolis are alarmingly gorgeous; large-boned, white-toothed, high cheek-boned. There are Scandinavian beauties everywhere you turn. Every third woman you see is a giraffe whose name is probably Greta or Inga. Pretty blondes come a dime a dozen, they blend into the landscape like dandelions on a lawn. The people of Minneapolis look so different from the collection of gritty Diane Arbus–photographed faces I encountered in Chicago when visiting my girlfriends during their first stabs at careers. The faces on Martha's Vineyard were distinct, handsome-plain and blue-blooded or dark and Portuguese. Madison is a grab bag; there's a constant population of multicultural students with a jumble of city kids and farm kids mixed together for flavor. There is an unspoken reserve to the people of Minneapolis that makes it feel chilly even in summer; the thing they call "Minnesota nice" should be called "Minneapolis ice." People don't talk to you just because you're there like they do in Boston. Everyone looks away at the exact second when eye contact would normally occur. No one goes out of his or her way to make you feel at home.

The traffic and parking laws are random and confusing; no parking after 4:00 P.M. and no parking between 2:00 A.M. and 6:00 A.M., and reserved parking for employees only, even if the building is closed, and no parking on the odd side on even days, or something like that. There are no turn arrows at stoplights, so you waste an entire green light not moving. I spend my first three weeks in Minneapolis in the impound lot bail-

ing my towed Nova out of car jail. This is not my idea of a
Welcome Wagon.

W HAT do you wanna do?" Phyll and I ask each other
every afternoon at four. Phyll has secured an office job
at an insurance company next to the Walker Art Center in a
building distinguished by a giant statue of a bison in front.
Completely uncertain of my qualifications in the professional
world, I've been dragging my feet seeking employment. I assume that future rock stars don't have time for jobs. Unfortunately I don't have a boyfriend to sponge off. I don't think I'm
girlfriend material just yet. I'm tubby and my hair is bleached
white and it looks like I cut it with a butter knife. Hell, I look
half-crazy. Besides, I've never heard of a guy supporting his
girlfriend—letting her move into his apartment, urging her to
eat all of his food for free while being coaxed not to lift a finger around the apartment—so she can pursue her rock star
dreams. "There's a barbeque at Karl's," Phyll says. Sometimes
we go, sometimes I feel too intimidated at these tight-knit affairs. No one's unfriendly; they just seem content to know who
they already know.

"Let's go to Lyle's," I suggest. Liquor Lyle's is down the
block from my apartment. Lyle's is superdark. The walls are
covered with black Astroturf. There are booths, there is air-
conditioning, and there are two happy hours a day, one at four
and one at seven. Phyll and I usually show up at four, drink
cheap two-for-one bottled beer, and eat free gristly chicken
wings and cheddar cheese on Ritz crackers. I never eat the
pickled herring. We're usually still there through the second
happy hour, and sometimes we're still there at closing time. Acquaintances drop by and join us for a drink, then leave. Phyll
and I hold the booth for the duration. Being from Wisconsin,
this is not considered at all to be an unusual way to spend most
of the day and night.

And I have developed a taste for scotch. Is that grown-up or what? Johnny Walker Red on the rocks, to be precise. And what a wide-awake awesome buzz. Sort of like tequila but not as psychotic. It's a clean buzz—one that makes me biting, sarcastic, and full of lies (which is exactly what my personality needs to hurl me over the top in the charming department). "Yes sir, I am Irish . . . in fact, my grandmother lives in County Cork to this day." Lines like this spill out of my mouth for no reason, usually to old men sitting at the bar. A complete crock.

Alone in my apartment after Lyle's, I fill notebooks with songs-to-be, thoughts, plans, ideas. I strum my guitar in three-chord patterns. Living alone is something I both love and fear. I'm lonely. I'm lovelorn. But come to think of it, I've always been kind of lonely and lovelorn, with or without boyfriends and roommates. Even though I don't want to be with a guy in a band, when I long for a boyfriend he is usually in the form of an unobtainable rock star. This type of fantasy saves me the energy I might expend chasing actual boys (who I know should be referred to as "men" at this point, but somehow it doesn't quite fit). I write songs to this illusive him on my skanky orange shag living room floor, strumming C, G, D over and over again. On occasion I'll throw in an F chord for variety. Only F is really hard because it's a bar chord and I can't keep my index finger pinned down to form a bar across one fret and be expected to make a chord with the leftover fingers below my wobbly bar finger. *Every time I see your face, I turn my head, we're always in the wrong place . . .* He's nobody in particular, no one I know; though I assume if he's any good he's already taken. He's just an imaginary ideal, a composite of all my favorite music men, a little Mick Jagger, a little Keith, some young Dylan and Bryan Ferry to smooth the rough edges. Maybe I'm trying to love myself but I have it all mixed up.

OUR favorite local band at the moment is Soul Asylum. They have energy, exuberance, intensity, and humor. And they rock hard. Every time we go to a Soul Asylum show we get "punk rock neck" from shaking our heads so fast and hard. Soul Asylum is driven by abrupt rhythms, loud guitars, and our buddy Dave's irresistible stage presence. Dave is a likeable Axl Rose before there was an Axl Rose. With a wild mane of blond whips and ripped jeans, Dave is sexual and boyish at the same time. His songwriting is all over the map—twang, funk, folk, speed metal—which is something I really appreciate. How can you be in the same songwriting mood all of the time? We go to all of their shows and rock our asses off.

My personal favorite, the Replacements, are now on a major label, making them more of a national treasure than the regional heroes they were a couple of years ago. We don't get to see them nearly as much as we did back in Madison. They deserve the attention: I haven't listened to better lyric writing since Dylan's heyday.

Now that I'm trying my hand at songwriting, it occurs to me that it's the words, the lyrics that touch me the deepest. Dave in Soul Asylum sings, "Now what is the sound of snow falling down/On the tombstone in the dead of the night?" Paul in the Replacements croaks, "Try to free a slave of ignorance/Try to teach a whore about romance/How do you say good night to an answering machine?" I've never trusted poetry in books, or poets, for that matter. Poetry is so dense, pretentious, discourteous, holier than me. But the thing that is grabbing me and transfixing me is the words coming from the mouths of these lovely poets with guitars.

My friends and I could probably be classified as "band girls," not like halter-wearing classic rock girls, or intentionally superslutty-looking heavy metal girls. We're "indie rock girls" before the term or phrase is coined. We are attracted to and moved beyond reason by band guys in this hazy genre. Muscles—ew. Skinny and clad in a thrift shop sports shirt—ooo-la-

la. Naturally the best line of work for us is to be in a band ourselves, that way we're insured a work atmosphere that is pleasing to the senses (as long as you can block out filth in
beer-drenched caves that smell like b.o., puke, and piss).

When it comes to drugs of choice, we're drinkers and pot
smokers. These are friendly, social activities that often involve
sharing food, stories, and music. Almost wholesome.

"M Y boss is opening a new restaurant and they need cooks,
waitresses, and counter help. Get down there now!" implores our friend Carolyn. Before my interview I decide I want
to cook. My hands are too shaky these days to serve hot bever-
ages. "I was a breakfast cook on Martha's Vineyard," I lie to
the manager, a bony hippie woman with thick glasses, a kind
face, and a tough exterior. I'm instantly hired as one of two
morning grill cooks. The restaurant is going to be called the
Global Café, a breakfast/lunch/all-night coffee bar. It's located
on the west bank of the Mississippi River. The West Bank
neighborhood houses a theater/comedy district, a piece of the
University of Minnesota campus, and it's the home of the white
blues scene from the seventies that boasts ownership of
Koerner, Ray, and Glover and Willie and the Bees; the names
Bob Dylan and Bonnie Raitt come up constantly in reference to
West Bank music.

On my first day of work it is clear that many survivors or
hangers-on from the seventies sound explosion are still there,
still talking about their close personal friend Bob Dylan, grous-
ing about punk rock and how that's not music while opening
businesses of their own in cheap commercial spaces on the corners of Cedar and Riverside. Inside, the café has no distinguish-
able look or decor, just tables, chairs, a counter, and chaos.
There is a revolving rack of avant-garde greeting cards. Enormous Day-Glo paintings of nudes. A large steel espresso machine. A handprinted sandwich menu. Ice cream. A little

something for everyone. Our clientele consists of those leftover people from the seventies who never felt the need to move on, college students and hippies, as well as Somali, Middle Eastern, and Hmong men. The bars on the West Bank are reputed to be rough and filled with bikers, drunks, and cultural tension. It's the closest thing to downtown Madison that I've seen in Minneapolis and I feel right at home here.

My grill partner is a musician named Mark who is my age. He looks half-young Dylan, half-Johnny Cash; slouchy and nonverbal, he says "yup" and "well" with great big sighs. But he's cute; scruffy, buttless, deep dimples, a mass of greasy, curly brown-blond hair. Mark just founded a band called the Jayhawks. He clearly knows nothing about cooking, either. Indiscernible eggs and misshapen pancakes are Mark's specialty. Freaked-out by his ugly food, I assign him toast duty because we both really need this job. I quickly pick up the fine art of short-order grill cooking. It's a Zen job. Throughout the workday (6:00 A.M. to 2:00 P.M.), Mark educates me on the Southern California country rock scene past and present. He brings in music by Gram Parsons and Emmylou Harris. I mostly listen and, on occasion, we exchange comments about our coworkers and customers. "Ya, Mark, I guess she's cute," I say of the new counter help, "but she has a weird odor to her, that sinus infection smell." Mark chuckles, he's always chuckling, and says, "You know, Laurie, you're right." And we snicker.

Co, burned-out by her thankless job in Chicago as a photography stylist for the Spiegel catalogue (coffee running), moves to Minneapolis in September and our group relocation project is complete. A united group of three feels better; as a trio we qualify as a crowd. Phyll and Co rent an apartment one block away from mine. Instantly hired as a waitress at the Global Café because she knows the cook, Co and I ride to work together in the Nova at the crack of dawn, smoking cigs with the A.M. radio blaring, dressed in cut-off leggings and old rock 'n' roll T-shirts with flannel on top to keep out the early morning chill. "Andy Warhol is dead," laments a woman eating eggs wearing a maroon beret with hair down to her butt. I read *Edie*, I listen to the Velvet Underground, I know all about Andy Warhol. Had Co, Phyll, and I been born in another era and lived in New York, Andy would've liked us. Maybe.

Co and Mark banter like an old married couple.

"Pick uuuuuup," Mark calls like a train engineer, "I said, pick uuuuup."

Co, the busty brunette with sparkly green eyes, saunters up in no hurry. She stares at the plate of ugly food she's supposed to deliver. Stares back at Mark.

"I'm not serving this, Mark."

"C'mon, we're backed up, just serve it, they won't care," Mark reasons.

"No fucking way."

"They will live, Coleen," he says with Heston-like drama, "THEY—WILL—*LIVE*!"

In the time that their argument takes, I've recooked the eggs and scooped the old toast and potatoes onto a new plate.

When Co saves one hundred and twenty-five dollars, she buys a used bass guitar and amp from a regular at the café, a West Bank artist who looks and paints like van Gogh (this is not the Left Bank in Paris, but maybe he doesn't know that). After work we meet at her apartment, slinking around on the floor under open windows so that no one can see us. The neighborhood is teeming with people-in-band types, and we feel the need to hide. Seated on Co's folded-up futon, we cradle guitars in our arms that we don't know how to tune. We're like shocked, brand-new mothers faced with baby's first feeding. "I heard somewhere that the dial tone on the telephone is an A," I tell her. Tuning off the phone dial does not work so we tune to each other. We try to play Black Sabbath's "Iron Man" with both our guitars plugged into Co's amp, changing the lyrics to "I am iron girl, doing all I can all around the world." Our objective is still very much a secret; to be caught would be of utmost embarrassment.

Managing an instrument is overwhelming. Standing up and managing an instrument is the next big step. Standing up, managing an instrument, and singing is a few hundred (thousand?) miles down the road. This doesn't deter us; the private thrill we receive in just trying is extraordinary.

THE Jayhawks are playing at the Viking Bar, a tiny West Bank bar next to the Global Café. In a short amount of time, the Jayhawks have established a following that is too big and too enthusiastic to be contained in the tiny box that is the Viking. I try to dress according to the music I'm going out to hear. For the Jayhawks I'll wear a black cotton Betsey Johnson dress that has a plunging V down my back almost to my ass. The designer dress, several years old, is worn with cowboy boots. Soul Asylum is more of a ripped jeans and T-shirts band, and the Replacements are a strictly party dress band.

The Jayhawks are pioneers of a new genre of music that is about to be called "new country rock" or "alternative country"—their songs resemble Southern California's 1960s country rock, a mishmash of Gram Parsons, Neil Young, Ricky Nelson, and the Byrds. They sing modern folk songs that are a mixture of Southern Gothic ("Go to sleep, my dead end angel.") and the dark Scandinavian flavor of the North Country ("Each night when I go to bed I pray, take me with you when you go.")

Their guitar player, Gary, is a long-legged Ohio boy with a degree in architecture, and he has some of the fastest guitar-picking hands I've ever seen. He's a clean, precise player with long, tapered fingers and a melodic honey-dipped voice. My grillmate Mark is the real showman in this outfit, the beating heart, the one who's risking it all for his vision. Mark talks to the audience, saying nonsensical blips that charm much in the way that Elvis used to. On stage he looks and acts like Johnny Cash or Dylan with a low, perfectly wobbly contralto voice that is sometimes shrill and twangy in a good, not obnoxious way—which is hard to pull off. Cool and in-control Gary and passionate loose-cannon Mark are perfect foils on stage; their voices blend together turning straw into gold.

The girls and I love this band. Our social lives tend to re-volve around meeting members of the Jayhawks for drinks. Their bass player Marc, a dry-witted, insecure, dark-haired cutie, has become our greatest friend and supporter. We know all the words to their songs and we holler our requests from the floor. We all laugh and smile together in that "we've got brand new friends" love fest. It's kind of gross, but so fun when it happens; it's rare to find well-matched peers.

P HYLL and Co have casual unofficial boyfriends, minimally groomed adorable rock 'n' roll guys they make out with and occasionally ask to spend the night. I do not. An entire decade of my life has been spent chasing, obsessing over, and believing that my life would be happy if and when I hooked up with the right guy. I've had a trail of errors in the boyfriend de-partment. Here in Minneapolis, I've learned to look away be-fore eye contact is made. For the first time in my life, I'm focusing on establishing a (far-fetched, grandiose) career and can't be bothered. I'm too busy spazzing out in my apartment with my notebook and guitar. And, oh ya, I'm not confident about my dateability. This finds me wide awake in the middle of the night, flailing on my futon, filled with anxiety. To calm myself, I switch on the black-and-white TV with the butter knife attached to the back wires for better reception that sits on a kitchen chair in front of my futon. When day finally breaks, I dress for work and leave my lonely apartment. Okay, my apartment isn't lonely, I am.

On a stormy night I click on the TV, praying for a late show. I settle on an old movie that looks like a film noir; it's called

It's a Wonderful Life. I can't believe I've never seen nor heard of this movie in light of my old movie obsession and fondness for Jimmy Stewart. (It's still the eighties: the merciless airing of this movie every minute from Thanksgiving to New Year's has yet to occur.) With the thunder and lightning punctuating my mood, I cry real tears from the moment old man Gower slaps the young George Bailey on his sore ear until the middle-aged George Bailey is pronounced the richest man in town. No, I bawl my head off. Sob. And I never cry. Not about real things that are actually happening anyway. *It's a Wonderful Life* is dark and yet manages to be a sticky-sweet tale of love, hope, pulling together, bad things happening to good people, life is worth living, the little guy with scruples wins over the money/power structure, all that. And it strikes a chord deep inside me, like good art, like Nat "King" Cole singing "Mona Lisa" or seeing a van Gogh painting. It's no secret that I'm a sap, a pushover, highly suggestible.

While Phyll and Co are probably mashing the night away with some newfound honeys, I'm sitting there crying over old movies or jotting odes of loneliness into my notebook. It's not that I don't enjoy a good romp as much as the next gal; I'm just not feeling very saucy these days. I'm going out, making the scene, and partying on down like a righteous girl-rocker-in-the-making should. But I have issues.

4: I'm Sick Y'all

STAYING home alone while my friends frolic is not normal for me, but I lack the savvy to flirt. In fact, my entire m.o. for "how to act in the world" is pretty much shot. I was gunned down, figuratively speaking, on my way home from Martha's Vineyard:

Almost a year ago, when I left Martha's Vineyard to spend Thanksgiving in Madison, naturally I would fly into O'Hare, and of course, I had to make a pit stop to visit Phyll and Co, who I hadn't seen in almost six months. I took the el to their apartment and we plotted the perfect night on the town.

We strutted down the sidewalks of Chicago's Wrigleyville neighborhood like we were hot shit. Dressed in our rock show finest—various decades of vintage dresses layered with black tights and Jantzenwear mohair sweaters reeking of mothballs, leather jackets, and boots—we wouldn't be caught dead in anything involving shoulder pads (take that, Belinda Carlisle). Our hair was large and messy and our bodies were round and girly, just the way we liked them. The only thing weighing on my mind was getting Phyll and Co out of their jobs so that we could all move to the same city to start our band because we already looked and acted like we rocked.

It was a two-block walk from their apartment to the Cabaret Metro; we were on our way to see one of our favorite bands, the Replacements. I thought this show was a very lucky, happy coincidence; a convergence of my favorite people and my most-loved tunes in one night. As always, we were laughing and talking a little too loud.

"Carly Simon picked me up hitchhiking," I boasted.

"We know!" they shouted, tired of my brush with fame.

Co tilted her movie star face to the sky, holding her wrist close to her jade eyes as if to check an imaginary watch. "This is the international sign of sexual boredom," she purred.

We roared. I inhaled a drag off my Marlboro Red, such a satisfying act on a cold night walk. I could see my breath. The cigarette smoke from my slow exhale swirled over my head making a dusky halo. It was a snowy, slushy night on the street corner in front of Wrigley Field. The streetlights beamed down on us like spotlights. I was completely happy.

But then something went wrong. Really wrong. What though? I was abruptly halted. Stuck. My foot wouldn't go. Too weird. I couldn't lift my left foot to take my next step. Sensation and liberty of motion were gone on the left side of my body. Half of me was erased. It was like an invisible god stole my good side. Or an enemy with a voodoo doll just cut me in half. I don't have the apt words to describe it. It was inner, immediate, numbing shock. Or silent hysteria coupled with painless paralysis. This happened with no warning. Without a single sensation. My left leg was gone. But still there. I couldn't lift it up to move it to where I wanted to go. I couldn't feel my left hand, either. My cigarette unintentionally dropped from my fingers; it hostilely hissed its end on the wet sidewalk. I was neither in my head nor in my body. I transformed into a calm crisis counselor observing myself from afar. From right there.

"Um, you guys?" They were gabbing a couple of steps ahead of me. They stopped, turned around, their broad smiles framed by red lips. "I'm in trouble," I stuttered. "I'm so embarrassed. I can't move." My speech was even and quizzical; I didn't sound like myself.

"What do you mean?" Phyll casually hollered in my direction. I'd interrupted a song she was singing about dreams and wishes. We always made up songs while walking; none of us owned a car. The statement I made claiming spontaneous paralysis was out of our range.

I couldn't move or feel my left leg. Or hand. I like to joke around, but something in my face, probably a look of confusion and fear, made them double back. They could tell by my small foreign voice that I wasn't kidding. And I wished I were kidding because all of a sudden I felt like a burden. In a matter of seconds I'd become Someone Who Needs Help and neediness, we would all agree, was most unattractive.

Lost in a surreal dimension, I found myself remembering an incident from when I was twelve and I held a kitten against my chest while standing in my backyard. Scared, the kitty stuck a single claw into the swollen mound of one of my newly budding nipples. When she tried to pull it out, she panicked and stuck her sharp hook through the other side of my pink flesh, like sewing with a claw. The closest adult to hear my yelps was a neighbor, Mr. Huggins, a heavyset father with slicked-back hair and black horn-rimmed glasses. He lifted my T-shirt and gently jimmied the claw out of my too-soon-for-a-bra nipple. It probably hurt, a lot; I still have a scar. But all I remember from that uncomfortable moment was mortification.

"My God, what should we do? What do you want to do?" My friends gathered around me with concern, fearful with knitted brows and narrowed eyes. Our entire tone, our "who gives a damn, take nothing seriously" stance had been badly shaken. Their black-gloved hands covered my shoulders and hands. This love, not my predicament, made me feel like crying. They surrounded me like a leather-and-hair cocoon to protect me from another strike from the invisible force that attacked me.

"Let's go back to the apartment; I'll call my mom in the morning and take the Alco bus to Madison like I had planned. I'll need some help, though. Sorry." Update: I was a burden.

Though no one said so, we were annoyed by this inconvenience, this thing thrust into our freewheelin' lives, this Situation, this menace messing with our collective joie de vivre. With a girlfriend on each arm, I was escorted back to their apartment dragging my lame foot through the freshly fallen snow. My black lace-up boots looked like special shoes made for people with problems.

Their apartment was on the third floor in a brick house cut up into six units on Roscoe Street. I limped up the stairs with what felt like an anvil dangling from my hip; when not working, legs are surprisingly heavy. Inside the windows were steamed up. Christmas tree lights twinkled across every wall year-round in single-color strands, mostly blue. The floors were littered with piles of record albums. Fifties moderne sofas, lamps, and kidney-shaped tables from thrift stores furnished the bohemian palace.

"Fill the bong, fetch me a beer," I commanded from the couch. My clumpy brown-and-blond hair fell into my face; mascara and eyeliner ran down my cheeks in black streaks. The snow's fault. Suddenly I was Bette Davis after a stroke, which maybe I'd just had. Sedentary on the couch, I could momentarily ignore the fact that I couldn't really walk. I hoped my friends would, too. I needed to numb the rest of me. Inside I was losing the feeling in my feelings; I was flattening out. I was thinking in mono rather than stereo.

"Are you sure you don't wanna call your mom or go to an emergency room?" I was so sure. I was in no mood to switch gears and freak out about my sudden freak accident. I wasn't ready to go home and deal with it. Wherever I was going next would not be a place offering bong hits and beer. I knew somehow that I was headed for pills dispensed in tiny white Dixie Cups that were brought in on stainless-steel trays. And bedpans. A deep sense of regret came over me, an "I wish this hadn't happened" sadness. My Situation was making me far more serious than I cared to be. Ever.

"What do you want to hear?" Co asked from the floor where she was sitting among the albums. This was, perhaps, the only way she could be engaged in this bummer. "What do you want to hear?" was how we dealt with heartbreak, confusion, disappointment, celebration, and everyday life. Maybe she hoped that music could make sense of that night and hopefully cushion our discomfort.

Co had always been the most innocent of our gang. She was a Madison townie like me, but she came from the good side of town. Her background involved university professors, theater, ribbony pigtails, and all-American boyfriends. But that was years ago. Most people would never guess this of urban Co with her frosted lipstick, paisley shirts, and half-slips. Had the circumstances been reversed, I don't know how I'd have dealt with Co incapacitated on the couch.

I sucked in a hit off the purple bong. "Johnny Cash or Hank Williams," I choked out through a strangulated chest, trying to hold the smoke and speak at the same time. Surely Johnny and Hank had had their share of confusing evenings. I had to light and smoke my cigarettes with my right hand and it felt all wrong. We all got sleepy trashed—what else was there to do really?

Hank Williams was so lonesome he could cry, and so was I. Hank Senior momentarily located the access to my emotions. "I'm gonna crash," I whispered, rolling over on the couch, my nose to a cushion. I didn't want anyone to see me cry, so I faked sleep, squeezing my wet eyes tight with my lips clenched and my shoulders shaking. The lump in my throat felt like an obstruction. I knew I was fucked. My girlfriends tiptoed to their bedrooms, I assumed with relief. Crazy vibrating electrical currents pulsed through my body and I thought I'd never sleep. But I did.

In the morning I woke up fuzzy-headed, still in my party dress, still on the couch. Damn. Nothing changed overnight. From the top of my head to the tips of my toes on the left side, I was paralyzed. The other side was hungover. I fumbled for the phone on the coffee table and dialed my mom's phone number in Madison. Catching a whiff of old beer and a full ashtray, I thought about chocolate milk with great longing.

"Hi, Mom."

"Well, hello there. When are you coming in?" She sounded excited that I was finally coming home. Not that my Cape Cod adventure bothered her in the least; I was nurtured with wanderlust. Whenever my family didn't know what to do with ourselves, we tended to take a trip with the hopes that the answer or solution would become clear.

"Well, there's a problem. I can't seem to move my left side; I'm all numb and nothing works."

"What do you mean, nothing works?"

I wanted to cry or disappear, but I caught the sob in my throat. I felt sorry for my mom. If I were a mother receiving this call from my daughter, it would kill me. I covered up with practicality. "I'm gonna need to see someone right away (in our family "seeing someone" always meant "a doctor"). Call the clinic. Can you pick me up? The first bus comes in at ten. Phyll's coming with to help me."

"My God, you need help?" I never need help.

"Ya, I'm, like, crippled."

To catch our bus we needed to hop the el to O'Hare. Phyll assisted me, carrying my bags with her arm firmly around my waist. She wore a somber brown skirt, cowboy boots, and a fierce "don't fuck with us" look on her face. We looked like female Midnight Cowboys. Helping me maneuver my one-sided existence onto the bus, she settled us into our seats and rifled through my purse for gum because I asked for it. She was Florence Nightingale to my Baby Jane Hudson. I was crippled like Joan Crawford's character Blanche, but I looked and sounded more like Bette Davis.

"Thanks, Phyll. Are you sure you don't mind?"

"Don't be ridiculous," she cut me off, "you're my friend. This is what friends do." I honestly don't know if I could've done this for a friend.

In ninety minutes we descended from the bus in front of the Memorial Union on the University of Wisconsin campus. It was the sight of countless beer-soaked pseudo-intellectual conversations and skipped classes in my past. That past felt very distant that morning as I watched my mom's heart sink to the sidewalk. I had forgotten how small my mom is, five foot one, ninety pounds, frosted textured hair that never behaved. We're neither close nor not close, but I was relieved to see her.

"Dr. Dominski's waiting for you," she said. Dr. Dominski is a neurologist. On the way to Dean Clinic, my mom dropped Phyll off at our friends Dan and Anita's house.

Alone together, my mom and I had little to say. I recapped the night before nervously tugging on a Marlboro. My mother took hard, raggedy pulls on her Tareyton 100. She and my dad had been divorced for two years. My dad was remarried to his former receptionist. My mom had recently entered the workforce. I thought she looked old for forty-five, but I didn't know how forty-five looked on women.

I had seen Dr. Dominski a year earlier on the day I woke up completely blind in my left eye. Where there was once a seeing eye, there was a black hole. I thought I was hungover or having my first migraine. But no, half-blind. Tests proved inconclusive, though a few choice terms like "multiple sclerosis" and "brain tumor" were bandied about. I was given the steroid medication prednisone. In a couple months' time, the claustrophobic darkness of being partially blind resolved into a chocolate-milky haze over the lens of my left eye. Looking through the healed eye is like living inside a photographic negative. I rely on my right eye; it's something I don't like to think about. In fact, I'd completely forgotten about the whole thing until I found myself returning to Dr. Dominski's office with my entire left side wiped out. But not really.

Dr. Dominski called me "honey" and "dear", which I found comforting. She worked hard, poring over files, ordering tests, touching every inch of my left side, looking for a sensation, for a clue. I would guess her age as not yet forty; a wisp of gray peered out from her pulled-back dark hair, her plain face set with determination. After an EKG and a CAT scan, she performed a lumbar puncture. *This* is Spinal Tap, I thought, as she shoved a needle as thick as a rod between two vertebrae in my lower back while I was curled up in the fetal position. She tapped my spine like it was an old maple tree full of sap. The pressure from the rod was unspeakable; I wanted to puke. And as much as I thought I wasn't in my body at the time, I was. And my body had something very wrong with it.

"Honey," Dr. Dominski sighed heavily, "it looks like you have multiple sclerosis. Your CAT scan shows a large patch on the right side of your brain called a 'plaque.' Plaques are indicative of MS. I have many patients who do very well managing this disease. My own father has it. That's why I went into neurology . . . " I couldn't hear her, the buzzing in my ears drowned out her speech. Plaque? On my brain? Did it come from not flossing in some symbolic way? I thought of a T-shirt I once saw of a cartoon man holding a string that had been pulled through his ears; the caption read "Mental Floss."

I curled up in the backseat of my mom's dilapidated orange Chevette, still fetal. We went from Dean Clinic to St. Mary's Hospital on a gray, looks-like-snow day. I sobbed; it had finally hit me that my life had changed, irrevocably, for the worst.

"We're here," my mom quietly announced while letting go of the clutch. The Chevette jerked and died; she's never gotten that motion down. A nurse gripping a shiny silver wheelchair greeted me. We rode up an elevator and I was wheeled down a hallway into a room, then helped into a hospital gown and laid out on a bed where they prepared me for an around-the-clock IV of the steroid ACTH, the strongest potion they had. This stuff, according to Dr. Dominski, made prednisone look like child's play. ACTH, I gathered, was the Jägermeister of steroids. It was supposed to abate, if not reverse the damage. Stop the bleeding, so to speak.

Assessing symptoms and categorizing them are how diag-noses are made. Multiple sclerosis was a harsh toke at twenty-four. If I allowed it to sink in too deeply, it would destroy me. I pocketed a handful of pamphlets at the neurologist's office. Along with *Multiple Sclerosis* I grabbed *Cerebral Palsy* and *Epilepsy,* just in case I needed cheering up.

MS is a degenerative disease that affects the central nervous system. The damage to the brain and spinal cord occurs in many widely scattered areas. Contributing factors include stressful events, fatigue, fever, emotional upsets, heat, and in-jury. Symptoms may include: complete or partial paralysis, diffi-culty in walking, dragging either foot, loss of coordination, loss of or distorted sensation anywhere in the body, double or blurred vision or temporary blindness, slurred speech, inconti-nence.

M Y hospital stay was a series of surreal vignettes, a slide show for the morbid:

"Hi! How ARE you?" a cheerful nurse bubbled while plung-ing a needle into the top of my right hand.

"Okay, but I can't really move or feel anything on my left side."

"Well, THAT'S no fun!" she sang, not looking at me. The needle was attached to rubber tubing. The tubes led to a gal-lon-size Baggie filled with saline solution and a clear thick serum, the ACTH that floated on top like oil in a salad dress-ing. The Baggie hung on something that looked like a coat rack on wheels. The needle popped out of my hand.

"Uh-oh," she chirped, "you have disappearing veins." A plaque on my brain, disappearing veins, shame on me. After an-other unsuccessful poke on top of my now sore hand, she jammed it into a vein in my soft inner forearm. The fluid burned under my skin as it rhythmically drip-dropped into my arm.

In the bed to my right rested a heavy woman of maybe thirty with long dark hair. I said "hi" weakly and she stared at the wall in front of us and said nothing. She then picked up her little remote box and buzzed for a nurse.

A less perky nurse stepped in. "How can I help you?"

"I can't really move or feel anything on my left side," she said morosely, parroting my symptoms. As if she wanted them, as if I were contagious.

"I'll call a doctor," the nurse replied. A doctor entered with the nurse, and they pulled the curtain separating us. I heard a series of muffled questions that went unanswered. My roommate was then wheeled out of the room never to be seen again.

Before this catastrophe I had a dramatic flair for hypochondria. A headache was an aneurism, a hangover a bleeding ulcer; chronic bladder infections were, no doubt, cancer. But that was just the theater of boredom. As a child I found a mad comfort in being sick; my mom took extra good care of me, she brought me things, I got to lie around all day in my pajamas eating cinnamon toast and watching *Match Game*. I wondered if I had brought this all down on myself. Karmically. According to my newest pamphlet, given to me by my nurse, *The Miraculous World of Steroids*, large doses of steroids could cause dementia and extreme bloating. Just like menstruation, or as the middle school teacher called it, men-stroo-*a*-shun. Another thing I learned about in a pamphlet titled *You're Changing!*

A NERVOUS stream of friends dutifully filed in. Nobody knew how to act or what to say. "Cheer up, why the long faces?" I scolded with a jaunty pout. "I'm gonna be just fine, just you wait." I'd transformed into a mixture of Shirley Temple and Little Orphan Annie with Phyllis Diller hair.

During one visit my uneasy well-wishers and I watched *Jailhouse Rock* on the TV on the wall. I chattered useless Elvis trivia; "Russ Tamblyn—you know, Riff from *West Side Story*—

helped Elvis choreograph the big number . . . see him there in the chorus? The movies ruined him, you know." But no one was taking my bait. On that sunless Thanksgiving weekend we passed around a smuggled warm beer in silence.

The hospital was so quiet. It seemed like no one was there but an occasional orderly and me. I was on an old wing, depressing and yellowed with age. It smelled antiseptic and rotten, all worn-out from years of constant sickness. In my head, next to "shock," was a seething compartment labeled "complete intolerance for this disease"; I guess another term would be "denial." I found my predicament unacceptable. I was in survival mode, a mode devoid of deep thoughts. But that might've been going on for a while. It was hard to say what was steroid-induced, what was illness, or what was just me.

ONE evening my dad and his new wife dropped by the hospital for a visit. He had a new house and a new family, too. Neato. Before all this hospital business we'd been at odds. I don't think he liked who I'd become, didn't like my strong opinions, my assertiveness, the funny way I dressed. I didn't like the choices he'd made with his life; when he left my mother, he essentially left us. He felt no need to provide financial assistance once we turned eighteen and he rebuffed all of my appeals for monetary help throughout my young adulthood. My three younger siblings had much better relationships with him. I felt like little more than an irritating reminder of a past he desperately wanted to leave behind. I think I reminded him of my mom. After a couple of days of IVs, I was in no mood to receive him or his new wife. I hardly knew her. I wasn't invited to their wedding. My dad is a large handsome man, a Swedish Rob Reiner. As a younger man he looked like Glen Campbell. His wife was a younger, but less pretty, version of my mother; small boned, of Irish descent, bespectacled with textured reddish brown hair.

"Excuse me, I have to pee," I announced. Getting to the bathroom involved dropping myself out of bed on good faith, hoping to land on my good foot, and dragging my IV on wheels and my lame limb across the floor like Quasimodo. I probably did it intentionally so that he had to see me in all of my handicapped splendor. Limping my return from the bathroom, my dad flashed his salesman grin and announced, "There's nothing wrong with you; you're fine!" Okay then.

AFTER one week of hospitalization, my visitors waned and got on with their lives while I dictated answers to my mom, who frantically filled out forms for Social Security, Disability, Unemployment, and Handicapped benefits. I was uninsured. My bills promised to be hilarious. I couldn't fill out the forms; I'm left-handed.

"We have orders to take you up for a CAT scan." At 7:00 P.M. on a Monday, life in the dead quiet of St. Mary's got interesting. Upon reviewing an X-ray of my head, a bold, perhaps bored, radiologist became concerned that I was harboring a sizable brain tumor. I thought, Please, oh please, let it be a brain tumor! I would rather have something removable at great risk than an incurable degenerative autoimmune disease. Dr. Dominski couldn't be reached. *Dynasty* was on my TV on the wall, and I couldn't get over how spineless Krystle (Linda Evans) was.

After a flurry of excitement, the on-call neurologist visited my bedside. "That large white patch on your X-ray is something called an MS plaque, and not a brain tumor after all." Plaque again. My heart sank. I really wanted a brain tumor. "Oh, Blake," Krystle whispered on the TV in her usual wimpy, helpless manner before she tiptoed up the stairs to softly slam her bedroom door.

A FTER a week of IVs, tests, physical therapy, and a course in cane management, I was set to go. Go where? I needed ACTH shots twice a day for six months. I needed physical therapy indefinitely. Nothing in my body had changed since that night in Chicago, except for the disturbing bloating caused by the steroids. I would have to move back into the house I grew up in. The house I moved out of the day after graduating from high school.

N EITHER of my parents had two hundred grand to cover my hospital bills. I doubt either of them had two grand in savings. After their divorce, finances were in an awful mess. Being a middle-class white girl, I (foolishly) assumed that I would always be safe and cared for. I thought—no, knew—that food, clothing, and shelter—as well as transportation and a little money to shop—were a given. I recall being told as much. My parents, the people who told me such things, also used to reassure me as a little girl—anxious after a parental argument with raised voices—that they would never divorce. So why was I surprised to find myself sitting in the welfare and social services offices in Madison pleading my case?

"You're living in your mother's house and you're unable to work. Your living expenses cannot be too great," an immensely overweight red-faced gentleman decided while glancing at my paperwork.

"She has two dependent children and gets very little in child support; I need to help her out, and, um, get back on my feet," I offered while trying to sound clear and respectful. Everyone there looked poor or crazy or very sick. Like me.

"Does she have the resources to assist you?" he challenged, whistling air through his nostrils.

"I'm an adult, I would like to move out as soon as possible and get my own place."

"Are you interested in assisted living or a handicapped residency?" he then asked.

Jesus, no!

He continued, "It says here you were living and working at a Martha's Vine-yard. Is that a place? And you were a waitress; you may be eligible to work in one of the hospital cafeterias where we have Employ the Handicapped programs. Wait a minute, this might be the state of Massachusetts's responsibility. How long did you work there? Is there proof that you have multiple . . . multiple skerlosis? That will have to be confirmed by one of our medical assistance doctors."

I focused on the large sweat stains under the armpits of his short-sleeved permanent press workshirt while dying a little inside.

"I'm not trying to rob you or the government or anything," I said, trying to assert myself, "I just need help figuring out how to take care of these hospital bills." My face was twisted in a wince of disbelief and embarrassed pain.

"Were you sent to the hospital by a referring physician in our directory? How long do you intend to need physical therapy? I'll need these forms signed and verified that your medication is necessary."

Another medication was necessary, something to help me mentally and emotionally, but counseling was never suggested or encouraged. After all, it cost money. I sat there wondering what I used to be like; I couldn't figure out how I got there.

Faced with an unacceptable situation (disease), I purchased an Exercycle with my first welfare check and rode the bike to nowhere until my gait smoothed out to almost normal. In June, following twice-a-day injections of ACTH for six months, Dr. Dominski announced my disease was officially "in remission." Remission is like purgatory, somewhere between heaven and hell, a place I can uncomfortably wait until my disease decides to reclaim my body. But I can't let myself wallow there; it works far better to act like the whole thing never happened.

✸

WHEN I moved to Minneapolis my condition was unde-
tectable to the untrained eye, yet I was still considered
handicapped, therefore eligible for disability benefits and Social
Security checks. The problem was the social services building
in Minneapolis made Madison's social services office look like
an enchanted kingdom. The offices in Minneapolis are on the
corner of Franklin and Chicago and the old brick building is
teeming with loitering jobless and homeless people with hard
faces, with African-American teenage mothers, with Native
Americans ignored by a country rightfully theirs, with margin-
alized Americans who have become stereotypes. I felt guilty
only to be recovering from a bad patch of debilitating health.

WHEN I was home recovering from MS, my symptoms
improved so gradually it was impossible to track if or
when recovery occurred. The day-to-day difference was unremarkable. When the lack of society became unbearable after
two months of voluntary exile, I set about the difficult task of
acting comfortable and defiant about my yucky state of handicap. Apart from Dan and Anita, who offered refuge on a regular basis when life at Mom's got too depressing, and of course
Phyll, who visited on weekends, I hadn't seen anyone. I wanted
to see a band. I needed to resume my education. Barely able to
manage my mom's stick shift with my gimpy left foot, I went to
O'Kayz Corral sporting a fifties housewife dress and a decora-
tive cane. "If I'm dealing with it, they can," I said to myself re-
peatedly in hopes that it might sink in. This was coming from
the person who was unable to make eye contact with a dis-
abled person. But now I did it every day—in the mirror.

Downtown on a frigid night, hobbling with my cane, pretending that everything was a-okay, became part of my life-
back-to-normal regimen. I died a little inside with each benign
stare or piteous glance, with each avoided eye contact. "Oh, hi,

I'm great," I'd lie while my inner dialogue would complete my greeting with, "though you have no idea how frightening and embarrassing it is to be in my skin."

The Comic Strip bar was separated from O'Kayz Corral by a wall—these were two throwback bars from the fifties with thematic motifs on an old forgotten block near Madison's deteriorating downtown. O'Kayz had a cowboy and Old West decor, while the Comic Strip looked like a white trash living room, complete with bean bag ashtrays and a bar in the middle of it. There was nothing funny about the Comic Strip; it was a bar that cashed monthly public assistance checks—which I was receiving—for its regulars who spent every penny in the bar. In between band sets at O'Kayz, the Comic Strip filled with showgoers out for a break from the sweaty smoky air inside O'Kayz. The well-oiled regulars laughed at our bizarre hairstyles and get-ups. On a mucus-freezing January night, I found myself sitting in the Comic Strip for an intermission, talking to an old friend named Steve, who was close with an old boyfriend of mine. Steve was a shy, kind, quiet man with a white Afro and black glasses. He's a great musician. He would be considered officially socially nervous, and even though I was a cane-wielding housewife from hell, Steve looked me in the eye. He had visited me in the hospital. "How are you?" he asked without his usual embarrassed stutter. "How do you spend your days?" he wondered. I admitted that I needed to keep busy to preserve my sanity. "Hey, would you like one of my guitars?" he asked. I loved it that he linked "something to do" with fiddling on a guitar. A couple of days later, Steve brought me his first electric guitar, a 1974 Gibson SG (a really good guitar). I considered this a Sign.

5: When I Was Twenty-five, It Was a Very Good Year

ALMOST two months into my Minneapolis residency, my twenty-fifth birthday is celebrated in the CC Club, another bar in our neighborhood. The CC is known as the house of rock stars. At any given hour you will be drinking in the same room with members of the Replacements, Soul Asylum, Man Sized Action, Rifle Sport, or the hundreds of us forming bands at the moment. I am overdressed in a dramatic, tight navy blue Ava Gardner cocktail dress looking around miserably, wondering why I feel so empty and unaccomplished.

By twenty-five you're supposed to be well on your way to where you're going. Twenty-five is the approximate age when a pop star peaks. A twenty-five-year-old rock 'n' roller could easily already be washed up. What am I thinking? I have my hopes hung on eclectic independent record labels that don't overly concern themselves with shallow, limiting views of artists (not too much anyway). "Creating and performing" needs to happen to justify my rock 'n' roll lifestyle. I'd better get this band project off the ground or else I'm going to wind up being a total rock hag. I could spend the rest of my life as a spectator. This is another level of purgatory, the endless waiting for something to happen. Co and I can almost stand up and play our instruments.

BACK in Wisconsin, my mom has sold the house I grew up in and purchased some new real estate, something she insists on calling a "farmette." Farmette? What the hell is that? Teeny-tiny farm? "Oh, it's just darling," she insists. Evidently a farmette is a farmhouse with an abandoned nonfunctioning barn on the property. The farmette is located forty miles outside of Madison in the middle of nowhere in a town called Rio, pronounced "Rye-o." I have no idea what she's thinking leaving Madison and moving into a farmette. In spite of messy finances, my mother only shops at high-end department stores and boutiques—not Fleet Farm. Does Rye-o even have a dry cleaner?

Sometimes my mom comes up with strange ideas that I think she thinks will improve the quality of her life, which is a fine thing to do; I just think she tends to focus on exterior solutions. One summer when I was in middle school she rented a plot on a farm outside of town not too far from our neighborhood. On summer evenings we had to go out there after dinner and pull weeds in the endless rows of easy-to-grow green beans that we let grow too big and tough. That was a seventies phase when granola, ecology, and earth shoes were all the rage; getting back to the soil was part of that fad. My mom actually canned pickles out of our misshapen cucumbers; those same pickles sat on dusty shelves in our basement until she moved to her farmette. I'm not sure what she got out of it. And I don't know what she thinks she's going to get out of moving to Rio.

The farmette might have something to do with her new boyfriend, who has moved from Honolulu to Rio to save her from the Trauma of Divorce. This man's name is Jack and he claims he was an intelligence agent in Vietnam. Jack grew up with my parents in the tiny town of Canton, Illinois, home of the state penitentiary. Mom ran into Jack when they were both in Canton dining in Canton's only restaurant (that wasn't attached to a bowling alley) while visiting aging relatives. They spoke, exchanged addresses, wrote letters, she visited him in Honolulu, and then he moved to Wisconsin. Why didn't she move to Honolulu so we could get some sun over the holidays? And this is the part that freaks me out: apparently Mom and Jack "went together" in eighth grade. Whatever. I'm not exactly up for following my parents' postdivorce stabs at love lives. But regardless of what I think, Mom and Jack now occupy a farmette.

Which means that Rio is where I'll be spending Christmas because I'm not quite old enough to have legitimate reasons for why I can't come home for Christmas. Walking through the farmette's threshold the first time, my eyes are assaulted by tacky linoleum, fake wood paneling, and avocado shag carpeting. This place is the product of several 4-H projects gone very wrong. According to my mom, Jack looks like Jimmy Stewart. All I see is Senator Bob Dole, only he doesn't clutch pencils with his gimpy hand, he clutches cocktail stir sticks to keep track of his highball intake. And his hand isn't gimpy, but he could play a competitive game of pickup sticks with the pile of straws he's fisting upon our first meeting in a dive country bar where he plays "American Woman" by the Guess Who on the jukebox. I assume this is part of some sort of Nam flashback.

On Christmas Eve, my brother, Chris, back from boarding school, my sister Hillary, home from her first semester of college in Eau Claire, Wisconsin, and I stand silently in the eerie farmette kitchen. My other sister Megan has the good sense to make other plans with her boyfriend's family; she still lives in Madison and has clearly been exposed to the farmette on more than one occasion. There is no Christmas tree waiting for us, so my baby brother Chris and I trudge out to a cut-yer-own tree farm located on the county road between Rio and Madison. We drag the tree through the snow without exchanging words. I think going away to boarding school on a hockey scholarship, far away from our parents and the fallout from their marriage, is the best thing that could've happened to him. He was traumatized and homesick when he first went, but now he seems happy and relieved. Especially with our new "home" and "new daddy." I'm sure Chris would rather die than live in the farmette and go to Rio High. I know I would.

Midnight on Christmas Eve, Chris and I watch *It's a Won-*

derful Life together because it's the only thing that's on. When the real Jimmy Stewart slip-slides around Bedford Falls stammering, "Zuzu's petals!" I wallow in a puddle of tears on my mom's orange corduroy sectional couch. "You know, Laur," Chris says, "that's what you should call your band." Of course: Zuzu's Petals. The symbol that indicated to George Bailey that he was back in his flawed life. Just like the idea of the band is the thing that has put me back in my life after that hellish year of my untimely crippling.

R EADER, I have a boyfriend; his name is Rog. He's over six feet tall with floppy brown hair and big brown eyes. He frequents the café and shyly flirts with me while wearing plaid Bermuda shorts and long sideburns. As I get to know him I learn that he's kind, mentally healthy, hilarious, and well parented. His parents patiently tolerated his high school experimental persona with love and patience and he was involved in a youth church group (which I'm learning, living in Minnesota, is an expected Lutheran activity). Rog is a college student with a rock band in his basement called Full Metal Hangover. Rog is nineteen to my twenty-five. I'm experienced and ambitious; I've lost the steroid-added girth and my hair has grown out. For him, I'm a dangerous lady, a walk on the wild side because I hang out with people in bands and know the perceived "cool people." For me, he's safe. We get along famously, though his Hawaiian shirts and immature friends who still make erect penises in front of their shorts out of garnishes embarrass me. Rog is chronically nervous and he talks fast like a little boy who needs to pee really badly.

Since our fling kicked off in the summertime (we officially hooked up at an outdoor keg party), Rog and I vacation at the Wisconsin Dells. The Dells, as we Wisconsinites call it, is a dramatic swatch of land sculpted by glaciers. A river runs through them, and they are green, cliffy, craggy, and lakey all at the same time. Perched upon this unlikely parcel of real estate is Wisconsin's idea of a good time: Xanadu, foam house of the future; Fort Dells, a reenacted Old West town; a wax museum, minigolf, water parks, themes galore—everything from the Bible to science fiction—all situated near blocks upon blocks of taverns with cold beer on tap.

Rog and I frolic through the Dells dressed like tacky tourists circa 1963 in golf hats, big old shorts, and bowling shirts while documenting our "aren't we fun and ironic" hijinks on film. Camping at nearby Devil's Lake, the scene of countless field trips in my youth, we share a tent and zip our sleeping bags together. We tend to drink so much beer that we don't make out all that often. I'm no camper, but Rog was an Eagle Scout and handles all of the naturey stuff. I provide the wheels. During one nightly commute from the Dells back to our campsite, I pull the Nova over to vomit (too much beer), and then I hop back in and continue driving. When in Wisconsin . . .

Two things I do at the Dells in semiseriousness, though I pretend it's all a big joke: 1) I have my picture taken for a mock cover of *Rolling Stone* magazine wearing a leather jacket and mirror sunglasses; and 2), I record myself singing Joan Jett's "I Love Rock 'n' Roll" in a make-your-own-record tourist-trap recording studio. An "engineer" records me singing along into a mike hooked up to a karaoke machine while wearing headphones, a simulated rock star. Only this isn't some hokey wish-fulfillment fantasy. This is me seeing what it's going to be like. I sound nothing like Joan Jett.

I spend many nights throughout the summer at Rog's house, a two-story rental that he shares with a gang of young dudes. They're all still young enough to be going crazy with their first years of freedom. And though I've been through it already, I'm more than happy to sit through it again; these guys are funny, they play Roger Miller records and collect metal conquistador wall hangings and colorful plastic-tiled seventies lamps that hang from the ceiling. One night there's a doozy of a storm with hail, thunder, lightning, torrential downpour, tornado sirens. When I return to my apartment the next day, I am greeted with bright rays of sun streaming through a skylight I didn't have the day before. The roof and ceiling of my apartment building collapsed into my apartment under the weight of last night's rain. Everything I own is destroyed under rain-soaked fallen plaster, wood, and roofing. The stench of rotten wood is gag inducing. I've never heard of renter's insurance and my landlord is protected under an act of God clause. Ho ho ho. I don't feel one way or another about this turn of events for some reason. It's nothing compared to being told you have an incurable autoimmune disease.

Most people are good. When something bad happens, they gather up their resources and lend a helping hand. I'm given bags of clothing and linens, and my workmates Rob and Sweetpea offer me their sun porch for the remainder of the summer. I feel oddly liberated by losing it all, but don't dare tell anyone that. Fortunately my guitar is salvageable—my friends take it to Benedict's guitar shop and it is completely repaired and refurbished by a thoughtful man who will one day be my boyfriend. I lose all of my diaries—in essence, my past—and I take this as a good sign, the mark that I'm completely reinvented from sick girl to rock girl. The MS thing is always on the tip of my consciousness, but I've mastered the art of shooing it away, since it's such a drag to think and worry about.

At summer's end Phyll, Co, and a woman we don't know rent the house Rog and the boys occupied near the Mississippi River. Rog moves closer to campus. Our new house has an upstairs, a downstairs, and a basement. It's a real house with a yard. What this means is a practice space for Zuzu's Petals.

WHICH one is Laurie Lindeen?" a woman says to me as she enters our back door to attend our September Gurls birthday party.

"She's in the living room. Why?" I say.

"Oh, I know someone in Madison who hates her."

"Why?" This is a fine how do you do, though I don't need to ask. Clearly a friend of someone who went out with the guy I loved in college. He screwed a lot of girls, and instead of deciding he was no good for me, I tended to flash seething looks at the other women. I like to think I'm past that behavior; I have a young hottie and Priorities.

Phyll, Co, and I love the song "September Gurls" by Alex Chilton, which is why we are throwing a September Gurls birthday bash in our new house; there are six September-born girls in our constellation, including myself. Not that we need an excuse, reason, or theme to throw a party. I'm turning a very agitated, impatient twenty-six. I want to be on the stage already. This is a very wild, well-attended party that features a twelve-foot bong running up the basement staircase, compliments of our new roommate's boyfriend, who seems to also be living with us. Our new roommate is an artist of sorts, and our new home is filled with her pottery shaped like bleeding vaginas and mutilated breasts. At some point I'm upstairs making out with my friend Gary while Rog is passed put on my bed in a Hawaiian shirt. As Ted Nugent would say (before I knew he was such an avid hunter), "It's a free-for-all." As Frank Sinatra and Bing Crosby would agree, "What a swell party it was." And why aren't any women singing these songs? I intend to change all that.

Co and I have fashioned our basement into a rehearsal space. My Sears amp from Goodwill sounds like it's been submerged in a swamp, but at least I can finally hear what I sound like. I've bought microphones that we duct tape to the ceiling by their cords like a couple of long, skinny art nouveau lamps. My greatest investment to date is in a guitar tuner, a little battery-operated rectangle box with a finicky pin that

swings wildly from side to side until your string is tuned properly; when it's finally in tune, the pin hovers nervously in the
center of an arc that lets you know that you should not be entirely secure about the in-tune status of your guitar. Standing
side by side in our damp, cat-pissy cellar, tingling and making
noises, Co and I work on the standing-up-and-singing part of
the equation. We chase our swinging microphones around or
stand dead still so as not to jar them. Phyll works constantly
and is in trouble with her student loans and has become tight
with the vaginal potter, which we find slightly off-putting. She
rarely joins us, and when she does, she complains about our
lack of patience and acts all flustered.

We still need a drummer, so we talk about that need loudly
at the café because on the West Bank our band is no secret.
"Hey, I used to drum in my high school marching band,"
shrugs Vicki, our counter jockey coworker. Vicki is a shy, quiet,
broad-smiled, big-boned farm girl from southwest Minnesota.
Impressed with her credentials, we invite her to our basement
lair. Vicki is probably four or five years younger than Co and I;
she has a pierced nose and reeks of patchouli oil, which I politely overlook (but abhor, coming as I do from the patchouli
capital of the world). Vicki is a slacker at the café, getting by
doing as little work as possible, which to me appears to take
more effort than seeing what needs to be done and doing it. Co
and I tend to be bossy workaholics. We all call one another
"Buddy" because that's what the Somali men must've been
taught to say in greeting by their English as a Second Language
teacher. "Hello, buddy," they say to Vicki and me. "Hello,
pretty lady buddy," they say to Co. They never, ever look us in
the eye. We enjoy imitating these men at the 400 Bar after
work, and Co and I evolve into "Betty" while Vicki remains
"Buddy." "Hello, Buddy, hello pretty lady Betty, do you want
to jam?" I love having a reason to leave the bar. Vicki gathers
bits and pieces of a discarded drum kit from Full Metal Hangover.

Trying to make songs is a baffling prospect; there is no right answer. Trying to communicate in a language you do not know, to others who do not know the language either, is comical at best. We think it might help to learn easy-seeming preexisting songs first; Kiss's "Rock and Roll All Night" and any other three-chord rockers we can think of. When we attempt Jefferson Airplane's "White Rabbit" because it only has two chords, we change the words, "Go ask Alice . . . she's the Brady Bunch's maid." And we crack ourselves up, fully aware of our deep level of dorkiness. Or we say, "It goes like this; *boom-chick-boom-boom-chick*," punctuated with a frantic chord change and inserted lyrics. And we laugh our asses off again. This goes on all winter and spring.

Sometimes it seems like the more you do, the more you're capable of doing; during the winter I enroll at the University of Minnesota to finish my degree in the wide-open field of English lit. It's a logical decision if I want to hang out with my young boyfriend. I'd like to finish something for once. Not only that, I have to be ever mindful of my health insurance situation. I'd like to hop off Medical Assistance and onto full-time student coverage, which will make the university hospitals and clinics easily accessible should I get into any trouble healthwise. Besides, college is a great thing to do while waiting to become a presentable musician; band and college work well together. The University of Minnesota pales in comparison to the University of Wisconsin; it lacks the old brick-and-ivy opulence, something I find essential in feeling "university." Like the city, the campus is spread out all over both sides of the Mississippi, and it even spills into St. Paul. Rog is a janitor at Coffman Union. I'm older than most of the students and I'm stuck taking all of the courses I avoided back in Madison, things like geology and logic.

The owner of the café, a Grizzly Adams lookalike, has decided that I should add cooking a full-course Indian dinner to my breakfast and lunch duties, where I have to make soups and chili from scratch between breakfast orders, so I quit.

Mark is long gone because the Jayhawks have begun touring, and Co is considering bartending over at the 400 because we have some psycho coworkers who storm out in the middle of their shifts and throw knives around in threatening passive-aggressive ways, and because our grizzled boss hasn't a clue about restaurant management and he accuses us of stealing cash from the till on a daily basis. Instead of the chaos of a poorly run restaurant, I take a student job at the Wilson Library in the circulation department. I love libraries and the smell of old books, but this might be the most boring, dead-end, depressing job I've ever had. The library is filled with lost dreams civil servants that sigh and moan all day, gray with frustration. My fellow student employees commiserate and gossip while shelving books or filing cards into a massive color-coded card catalogue. On occasion, a pervert flashes one of us in the stacks, but that's not exciting, it's pathetic; it's such a strange expression of anger.

Zuzu's Petals practices several times a week in our basement. Phyll never joins us, but slowly, slowly we're making progress.

THE summer of '88 is so damn hot that I buy a child's blow-up pool at pre-cool Target so as not to perish. I lay in my little plastic pool in our backyard after work, sometimes fully dressed, lacking the patience and energy to go inside to change into swimwear. Steam rises off my body, dead bugs and grass clippings float on the surface. The gutters in front of our house on Forty-second Avenue are littered with dead sparrows. This I take to be a bad omen. Heat can exacerbate MS and even before MS I hated the feeling of being inescapably hot, such a hopeless, claustrophobic type of discomfort. Whenever we open our back door in the late afternoon to head outside, it feels like we just opened an oven door; heat blasts in our faces in a hot *swoosh*. I'm melting; the hot air feels like it could singe my eyelashes and hair.

I work, sit in the pool, hang out with Rog, and make music—a full life for an extra-hot summer. Phyll and our other roommate, who I've not bothered to get to know after taking in her artwork, have formed a friendship based on occasionally dropping acid and entertaining guys with missing front teeth. These upstanding fellows steal pot and money from our house. Almost a year into my lease, Rog decides that the time has come to tell me that a toddler accidentally strangled himself in the blinds in my room and that he originally thought it was best not to tell me. He was right. There's nothing in the world more angry and unreasonable than a baby ghost and I'm afraid of ghosts; to avoid this scene, I stay at Rog's as much as possible. To avoid the sad state of affairs within our household, Co bartends late into the night. Co, Vicki, and I meet at the 400 four afternoons a week before practice; "Bye-bye!" we say to our fellow regulars, relishing the fact that we have a purpose.

I'm out of here. I can't take it anymore. The drought of my soul, like the drought this summer, is unbearable.

This is the gist of a note left on our Formica dining-room table by Phyll. One stifling August afternoon, after a day of doldrums in the library, I return to a house devoid of all of Phyll's belongings. She had a lot of stuff and every bit is cleared out. An oil stain on the driveway left by her rusty rust-colored Camaro is all that's left. We never saw any signs of the possibility of this happening. Sure, we weren't getting along, but I didn't take that too seriously. We—Co, Phyll, and I—often go through phases of estrangement. It's never lasted more than a year. Our little cowgirl packed her duds and left Dodge, left us eating her dust, left me feeling responsible for her heartache.

Phyll, the fiery loyal friend who initiated our migration, the woman who commuted to Madison when I was sick and learned how to administer my ACTH shots so I could take weekend trips, felt so hopeless and sad that she had to flee. She was clearly having a tough time with finances and student loans and anger (like all of us), and I wasn't there for her. I bought her a guitar, but she never joined in, didn't attack the music with the same vigor that Co and I did. Maybe I should've spent more time with her and tried harder to help with her problems. I could've been more encouraging and made her feel like a part of the band. I might've asked what I could do to help. The problem is, there's a hard husk around me after being so sick and becoming well. I can barely take care of myself.

"Phyll's gone," I say to Co when she tromps through the back door after work.

"What do you mean 'gone'?" she says with some annoyance. "Gone where?"

"I mean gone, as in packed her stuff, left a melodramatic note, and took off with no forwarding address."

Co stands there with a surprised, confused twist to one side of her mouth. I hand her the note. This is weird, tragic, and funny all at the same time.

I stand encased in a crust that prevents me from absorbing the sadness of this situation. Co does the appropriate thing and gets teary. She's sad and worried about Phyll and feeling bad that we hadn't been getting along with her. I'm feeling guilty and pissed off so I wear a hard face—after my parents' divorce followed by being ill, I've lost the key to properly processing grief and loss. I told Phyll on countless occasions to pay attention to her own troubles instead of catering to me; her selflessness was causing her to lose track of her own financial, professional, and personal crises. It seems to me that in caring for me she was avoiding her own issues. And now this whole thing feels like my fault.

In an effort to shake the shock of this moment, ever-practical Co says, "What about her bills?"

Relieved at the invitation to move on from my inability to process this whole thing, I say, "She says on the back of the note that she'll send money, but we shouldn't try to track her down."

"Okay. Whatever."

"Ya. I guess so. I have a new song; wanna practice?"

We need to practice because in a few weeks we have our first gig.

N EEDING to move out of the haunted house that Phyll abandoned because the rent is now unmanageable, I rent a floor of a house chopped into apartments close to campus with an acquaintance from Madison, a younger woman who uses political activism as her stage. She's into El Salvador; I'm into Elvis. Because our worlds rarely intersect and our apartment is little more than a crash pad, we get along well. Co rents an apartment by herself on the edge of downtown near Loring Park. We're so used to packing up and moving on a regular basis that it's no big deal. Like Phyll, we're always ready to leave if need be.

Co, her younger sister Molly, and I drive to Madison for a weekend road trip. Co and Molly want to visit family; I plan to stay downtown with Dan and Anita, our first married friends to own a house. If I feel like it, I'll let my family know that I'm in town. The Nova, being born in 1969, lacks air-conditioning. And because it's still the summer of the dead bird, it's suffocatingly hot. It's open-windows-melted-tar-and-burnt-tire-smell-blasting-in-off-the-highway hot. Parched hills and farmland, all-bleached-yellow-by-the-sun hot. Not the lush, green hills one normally encounters on this pleasant stretch down 94 East.

Just past Wisconsin Dells, at the Lyndon Station exit, traffic is at a standstill. I inch my way around on the shoulder trying to figure out the cause of the traffic jam. Up ahead we see yellow and orange flames. Trees ablaze. Burnt and burning grass. Smoky black wind. Flames blowing and licking across the highway. And it's hotter than the earlier hot. It's panic hot. We instinctively roll up our windows, and I take the Lyndon Station exit. We've traveled 210 of the 253 miles needed to reach our destination. At the nearest gas station we learn that traffic is being sent back the way it came until the forest fire is contained. No way in hell am I turning back, we're almost there.

There's a side road that runs adjacent to 94 East that must eventually feed back onto the highway. Turning back never occurs to me. I speed down the side road trying to get this over with as quickly as possible. To the left of us, a forest is burning down. The closest tree to the road catches the flame and it instantly spreads across the ground up to the pavement. Red and yellow fire blows across the road while I drive over it. We can't dodge it; we're on it. No one is speaking; the incinerator outside is loud with the white thunderous noise of burning wood. Burnt trees crash to the ground like ashes off a flicked cigarette. Burning trees are close enough to fall on us. It occurs to me that I'm driving a gas tank over an open flame. There is no air to breathe. Even the steering wheel feels hot.

In a minute's time we are past the wildfire and our faces are smudged with cinders and sweat and the dashboard is caked with sooty dust. "Holy shit," we all whisper. More silence. Then we laugh hard with grateful relief, like we just pulled off a jailbreak. We are strong, we are invincible, we are morons.

6: My Musical Résumé, or I Sang Alto in the Choir and Other Confessions

How does a music lover transform into an actual music maker? What are my qualifications? I can earmark a series of revelatory moments in my life that explain my passion and that will aid in Zuzu's Petals' progress. God, I hope so:

This is a snapshot, an old faded Kodak color print that I've carried around from apartment to apartment. It's a picture of me in kindergarten in Peoria, Illinois, sitting on my bed with the white wrought-iron headboard. In it I'm wearing a flowered quilted robe that matches my bedspread. My hair is fashioned into a pixie just like the English supermodel Twiggy's. I'm clutching my favorite record, *More of the Monkees*. I listened to that album incessantly, thinking that Davy Jones might "forget that girl" and find the kindergarten siren of his dreams. I look like a five-year-old mod with dark circles under her eyes.

In first grade we moved away from extended family in central Illinois to Madison, Wisconsin. The Larson twins were my first Madison friends. They were dominatrixes in cat-eye glasses; I gave in to their orders without hesitation because there were two of them, and being the oldest in my family I had never been bossed around. At first their demands were wholesome, gymnastics and figure skating that I joined with them; they were gifted natural athletes and I always made them look good. Things evolved as their tastes matured; I was forced

to steal my mom's cigarettes and make prank phone calls for
their smoking and listening pleasure. The Larson twins had a
barely speaking older brother two years our senior who had an
electric guitar and amp in his bedroom. The summer before
middle school, their brother joined a band called Lucifer, and
they played this incredibly crotch-tingling song that ended with
the words "wham, bam, thank you, ma'am." I was moved beyond words. (I won't trace that song to its origins until I purchase Bowie's *The Rise and Fall of Ziggy Stardust* my freshman
year of college.)

WHEN I was in fourth grade my parents hired a babysitter to take me to a David Cassidy concert. Once my
eyes and imagination feasted on the Partridge Family on Friday
nights, David replaced my Davy Jones, Bobby Sherman, and
Donny Osmond posters on my closet door quickly and completely. When I got to his rescheduled concert (he canceled for
emergency gall bladder surgery, and I had to wait half a year),
ten thousand other girls knew all of the words to his songs,
too. And even more threatening, some of the girls were
teenagers with breasts. David didn't belong to me at all. I felt
betrayed. Bitter. All of that energy invested into nothing. I
knew it wasn't going to be a private concert in my logical
mind, but I guess I thought I'd meet him and he'd somehow
know me. That's the deal with pop stars; you're expected to
share them with the masses. I hated the idea.

THOUGH my forays into popular music were sometimes
disappointing and confusing, there was one thing I could
always count on—musicals. I loved them. Everything by
Rodgers and Hammerstein (except *South Pacific*), Rodgers and
Hart, all Disney cartoon film music (though that went down-
hill after *Robin Hood*), everything from *The Wizard of Oz* to

The Wiz, anything starring Bing Crosby, Frank Sinatra, Elvis, Julie Andrews, anything involving Leonard Bernstein or Irving Berlin, everything choreographed by Busby Berkeley, Fred Astaire, or Gene Kelly. But in a category all its own is Meredith Willson's *The Music Man*.

The Music Man revolves around a scam, a premise that the lead character Professor Harold Hill—a con artist—calls the Think System. The Think System is today's equivalent of creative visualization. "Hear the music here," says Professor Hill (brilliantly portrayed by Robert Preston) while pointing to his ear. "Think the music here," he advises while tapping his forehead. "And the music comes out here," he says and holds up a trombone and breaks into "Seventy-six Trombones." Professor Hill was the man who could transform doomed idle youth into accomplished musicians. This all sounded very good to me. Hill's pattern was to slip out of town and move on to the next gullible village to sell the next band fantasy to the next flock of suckers while pocketing large sums of money collected for his services and nonexistent uniforms and musical supplies. Until (!), Shirley Jones (a very young and lovely Mrs. Partridge), as Marion the Librarian, snagged Hill's heart, and Professor Hill stuck around to face the music. But as the youth of River City, Iowa, gathered together to show the disgruntled townspeople their musical skills, it was proved that the Think System kind of actually worked. You've got to have heart, and you've got to believe.

I would set my wind-up granny alarm clock to go off at all hours of the night to catch the late-late show; *42nd Street, Holiday Inn, Carousel*. My family listened to soundtrack albums like *The Sound of Music, Mary Poppins, Oliver!*, and *Oklahoma!*. My dreamy formative years revolved around conflict resolved in less than two hours, usually resulting in the ultraromantic connecting of star-crossed lovers (except in *Jesus Christ Superstar* and *Fiddler on the Roof*, through which I received my religious education). That's life in a nutshell, isn't it? Need-

less to say, the Think System was internalized like a prayer. I
believed Professor Hill. Forever and ever, amen.

I DISCOVERED Elvis in sixth grade. The CBS Friday night
late movie at 10:30, when not airing scary movies like *Village of the Damned*, showed Elvis movies. My favorites were
Girl Happy and *Blue Hawaii*, movies where Elvis was young
and unpuffy and his female costars (Shelley Fabares) weren't
threatening with their sexual energy (Nancy Sinatra, Ann-
Margret). There were a lot of beach parties with spontaneous
dance numbers and vacationing unescorted teens ready for a
song at the drop of a beach ball, and life was simple. I ordered a *Best of Elvis* two-record set off the TV without
parental consent. The albums arrived COD, and my mom
paid for them, but I got in trouble—probably grounded. I
didn't care; I could listen to my Elvis records in my room un-
interrupted.

I SANG in the choir every day for four years in high school.
When you practice something every day for an hour, you
can't help but learn and improve. To be allowed to open my
mouth wide and let out a song every morning probably spared
me from what so many call the Hell of High School. I had a
daily release, a vocal venting, a melodic scream therapy. At the
end of second period I felt cleansed.

I was a second alto, the lowest female voice in the concert
choir and the a cappella choir. I stood in the front row, left of
center. At LaFollette High School, the choirs were great. They
were invited to Europe to sing in cathedrals. We sang madri-
gals, pop songs, musical scores, and classical choral arrangements, everything from the Beatles to Bach. In madrigal we
sang a fifteenth-century ditty with the lyrics, "I sit, I sigh, I
weep, I faint, I die: In deadly pain and endless misery." We

learned that when you express sadness and hopelessness in a song, it is released.

The hardest part about choir was sight-reading music because I couldn't read music. To cover my handicap, I listened carefully to the other second altos who could read music and immediately memorized my lines. I developed a photographic ear. Off the choir risers, I picked up songs in their entirety off the radio. Oh, how I loved harmony; eight different parts rubbing against one another to make a beautiful coherent whole.

The choir teacher, Mr. Witte, was one of those rare inspired and inspiring *Dead Poets Society* types. He pushed us, demanded greatness, and made us laugh. He taught football players to sing without embarrassment; he improved our withering adolescent quality of life. Bald and Nebraskan, he leapt about the room in a hunched-over stance, teasing, singing in a big tenor voice. Songs were pulled from the repertoire minutes before a performance if we weren't singing well. To be liked by Mr. Witte was an honor; he had pet students. I was not one of them. When I inquired as to why I was not chosen for the Europe-bound choir my junior year, Mr. Witte sighed and told me that the trip would be the highlight of most of the chosen ones' lives. He felt that I had a great big life ahead of me and that missing the European trip in high school would not greatly affect me. I believed him, which was preferable to assuming that I wasn't going to Europe because I sucked.

HOPING to capture the fun I watched in Elvis movies, during my senior year of high school I went to Daytona Beach with a large group of girls for spring break. A couple of my fellow travelers were close friends; the rest were casual acquaintances whose habits I did not know. We had two hotel rooms overlooking the ocean, and we crammed six to a room. My travel companions had itineraries, wholesome places to go, day trips to Disney World. I, on the other hand, wanted sun, drink, and *Led Zeppelin 2*. On the pier was an enormous nightclub called the Pier. A band calling themselves Merlyn were the house cover band. I went to the Pier every night, first with some of my group, then alone. The drinking age was eighteen and I was seventeen, but that hadn't mattered for over a year. Merlyn was my first dose of a bar band.

The men of Merlyn had big hair and spandex pants. They did a lot of Bad Company covers, which was all right by me. They played a Led Zeppelin song called "The Ocean." I loved it. I played my Zep tape obsessively on a portable cassette deck in our hotel room, though I had friends who preferred Barry Manilow (who was also all right by me). No boys from other parts of the country wanted to make out with me. There were no girls going wild, no boob flashing. Everyone in our room wore respectable pajamas, remembered to take out their contact lenses at night, applied Clearasil, and wore their retainers. Sometimes some of us passed out in our gym shorts. I went home and bought the Led Zeppelin album *Houses of the Holy* so I could listen to that song from spring break over and over.

In high school I didn't know any other girls who were as strangely into music as I was. My friend Sarah quietly listened to Bob Dylan. Our Steve Miller Band listening contemporaries did not consider Dylan cool. Another girl, named Deb, was a foaming-at-the-mouth member of the KISS Army. She was made fun of. I learned the truth at seventeen: Keep your obsessions to yourself.

I WAS still seventeen when I started college and went through sorority rush because I thought that was What One Did. The greatly desired top-shelf houses passed on me. Not used to being asked what my father did for a living, instead of telling the truth, which was "I have no idea," I responded with "sales." My mother's own sorority rejected me even though I was considered a legacy. I wasn't used to personal or socioeconomic rejection. A sorority with a reputation for housing heavyset blondes invited me to join. Ridiculously drunk at a frat party, I saw a girl screaming in the large locker room–style shower while two boys sang, "She wants a gang bang, she always will, because a gang bang gives her such a thrill." I'm not sure what I saw, only what I heard. Her screams did not sound gleeful. I didn't understand what was happening because I didn't know it existed. I was only looking for a community at an extralarge state university. I returned to my dorm room and put our phone receiver in my underwear drawer off the hook. After a week of attempted rescue, the sorority gave up on me. If those were the types of guys I was supposed to date and eventually marry, I needed to reassess.

Freshman year in college, my roommate Lisa and I slept until *All My Children*, then shuffled off to the bathroom in our robes to change the bong water. Musically we found common ground with Neil Young, the Rolling Stones, the Beatles, and Led Zeppelin; I silently endured her Kansas fixation. We never went to class. Instead we fancied ourselves bon vivant hostesses entertaining intriguing artists and thinkers who usually consisted of three rooms' worth of girls with a propensity for overeating and boys with braces and a flair for science. To amuse ourselves we engaged in creative play; Lisa dressed up in summer gear and transformed our tiny room into a beach in the dead of winter. I strutted and pouted into a hairbrush microphone on top of my bed doing my best Mick Jagger singing "Shattered." In the spring, when we refused to attend classes to honor the TA strike, we went to *Grease* at the drive-in five nights in a row where we reenacted scenes and dance numbers on the hood of my '76 Impala. We gained a lot of weight and then went on strange Diet Dr Pepper and strawberry yogurt diets that never lasted into skinniness. "Druggies!" was written on the message board on our door. I never had to study in high school and hadn't a clue how to do college. I assumed I was there to have a good time.

✲

THE first punk rock nightclub I entered was called Merlyn's—the same name as the Florida bar band. Merlyn's occupied the space that used to be the Red Rock Lounge in Madison. I went to see Iggy Pop three nights in a row. Still technically a freshman in my second year of college, I didn't know a thing about Iggy. But I did know that Chris, the cute neighbor who I very much wanted to go out with, was attending these shows. I entered Merlyn's at street level on State Street through an unmarked door in between a gyro restaurant and a clothing boutique. Inside everything was black and barely lit; to get into the club itself you had to climb a flight of black, grimy stairs. Inside were giant boulders spray-painted black, a weird postmodern decor. Bored-looking people with neon-dyed hair, safety pin piercings, and Ramones T-shirts loitered about. Women with ripped fishnet stockings and white pancake makeup posed for one another.

When a shirtless, small-framed, skinny, skinny man with long brown hair and enormous blue eyes took the stage the crowd exploded with cheers of appreciation. I divined that he must be Iggy. He howled into the mike, singing rip-it-up punk songs and low crooning ballads. He fell on the floor in bratty tantrums; he cut his arm with a shard of glass from a broken beer bottle hurled on stage. I stood there in black baggy trousers and pointy shoes with silent repulsion and fascinated attraction.

Lisa, my roommate for the second year in a row—though we'd abandoned the dorms for the first floor of a house— thought that she was going out with our cute neighbor Chris. But she happened to be out of town for the Iggy Pop shows, not that she would've gone had she been around. She never went out. Chris was a smiley, friendly cross between a young Rod Stewart and Sting, and he wore old man suit coats and skinny ties. I rationalized swooping on my best friend's new sort-of boyfriend by deciding that they were a bad match; Chris loved to go out every night to dance and watch every new band that blew through town like XTC, the Police, X, and the Blasters while Lisa was a homebody. I, on the other hand, was always ready for action. When she returned to town, Lisa ceased speaking to me so I spent most of my time two doors down at Chris's.

Spooner was Madison's favorite rock band, and Chris's older brother Butch happened to be Spooner's drummer. I was a baby in a crowd of older, more sophisticated, knowledgeable musicians, aspiring filmmakers, and actors. Butch was a midwestern Warhol, attracting everybody who was different, expressive, wildly attired, or just dying to be Somebody. At parties after shows I loved snorting cocaine that was offered to me because I was Chris's girlfriend. A cranked-up new wave angel in elf boots, I loved this scene and these cool older people thrown into my orbit by association. I listened carefully and learned about music. Chris introduced me to the Hollies, the Ramones, Roxy Music, and the Clash. My young wasted head spun with that warm feeling of belonging. One thing about Chris that I had to ignore: he called me "lady," like, "Lady, you're the greatest." Ew.

This is how he dumped me: "Are you seeing someone else?" I asked one night after he returned to the apartment we now shared with Butch and his girlfriend. I could smell it; I could taste it. "Yes," he admitted. At least he was honest.

7: Wedding Belle Blues

My sister Megan is getting married to Dale, the guy she's been dating and living with for the past couple of years. Dale's a security guard at Sears, he's quiet and sullen, always sneering, and considerably older than my sister. The wedding is to be an elaborate affair with bridesmaids in poufy gowns and a reception at a yacht club that nobody belongs to. I'm ambivalent about marriage in general, and this one in particular. You would be, too, if you had to wear a powder blue satin dress that would not look out of place with a hoop skirt underneath. Besides, isn't a younger sister's wedding the event that brands you an official spinster?

I have no desire to get married. It's never even occurred to me. It's not my idea of a good time. Look at my parents: Dad, remarried with a new family that's not as fun or cool as the family he helped create, and Mom, shacking up with an eighth grade beau. What's the upside of being married, somebody please tell me. The one good thing about Megan's wedding is that she's invited a bunch of my friends; I will have human insulation from my can't-stand-each-other parents and the throng of relatives I've not seen since my transformation into up-and-coming rocker.

As a bridesmaid, I assume the duty of driving the bride to the beauty parlor for her wedding day updo. "Are you Laurie?" asks a Wisconsin hairdresser who still has a Kristy McNichol shag twelve years after the fact. The part about my sister scheduling a hair appointment for me was not conveyed until I was within striking distance. Evidently my antihairdo embarrasses Megan. I walk out with ringlets akin to Nellie Oleson's on *Little House on the Prairie*.

Before the wedding we gather in the basement of the church to change into our costumes. The first person I see is my grandmother, or Gogi, as we call her. I haven't seen her in years and she bursts into tears at the sight of me. I don't think it's because of my hair. I decide that I must cry, too. I was the first of her many grandchildren. It never occurs to me that she might be weeping because I have MS and she hasn't seen me since my diagnosis. I cry because I'm seeing my Gogi, and because of my dress and my hair and the heat. Gogi's my grandmother; why don't I see her very often? Maybe geography; she lives in central Illinois while I'm in Minnesota. Gogi beholds me at arm's length to get a good look at me. "Laurie's gained weight!" she announces with more than a little glee. Gogi has sharp good looks, a square chin, dyed beige hair, unwrinkled skin, and clear turquoise eyes unfettered by other shades of blue. Gogi is my dad's mom, thrice married, and a tough and vibrant old cookie. She rocks in a slightly sour way. Gogi pulls my Bo Peep gown off my shoulders so now I'm a total belle. I'd rather be little Bo Diddley, of course.

In the back of the unair-conditioned church on a ninety-five-degree day, I wait to walk down the aisle with the groom's brother, a portly fellow with a handlebar mustache and mutton chops. Up in the balcony someone is singing "Ave Maria"—it's perfection; it's Megan, my sister, the bride. Her clear voice is strong and soft with just the right amount of vibrato, not too much, not too little. Her voice cuts through silk, through the suffocating air. The true singer in our family, her voice is gorgeous. I begin my step-together/slide down the aisle with tears falling onto my cheeks. My friends, occupying a pew and smelling of hops, burst into suppressed giggles at the sight of me in wall-to-wall taffeta, bare shouldered with Shirley Temple hair. When Megan is escorted down the aisle by my parents, who hate each other, my tears come down with a vengeance. I watch in silent sadness as they hand her over to her new husband, the security guard at Sears.

At the reception, a swirl of aunties and alcohol, I tell my great-aunts and parents' friends about returning to college to complete my degree. I tell Mr. Witte, my former choir teacher—the man who chose my sister Megan for a European choir trip—about the band. I have that split, the need to seem on the up and up in front of older people and the need to be an artist on the fringe in front of peers. Rog and I polka across the dance floor, I do the chicken dance with Gogi, and my sister the bride is whisked off to her honeymoon in Nova Scotia. I have no idea why they're going to Nova Scotia; I doubt it was my sister's idea.

To prepare for our first gig, Zuzu's Petals needs enough songs to fill out a set. Because we are the opening act, we only need thirty minutes of material. We'll be lucky if we can stretch it into twenty minutes. I have written a song about unrequited love, another song about an aching yearning (unrequited love), one about the malicious nature of gossip in Minneapolis ("this town's got eyes in the back of its head") that is about the imagined origins of unrequited love. Co has written a song about female drifters, one about a wasp nest in her apartment ("you killed my brother the wasp; now you've got to pay"), and one about unrequited love. Together we've cowritten a song about freaks called "Freaks" (which will evolve into "Jackals" as we become more jaded), and a song about the café entitled "Café Song." We also offer loose interpretations of songs by other bands; a Butthole Surfers song called "BBQ Pope" and a song by the Gun Club called "Sex Beat." Because we're nervous amateurs we will most likely shout rather than sing these tunes.

Our first gig is set for Labor Day, 1988 at the 400 Bar. No one goes out on a holiday Monday night, the night before school starts; the bar has little to lose in throwing us this bone. It helps immensely that Co works at the 400 and that we spend a great deal of time there. We've proven to have many friends willing to spend money on booze—a prerequisite for a booking in a bar. The headliner, none other than Rog's Full Metal Hangover—had to send demo tapes and hound the manager mercilessly to secure their spot on the roster. Full Metal Hangover is a perfectly good-enough jokey band heavily influenced by R.E.M. and the popular Minneapolis bands. Their set list relies on cover versions of terrible songs played with irony, songs like "Margaritaville," "Hot Blooded," and songs from the *This Is Spinal Tap* soundtrack. Zuzu's Petals has been practicing in the basement—standing, playing, and singing all at the same time—for six whole months.

The 400 Bar is a long thin alley. Not a large place at all. Picture van Gogh's *Night Café* cut in half. Behind a long varnished wooden bar accented with metal-and-vinyl stools rests a pool table covered by a sheet of plywood to protect it from the unpredictable music crowd. Against the wall between the bathroom and the pool table is a jukebox. The stage is an extension of the bar, though not of the same oak magnificence. The stage is a particleboard triangle attached to the end of the bar. Its dimensions are approximately four by four by six feet; one of the four-foot slices holds Willie Murphy's weathered honky-tonk piano that he pounds every Saturday night for the former hipsters. Neon beer signs provide light.

The night I've been subconsciously preparing for most of my life is finally here. And I'm not ready. This is nothing like a Mickey Rooney/Judy Garland musical where the young people exclaim, "Hey! Let's put on a show!" and an entire flawless production is whipped up on the spot. I am white-hot scared, nervous, unable to speak, visibly trembling. It's sticky hot, as most Labor Days are. I'm wearing a holey Rit-dyed pink T-shirt with no bra. On my feet are black old man's oxford shoes. Something old. I've changed the strings on my guitar because I heard somewhere that you should change your strings before a performance. Something new. I'm using a guitar strap and amp belonging to Full Metal Hangover. Something borrowed. I have on striped OshKosh B'Gosh overalls. Something blue.

This is my wedding night. I'm about to marry the stage. Now on the backside of my twenties, more and more friends are getting married and settling down. Not me, I'm acting up. A wedding is the staged production that gives the audience a glimpse at the bride's exquisite taste (or lack thereof). On this night, the night that would've been my parents' twenty-eighth wedding anniversary, I will publicly vow to love, honor, and obey the demands of the stage. For better or worse. For poor and for poorer.

Co is wearing a black-and-white wildly striped polyester dress circa 1966; it's short-sleeved, has a sharply pointed collar, and zips up the front. On her feet she wears red plastic low-heeled sandals that only she can pull off. Vicki is in cutoff overall shorts, high-top sneakers, and wears a variety of beaded earrings and bracelets. A blue bandanna around her forehead keeps her bone-straight dark hair out of her eyes. My unruly hair is contained in pigtails while Co's long chestnut tresses fall in a variety of bangs and layers onto her face. Here come the brides.

My partners and I have sent out invitations in the form of postcards, word of mouth, and posters we've made and stapled to telephone poles all over town. My belly gurgles and twitters with an anxiety that borders on nausea. To combat this feeling I order beer upon beer and chain-smoke while envisioning myself blacking out. The bar is filling from back to front. Something I neglected to imagine. Something I'm not prepared for. (Something I won't experience again for years.) There are a lot of musicians in the room. Shit. Co and Vicki try to talk to me, ask questions, make comments, crack jokes, and check in. I only half hear them. I'm in another dimension padded with fear, isolation, and concentration. Unable to speak, I nod my responses to questions I've not really heard. It's showtime.

The background chatter and jukebox music dims as I mount the three steps that lead to the world's smallest stage. I place my snap-front alligator skin purse on Willy's piano with irreverence, light a cigarette with trembling hands, and tune my guitar. Co and Vicki, seemingly unfazed, are nonchalantly setting up and talking to each other and to anyone else who approaches.

Somehow I am walking up to the mike with my guitar from Steve in Madison slung on my hips and I hold up a book for the audience to see. It's a self-help book titled *How to Start Your Own Rock Band*. My first rock 'n' roll performance begins with a reading; I read the highlights from the first chapter aloud. It's a laundry list of requirements that need to be checked off before starting your own rock band. "Number one," I say with a quivering voice, "have a gimmick." I look up and stare at the crowd with a curled lip of disgust and roll my eyes. To some our gender is considered a gimmick; my sneer says, "I'm not amused in the least." "Number two," I continue, gaining strength, "have a sound all your own. Um, no problem there." Sprinkles of laughter. "Number three," I say, clearing my throat, "perfect your skills on your instrument." Oops, forgot that one—now's as good a time as any to rip into this instrument that I hardly know and let them have it.

We begin and I exit my body. Nine short, mostly original songs are performed at breakneck speed on account of our nerves. While unable to feel my left hand on my guitar, I sing/shout in a strangulated flat voice. Mistakes are more frequent than the right notes. Vicki on drums is trying to hold it together with her tribal poundings while laughing hysterically. This is such a rush. Theater-trained Co is slinking around with her bass while looking very much in control. The rest is a blur. I'm living my dream, doing something that terrifies me. Like a skydiver who's afraid of heights, I feel completely alive.

The packed house is witnessing a god-awful din; many are cringing, laughing, not paying attention. Some stare in disbelief. Some have quizzical expressions like they're trying awfully hard to figure it out. Some clap and whoop out of solidarity, politeness, or intoxication. If we had waited until we were officially ready to perform, it would've taken years. I've waited

long enough. We've chosen to learn the hard way, on stage. If I
didn't have MS, I wonder if I'd be up here right now. I had a
hard time making things happen before I got sick. The panic of
potential incapacitation makes me want things *now*. I have absolutely nothing to lose.

It's over in an instant. Having no idea what happened
specifically, I'm walking down the steps and onto the floor. We
must be finished. A virgin bride of sorts, my cherry has been
popped in front of a crowd. Ya, it hurt. I bled. But I can tell in
no time I'm gonna like it. A lot. I hope. An audience member,
feeling obligated to comment on our performance, sputters,
"Well . . . *that* was fun." I'm too fuzzy to focus on Full Metal
Hangover's set; I hope it went well for Rog.

I T ' S difficult returning to your normal life the morning after a
gig. I'm not exactly a dewy-eyed newlywed with an after-
glow. More like a haggard mental patient following shock
treatment: After all of that adrenaline leaves your body, you
are left with a ferocious hangover. The counterchemical is as
down as adrenaline is up. Antiadrenaline is the darkest shade
of navy blue; it brings a sort of postcoital depression. Not only
that, I have an actual hangover. Having not slept well, I drift
through the day after going over the night before, rubbing my
memory for clues. I know it sucked. I wish we didn't suck.
That's the outwardest, most available response. But a little
deeper down, I think that it was great, that we have some
magic in there—somewhere. I just know it.

We need more gigs. More and more gigs. We need to record.
We need to practice. Zuzu's Petals world domination! I have
created an insatiable monster. For the first time in my life, I
have ambition. Tons of it. We've made it clear that we're willing to play anywhere; a house party, a dive on Lake Street
called Fernando's that doesn't pay, but allows you to play if
you show up with your stuff and a few people willing to buy

drinks. We visit the local record label Twintone, first home of the Replacements, the Jayhawks, and Soul Asylum. A hip-looking woman I've observed on the scene, a Twintone employee, politely suggests we make a demo tape for clubs, reviewers, fanzines, and prospective labels to hear.

We bug our friends in Soul Asylum for an opening slot at one of their well-attended gigs. Their girlfriends bug them on our behalf. "Sure . . . okay . . . fine; you can play on the bottom of the bill at the Cabooze!" they finally surrender while probably thinking, Now leave us the hell alone! For our fourth show we will be the first of three bands at a giant roadhouse called the Cabooze preceding Run Westy Run, a funky-bluesy rock band made up of adorable brothers, and headliner Soul Asylum. This is major.

I'm a mess. We show up in the late afternoon for sound check, and being on the bottom of the bill, we have to wait around for a very long time while Soul Asylum and Run Westy Run take long, luxurious sound checks. A couple of minutes before the doors are opened to the public, we are granted an abbreviated sound check of our own. Something is wrong with my amp. It doesn't work. I nervously jiggle cords and switches but I can't get a sound out of it. I walk two hundred feet through what resembles an empty airplane hangar with a huge bar set in the middle of it, to the sound booth, to tell the soundman that I can't hear my amp on stage. The burly house soundman, who looks like he just woke up, trudges two hundred feet back to the stage; he's very put out. With a cigarette dangling from his lips he flips the standby switch on my amp with disgust. I, like, failed to turn it on. I'm so fucking embarrassed. This sets the stage for the evening.

All I can say is everything goes wrong. Every little thing. The club is so large, and performing is so new to us, that we don't know how to handle ourselves when we can't hear anything. Sound systems, called PAs, project the sound on the stage out into the club through enormous speakers called mains. The bands hear what the audience hears through little speakers on the stage floor called monitors. But none of us can hear a thing through the mains or the monitors. I don't think the monitors are on; maybe the soundman is punishing me for my faux pas during sound check. And there are a lot of people out there. And we are angry shrinking wrecks. Playing different songs, starting and stopping at different points, getting completely lost in the material and song order and fluffing words and notes. I'm screwing up so badly on the guitar that I give up, quit, midsong. Co and Vicki are looking at me with bewilderment, they're still trying, but none of us knows what to do. This is my worst nightmare.

Our show business coffin is nailed shut. As we sprint from the stage in horror, a beer-bellied dude in a Vikings jersey hollers to Co, "The only good thing about that show was your tits!"

"Fuck you!" she screams, pushing her way past him. She must've shoved really hard because the guy stumbles backward and hits a cinder block wall. Onlookers applaud her performance.

Rog is there to show support (and to see Soul Asylum for free). I mumble to him in a failed whisper, "That was so awful. I'm so mortified. We have no business being up there. I suck. I'm never playing again."

Rog pats my shoulder and claims that it wasn't that bad, though he knows that it was. I know it was. We all know it was. Nobody feels obliged to tell us, "*That* was fun." It was not. I don't have anything to say to my bandmates, who appear to be over it—they're laughing and swilling beer backstage. I blame myself entirely. I drink scotch and howl all the way home, which I'm sure Rog is enjoying to no end.

Gigs trickle in in the form of "new band showcases" that take place on off nights in clubs that offer beer specials in an effort to lure an audience. I learn that I must always place my amp on stage left so that I'm able to see the girls through my good right eye, otherwise I'm isolated. Soul Asylum was an op-

portunity of a lifetime, a chance to get exposure and to entice
people into liking us, but we stunk up the joint. We've convinced a large local music-going audience that we suck. Really
suck. I think we need to record something to get a handle on
what we sound like. Still shell-shocked, I refocus on finishing
school. I call in sick to the library more frequently than I show
up. Zuzu's Petals is back in limbo land. Our current practice
space is in Rog's basement, but it's causing tension between
Rog and his roommates, who claim they need to study instead
of listen to us wail, which in turn causes tension between Rog
and me because if I had things my way, we'd be practicing
more than we already do.

Co, Vicki, and I learn how to go into music stores and guitar
shops to acquire the necessary tools of our new trade. Guys in
large chain music stores like Guitar Center usually have really
bad big hair or mullets. They might be wearing zebra-striped
Zubaz or pukka shells. They are all definitely frustrated failed
musicians who treat us like idiots. "You need a pick, it's used
to strum your guitar," he says, placing a hairy patronizing
hand on my shoulder.

"Oh ya?" I muse.

"Yamaha makes a very nice starter acoustic guitar and
Fender has a new pink (!) electric guitar."

"I play a '74 SG," I inform him, knowing it's better than
whatever he's wanking Van Halen songs on. "I'm wondering
about the price of a Marshall head and cabinet—with tubes."

The price for this coveted amp is so high that I sigh and
imagine myself continuing to play through my faulty amp that
causes electric shocks between my hands on the metal strings
and my lips on the metal microphone. I imagine this mild form
of shock therapy is not going to improve my outlook.

T HERE is another all-women three-piece band in town that
has become instantly popular, Babes in Toyland. They

regularly sell out local venues and are making records for an ultrahip record label out of Seattle called Sub Pop. They're already touring and garnering international attention. They did a good job when they opened for Soul Asylum. I see them with my own eyes and am transfixed with a mixture of confusion and envy. Their lead singer Kat snarls, howls, and screams; she sounds like Linda Blair's demonic voice double in *The Exorcist*. She is also quite fetching; picture Brigitte Bardot in a too-small schoolgirl dress. I don't think I feel the overt rage Kat is expressing. Well, maybe, somewhere in the tips of my fingers. But my anger is buried deep inside and comes out inappropriately like a good passive-aggressive. Babes in Toyland uses volume, anger, beauty, and sexual energy to get noticed.

Zuzu's Petals cleverly complains through sarcastic smiles. While Kat spits, "Vomit my heart, spread my legs apart," Co hiccups, "Boy, you better buy yourself a spine, cuz you ain't wearing mine." We're in an antigrooming phase, all sporting armpit hair and the biggest, bushiest eyebrows in show business. You might blame Madonna in *Who's That Girl?*, but we're too immersed in our immediate world to pay attention to Madonna and her career/image moves. I look like my brother, only not as cute. Maybe we're trying to look and act like boys, sort of dirty, greasy boyish girls not terribly obsessed with the rigors of beauty upkeep or fitness. It's an androgynous phase because we can, because I wore dress pants and high heels most days in high school, because it's carefree and fun for now. Vicki is being her natural self, a shy tomboy. Co and I are just in an antifashion phase.

To complete my degree, I've figured out how to incorporate my musical interests with academia while still telling my professors what they want to hear. For American Pop Culture 1970 to the Present, I write a major paper about the band KISS, arguing that they were a symbolic representation of America in the seventies. Because "symbolism" goes down big in academic circles, I point out that KISS's costumes, alter egos, and fascination with outer space mirrored America's mind-set that was absorbed in fantasy (*Mork and Mindy*) and in escaping reality (Studio 54). For a literary theory class I write a paper titled "The Replacements and the Use of Intertextuality in Songwriting." I dissect Replacements songs and cite wherever the Beatles are borrowed from, wherever other contemporary bands are mocked or challenged, wherever old lines are lifted and reinterpreted. For my senior project, I rewrite a piece of fiction written in the 1880s by Louisa May Alcott using a modern setting. Alcott's prefeminist painter in my version becomes a (guess what?) founder of a rock band.

Once again we visit the local record company Twintone, who's now added Babes in Toyland to their roster, and ask them what we need to do in order to earn a recording contract at their coveted label. We need a) a demo tape, b) "singles" (small 45-rpm discs made of vinyl that are played on "record players," an ancient contraption that spins these discs), and c) we need to play out of town and establish a fan base. In other words, we need money to buy studio time and a van. "Let's see," says the guy who's agreed to talk to us as we walk toward the door, "you already hang out with musicians, but it doesn't hurt to sleep around with tastemakers from other cities, it's done wonders for . . . " We need to whore.

"SPIKE on a round!" "Leonard on an oval!" "Short wally blues!" "Smoky dark!" This is the language of my new job. Exasperated by the doldrums of the library, I've secured employment at the famous fourteen-stool breakfast joint the Hi-Lo Diner. This is my kind of job. It's still dark out when I get there at six in the morning. To wake up, I mix hot chocolate with coffee and smoke pot in the back alley. Inside the Hi-Lo, behind each stool, people stand in line, hovering over each occupant, waiting for a seat. We abuse the customers in a mostly good-natured way. "Bourgeois, motherfuckers!" my boss calls out to a yuppie couple as they leave. They believe he has said "au revoir" and respond accordingly.

The Hi-Lo Diner is funky, it smells of bacon, and is run by actors, artists, and an assortment of Individuals who can't work for the man. Hi-Lo workers are marginally employable, too smart for their own good misfits. Like me. The narrow walls inside the diner are covered in grease-preserved foreign paper money and signs that say THERE IS NO FULFILLMENT HERE and the obligatory TIPPING IS NOT A CITY IN RUSSIA. A counter comic artist produces daily scenes from life at the Hi-Lo; his little three-by-five masterpieces are taped to the silver milk machine alongside outrageous photographs of the staff on costume day or hat day.

Through embalmed speakers and an ancient cassette deck, we listen to a library of old tapes by Jimmy Reed, Little Walter, Otis Redding, Smokey Robinson, and the Beatles. Younger employees bring in Ween, Elvis (the movie years), the Knitters, and Randy Travis. Everything sounds just right in this space.

I have gracefully accepted the role as the Mean Waitress, refusing to laugh at dumb jokes, giving sarcastic who-cares grins and nods to people who try to share their stories or get in on the act. I look at an imaginary watch while they blather on, and I offer phony staccato "ha-ha's" to their lame punch lines. I only get away with this attitude deluxe because I'm dreadfully—by Hi-Lo standards—efficient. One morning while treating Co to a free Spike—a goulash of scrambled eggs, garlic, cheddar cheese, and sauteed mushrooms—a young college student stares at us in disbelief. He turns to his buddy sitting next to him and utters with horror, "Oh my God, the Mean Waitress and the Mean Bartender know each other!" I write a paper entitled "Diner Poetry" for my folklore class.

WITH my second-to-last student loan, I pay for time at the Underground recording studio, located in an abandoned storefront on the corner of Twenty-fourth and Nicollet.

Inside is a gutted space filled to the rafters with musical gear, cords, and wires. The walls, windows, and ceiling are covered in soundproofing material that looks like squishy Styrofoam egg cartons. Everything is black or gray or yellowed white and it smells of smoke, stale beer, and b.o. This is the place where chaos can be turned into order for Zuzu's Petals. This is a new world for us and it is love at first sight for me.

Wally, the quiet and patient engineer, plays back each "take" into our headphones, and we make decisions and changes together. Our musician friends Dave and Gary stop in to offer assistance; I imagine them grimacing in the control room where we can't see them. We're allowed infinite takes to catch the best version of our songs, a version littered with as few mistakes as possible. After Co and Vicki finish the rhythm tracks, I'm allowed to play my guitar parts separately. The studio forces us to get in synch. It's fun, exciting, and a little heartwrenching to hear what we really sound like. Like mothers who are oblivious to the fact that they might have an ugly child, I blindly love what I'm hearing. We're raw and fearless, the essence of us.

"You don't gotta be a man to be outlaws like us," Co drawls. "Springtime came as a surprise, the pageant was marred by a crime," Co reports. "Be careful where you go, be careful what you say, be careful who you know," I warn, "this town's got eyes in the back of its head, you'll be sorry someday." Co and I are struggling to find our voices. Down in the basement alone with a microphone and wearing headphones, I feel like a dirty Barbra Streisand. We laugh, cackle, whoop, yelp, and groan. We overenunciate our Rs with hard upper-midwestern accents. My guitar playing is bold, unfettered, and strange, it gently cracks up and takes risks. We're on a rickety roller-coaster ride that swells and ebbs. The results are both awful and beautiful.

We peddle copies of our four-song cassette, the fruit of our studio experience, to independent record stores, and we mail copies to noncommercial radio stations, small record companies, night-clubs, and the local press. The Zuzu's Petals Demo Tape makes the

Top 20 at the University of Minnesota's radio station, WMMR, sandwiched in between the Beastie Boys' *Paul's Boutique* and Camper Van Beethoven's *Key Lime Pie*. We've hit the big time. Never mind the fact that WMMR is only accessible to students who live in the dorms. And no one in the dorms actually listens.

We continue to try to play whenever we can, wherever they'll have us. We can usually scrape up two gigs a month. Co and I continue to write songs on a regular basis and we've learned some new covers, like Melanie's "Brand New Key" and the Seekers' "Georgy Girl." I'm still nervous as hell, but that just might be the way it's going to be with me. Co is a natural on stage; I have no idea how I'm coming off even though I dominate microphone time during performances. My guitar playing is the best it's ever going to be in terms of taking chances.

I WISH you could strap on an electric guitar right now. Place your left index finger on the fourth string up from the bottom on the first fret. Now place your middle finger on the third string and wedge your ring finger right next to it, on the second fret, one down from the top. Now, bend your right arm and pull that hand up to your shoulder while pinching a guitar pick between your right thumb and forefingers. Don't move your left hand out of position as you swing back your right.

Release your right hand across the strings, strumming, down-up, down-up, all the while shimmying your right shoulder to the beat, any beat. Your right hipbone might help out by banging against the body of the guitar while you do this. Let it.

You're playing my favorite chord, an E. I call it the mighty E, the biggest, most rocking chord I know. Nothing in the world feels better than letting a big E chord rip. Go ahead, try it a few more times; you're hooked, aren't you? See, the Think System really works.

And somehow, I've survived my first year or so of "marriage"—it was rough, but I think I like it.

8: Here Comes Your Man

I'M not happy," I start.

Rog and I blurt in unison, "I don't think we should go out anymore."

Ours is a passionless union—my unconcealed zeal for my band is both a threat and a turnoff. Rog's band is a fun excuse to be with his friends; my band is my life. On a spring afternoon, Rog and I have the most civilized breakup known to me. We admit apathy, weep, hug, and part as friends. Regardless of our broken-up status, Rog drives to Rio in a pickup truck to help my mom move from the farmette back into an apartment in Madison. Mom's farmette experiment is a bust, and I've let go of one of the nicest people I've ever known. My mom and I fail in unison, never acknowledging failure, or even recognizing it. We never give it a second thought.

The Rog breakup leaves Zuzu's Petals without a practice space. Vicki offers the basement in the house where she rents a room from her friend Amanda, an older woman who "got the house" in her divorce.

After one basement session, Vicki meets us at the 400 with a stern expression. "Amanda says we can't practice at the house anymore."

"Why?"

"There was a fire in the basement after we practiced down there."

"Did we leave a cigarette or a candle burning? Does one of the amps have a short in it?" Co and I ask.

Then it sinks in. "Oh my God! How bad? Is everything all right?"

"Ya," Vicki admits, "it happened a day or two after we practiced. A couple of scarves burned and it was smoky and stinky."

"Oh, good. Well, not good, but at least we didn't start it."

"Our vibes. Amanda blames it on our energy."

As if.

A BOXCAR?" Co and Vicki are staring at me in disbelief. Yes, our next practice space is going to be a boxcar. We have no choice, having been ejected from Rog's house after our breakup. We can't afford to pay for an official space in a studio. This is our only option—a boxcar.

The guy I have a major crush on is a visionary. I think. To him nothing is more symbolically American than creating art in a discarded boxcar on forgotten railroad tracks. He's a painter, collage maker, and a musician. And, my God, he's gorgeous. Scary gorgeous. Scandinavian god gorgeous. His name is even Sven. He has those penetrating blue husky-dog eyes, long sandy wheat-colored hair, chiseled cheeks. Sauntering around in ripped jeans and a paint-splattered T-shirt, I am blinded by lust. I've never had an official drop-dead-gorgeous hunk for a boyfriend. Cute, yes. Interesting, sure. Even handsome. Sven is a different story altogether. In high school, my main boyfriend had a great personality and a bump on his nose from breaking it so many times playing hockey. Sven was a homecoming king and basketball star in high school. Now he's this out-there artist and musician. How cool is that?

I compromise myself, making it easy for him to be around me, fitting myself conveniently into Sven's plans, into his artistic vision. I offer him rides in my car—he has no license; drinks at the bar—he has no job; free breakfast at the Hi-Lo—he has no money. I marvel at his threatening, hubcap-riddled art and praise his mediocre band. My female friends and I whisper about Sven in schoolgirl giggles. He's new on the scene; his physical appeal is not ignorable, even to my friends with depth. I make it clear that I'm in pursuit, as in "hands off, let me have a crack at this one." Sven offers more than a pretty face, he's soft-spoken and gentle, with a quiet, amused giggle that can build to a roar. He's a former small-town Minnesota home-coming king turned bohemian squatter. The giant gap bridging these contradictions titillates me to no end.

Maybe I should think twice about pursuing someone who is originally interested in hooking up with my best friend Co. They always want curvaceous, sassy Co first. Until I can tap-dance my way into their field of vision with my fine sense of humor and availability. "It appears that he's hot for you," I admit to Co, "but please, please, please, can I have a shot at him?" "He *is* awfully cute," she sighs, but acquiesces because she already has a boyfriend.

Maybe I should take into account Sven's seriously creepy friends. Violent drunks. Directionless, unemployed losers with great hair. But they don't deter me, nor does Sven's vacant gaze or his inability to pay attention to what I'm saying. He is an artist after all, the real deal. Head in the clouds is a side effect of all that creativity. Besides, he loves my band and I'm in a big drinking and pot-smoking phase; I don't require a lot of sub-stance from a guy. I willingly let my guard down in the pursuit of beauty.

Zuzu's Petals is my main interest anyway, and Sven encour-ages me to be more absorbed in the band, to play my guitar all day and all night, like him. But I still need to work at the diner so I can pay for everything. In offering us his boxcar as a prac-tice space, Sven is our new enabler. I'm hoping he'll rub off on me and I'll become a real full-time artist rather than a hash-slinging student by day, rock singer by night. It's not like we of-ficially start going out or go on dates or anything. We just hang out, which leads to bed, which leads to more hanging out. Sometimes we even go out to dinner or a movie (if I buy).

I can't give Sven a voice because I can't hear him in my head. In my memory, Sven is silent, wordless. Just there. Completely passive, a leaf blown in the wind and dropped from place to place until it's raked up and bagged, or blown into a gutter, stuck, until it slips down into the sewer.

S VEN scouted the boxcar during one of his scrap-metal hunts; he funds his art, music, and drink by selling scavenged copper and tin. I've never met anyone like this, so original and so wanting to be outside of conventional society. The boxcar is Sven's studio/crash pad away from the chaotic house he shares with a revolving door of inhabitants on Eleventh and Franklin, a slum corner where I fear leaving my car to knock on his door. Sven needs wide-open space to assemble his trash heap collages and giant textured paintings. The fields behind the boxcar are abandoned. No one complains about noise. This might be the rock 'n' roll rehearsal space of the future, cultural recycling. I dreamily nod in absolute agreement, eager to align the band with this experiment.

Behind the University of Minnesota campus, in a former railyard surrounded by empty grain silos, stands the boxcar. This is Minneapolis's former boomtown ghost, its grain and mill industry. In a still-turned-on outlet outside an abandoned silo, Sven has discovered electricity. He runs a weather-resistant power cord from the boxcar to the silo. Electricity is needed to power lights, amps, and mikes. The boxcar is a weather-beaten red and has an enormous sliding wooden door that Sven padlocks shut when he leaves. He has landscaped his yard—a patch of dirt and weeds in front of the boxcar—with his urban artifacts, old painted doors and mannequins wearing large swatches of scavenged silk and printed fabric. Inside the boxcar, on the floor, rests a discarded blue braided rug. Old wooden crates are end tables topped with funky thrift store lamps. It's like a backwoods cabin, sort of. The railroad tracks are grown over with purple and yellow wildflowers and dry reedy grasses. How romantic. We can open the big sliding door and play our ramshackle punk ballads to the birds and the sky.

One thing Sven forgets to tell me about when selling the box-car dream is a large population of predominately alcoholic homeless men. The first afternoon we come bumping in on the dirt road, my ancient Nova stuffed with guitars and drums and amps, a half-dozen filthy, scraggly-bearded drunk guys greet us. They're sitting around a fire on a ninety-degree day, arguing and gesturing wildly about napalm. My hunky sort-of boyfriend is sitting around the campfire swilling Wild Irish Rose with these gentlemen. My inner dialogue is contradictory and confused: How cool that he can do that. Gross. This is good for me . . . somehow. Am I scared or repulsed? Both. I don't know if I can handle this. What's wrong with me?

And what *is* wrong with me? Where is my compassion? From the sounds and looks of it, these guys are discarded Vietnam vets. They're seriously addicted and/or mentally ill. They're shattered. Someone should be helping them. Their faces are old and haggard; their hands are swollen purple with a permanent layer of dirt and sweat that protects them from the elements. Their clothes are tattered jeans and flannel shirts molded to their bodies, a second skin with a lively stench. I know I should be doing something, offering assistance, performing that simple act of kindness so many bumper stickers urge. But I'm afraid of them. Reeling in inner horror, I unload our equipment in an effort to busy myself.

I wonder if Co is thinking what I'm thinking: How did we go from playing air guitar in a dorm room to this scenario? How did Co, the cute girly girl with ribbons in her pigtails and a Big Ten football player for a boyfriend, go from the Kollege Klub to a boxcar? Her current boyfriend is a Native American who gets pulled over on his bike by the police and questioned because it's after dark. We've stepped over that invisible line that separates the "normal" from the fringe. I feel guilty because I know I can step back and forth over that line whenever I feel like it. The group of men we're smiling at through gritted teeth cannot.

We say hi, and I assume that Co and Vicki are cool with this added ambiance. "Play some Jefferson Airplane, pretty rock mamas," a crazy-eyed chap with black stumps for teeth bellows in our direction.

"Is this okay?" I whisper to Co.

"Sure," her voice quivers, then gathers strength, "why the hell wouldn't it be?"

"Drummer girl! Hey lady drummer!" The hoboes really like Vicki; they pay her special attention, flutter their crusty eyelids at her. Vicki has gained a degree of self-confidence and assertiveness since joining the band. She laughs and hollers "What the fuck are you looking at?" and returns to her drums. There's something exotic and erotically charged about a female behind a drum kit. It must be that primal pounding thing, tough and sexy and slightly threatening. My only example growing up was Karen Carpenter, and she certainly didn't have any of that going on.

The hoboes like to participate in our practices. They love rock 'n' roll and Jesus and President Bush (Sr.). And they love to fight once the daily swill kicks in. "I saw Iggy and the Stooges at the '69 moratorium!" one former Marine howls, desperate to connect with us, dying for our attention, or at least an acknowledgment of his presence. We uncomfortably answer them with one word, usually "cool" or "wow" or "yikes." One guy looks like the troll in my *Three Billy Goats Gruff* storybook from childhood. They call him Cowboy and he's shrunken, with an odd underbite and a scowling red face. Cowboy has long reddish hair and a beard and he speaks mostly in grunts. There's another guy named Ed who stands about six foot five with balding blond hair and freckles; he looks like a runaway farmhand who never got found.

Sometimes they gather outside the boxcar, our homeless groupies, like anxious concertgoers waiting for the jams to kick in. We're working on new songs and trying to concentrate. I sometimes gauge our new material by the hoboes' reactions. When we play our new song "Shipwrecked" they converge on the boxcar, gathering inside and hopping around like Neanderthals. I've half written this song about them: "Shipwrecked in a bottle," I sing, looking away. I force myself to hang with this arrangement, though I feel threatened and scared. In the middle of the song one of the pirates collapses into a grand mal seizure, his body twitching and contorting and flopping on the ground. His shipmates, who conduct themselves like this is a daily occurrence, rescue him from choking on his tongue and carry him outside.

We can't deal with this. This is too serious. Rock 'n' roll is supposed to be fun. And it's supposed to be dangerous. But the way I see it, if one of these guys drops dead during practice, we're guilty of murder—and that's *too* dangerous.

I THOUGHT hoboes were down and out in a by-choice kind of way, you know, intentional dropouts. Hoboes were kind of romantic, a part of the American landscape. Like Red Skelton's Freddy the Freeloader, or Roger Miller's "King of the Road." Happy unfettered types. But I guess that's a 1930s perception, from back when panhandlers knocked on people's back doors and offered to do chores in return for cash or a meal. The dust-bowl and the Depression provided credible reasons for their circumstances. It could happen to anyone, and folks respected and acknowledged that fact.

But now we're so used to seeing them on the periphery that we choose not to notice them to avoid getting bummed out. These guys in the railyard are nothing like Judy Garland and Fred Astaire dressed in tattered old suits, singing, "We're just a couple of swells." Judy and Fred were talented song-and-dance people who were poking fun at the upper crust in their mock formal wear, back when hoboes were considered daring and cool. I was a hobo, a bum, for Halloween as a kid on more than one occasion. And here we are, dressed like the real hoboes on purpose in our tattered jeans, flannel, and work boots. We're here to make music, which is hard to do with all this grim reality in our faces.

And, I admit, I don't want to get too close to these guys. They smell, sound, and look nasty. Carone is their leader; he looks like a one-eyed John Phillips from the Mamas and the Papas. Farmer Ed smashed his eye out with a rock during a fight. Carone also suffers from diabetes and has a limp that I suspect has something to do with gangrene. He bellows insane stories about fighting in the Irish Republican Army. Sometimes people from the nearby university or Social Services or a church come down to the railyard to see if they can do anything for these guys. I'm skeptical about the researchers who come down to bear witness and record the conditions these men live under. But I'm no better: I'm afraid of them and embarrassed for them and ashamed of myself—a horrid combo platter of emotions. All I'm doing is sort of going out with an artist who has befriended them, who shares their space.

"Can you give us a ride to the liquor store?" Somehow they've pooled enough money for another bottle. I don't want to contribute to their alcohol consumption. I know that if I don't take them, they'll find some other way—they always do—and frankly, I don't want them in my car. "Sorry, you guys, we really need to practice." Summer is turning to fall; it's getting dark earlier. It's colder out. I don't like being in the railyard after dark. The whole place becomes haunted. I imagine crimes are committed down here at night, people go missing. The change in the season threatens their ability to survive out of doors.

A cold wind whistles through the boxcar. We practice in leather jackets and stocking hats. We wear gloves with the fingertips cut off so we can play our instruments. This is neither romantic nor fun. In fact, it never was. Practice is disturbed by the smell of burning. This burning reeks of materials other than the kindling and dried grasses used for the hobo campfire. It's heavier and chemical smelling. We hop down out of the boxcar to a stream of black smoke wafting out of the back window of my Nova. The backseat is smoldering deep down in the coils below the upholstery. We silently pour water from our water bottles onto the smoke. I fish a burning hand-rolled cigarette out of the cotton batting, foam, and metal. This is what happens when you don't give them a ride to the liquor store. They're in my car forever.

WE promptly pack our gear and move into the basement of my latest apartment, the first floor of a decrepit house on Como Avenue, a sleepy old street near campus, near the Hi-Lo Diner, near the boxcar. This basement is old and dark; it smells like my late great-grandfather's old hotel in Michigan, like musty green moss, stale cigars, and cement blocks that never dry. There is still a wooden storm door and concrete steps that lead into the backyard. This will do for now.

The big black hole and its accompanying smell in the backseat of my Nova, on the other hand, are unacceptable. And depressing. No one can sit back there without gagging. For lack of an alternative, I drive this dying vehicle for one more winter. I intend to use my final student loan before graduating on a van. I shop in the Sunday Minneapolis *Star Tribune*'s Motoring section and in an ad placed by Peterson Pontiac, our van beckons: a 1979 Chevy conversion van, green velour captain's seats and wood-paneling interior. I respond immediately, getting a fifty-dollar trade-in for the Nova. I love this van: Deep-pile green shag carpeting adorns its floors. The paneling reenacts a log cabin. It costs $1,999, an amount that will swallow my entire student loan. Who cares? It's Barbie's Dream Van and Scooby Doo's Mystery Machine wrapped into one. It's so cool; we'll be traveling in style. No bum's gonna burn this baby down.

Because our demo tape has been intensely circulated by us, a tiny independent record label in town, Susstones, would like to release a single by Zuzu's Petals. "People are really into all-women bands these days" is the tone of our invitation. I wish someone would say, "I really love that song of yours about unrequited love." Or, "You guys [meaning gals] have a cool sound." But if our gender is a fad, there's not much we can do about it. We would sound too cranky walking around saying, "Hey, man, so what if we're girls, it's got to be about the music." Susstones is operated out of its owner's apartment, meaning that Zuzu's Petals is responsible for paying for the creation of our single.

Butch, my former boyfriend's brother in Madison (remember him, "the midwestern Warhol"?), now owns and operates a recording studio, Smart Studios. Butch is making a name for himself as a producer of independent rock bands. Back when Butch and I and our main squeezes briefly shared an apartment before I was dumped, he and I used to tool around together in the afternoon—he was a cabdriver and I was a deli employee on academic probation while our partners were gainfully employed full-time students. Butch used to take snare drums into bus shelters in an attempt to find the perfect drum sound and made me listen to avant-garde Snakefinger records. "Laur-hoo, how are you?" He laughs, sounding happy to hear that I have a band that would like to record a single in his studio. Butch says he'll give us a deal and promises his involvement; his name on a record seems to Mean Something these days.

To make the Dream Van's virgin excursion worthwhile, we weasel ourselves onto the bill opening for the Madison band Poopshovel on the night preceding our recording session. My ex-roommate/Co's ex-boyfriend Bill fronts Poopshovel. Our first out-of-town show will be in the Wagon Wheel. It's easier to get a gig in Madison than it is in Minneapolis; there's not as much competition, and not as much hearsay about our level of sucking. The two main czars of club bookings in Minneapolis, Maggie and Steve, keep us at arm's length—Steve grouses about our inability to draw a crowd, pointing out that we've many dues to pay before we're getting anywhere near the coveted stage at the Seventh Street Entry; Maggie is always very nice but preoccupied with the profusion of talented sexy young male musicians in her midst who have an easier time of charming her than we do. Regardless, our dogged tenacity results in being thrown a bone in the form of a tasty gig on occasion.

Madison's Wagon Wheel is in the basement of a large building near the state capitol. Like nearby O'Kayz Corral, it has an Old West/cowboy motif. All of the benches at the tables are backed with actual wagon wheels cut in half. I've always found that kitsch helps when seeking refuge in a dark Wisconsin bar; it reminds you to be a cheerful, ironic drunk. I frequented the Wagon Wheel my final year in Madison; it was an untapped tacky haven of midwestern realism; the out-of-towners had yet to discover it. Now, I hear, it's *the* place to go. They didn't offer live music during my reign, only a deliciously dated jukebox and about six floor tiles that could be used as a dance floor if need be. The Wagon Wheel is the bar my dad sat in while waiting to drive me home from gymnastics when I was in middle school.

EVERY Tuesday and Thursday after a stress-filled day at Sennett middle school (mean girls, hormonal upheaval), I was shuttled downtown to gymnastics class at Madison Turners. Turners was an enormous gymnasium that specialized in torture and humiliation, as if I needed any further anguish after dodging tough girls who wanted to beat me up every day in school. I was an okay gymnast, not great. Turners prided itself on its German heritage and was highly regimented, disciplined, and anal. Each session was kicked off with a mass drill—the kind of synchronized, choppy choreographed floor calisthenics you might see in *Triumph of the Will*. I was one of three students from the east side of town; most attendees came from the more affluent west side (Co's part of town). The west side girls were superior gymnasts and showed no signs of awkwardness during adolescence. The matron in charge, Mrs. Johnson, clad in Lycra sweats and a baby blue cardigan with a constantly burning Virginia Slim, favored the west side girls. Their leotards and hair were always sleek and smooth. My underwear bunched up under my leotard; I didn't know there was special leotard underwear. My hair rebelled against barrettes and elastic bands.

In seventh grade I got my first period. Transporting my first period to Turners was a mortifying prospect. I had to haul a brick-size sanitary napkin attached to a belt underneath my flimsy leotard. To camouflage my condition, I wore a pair of stretchy shorts over my leotard.

"Lindeen, those shorts look sloppy; remove them at once," barked Mrs. Johnson.

My bulky horror was unmasked. After what seemed like an eternity of pointed fingers and snickers, I slunk next door to the Wagon Wheel, where my dad nursed a Budweiser while waiting to drive me home. Of course I didn't share my humiliation with him. My dad and I would never talk about something as normal as a first period. Nobody talked about any of that kind of stuff in our house. My mom and I didn't even talk about it; the supplies just magically appeared on my dresser a few months before I got "the curse."

My dad and I drove home not speaking, listening to the radio. I wistfully gazed at Lake Monona, remembering a game my friends and I used to play at Olbrich Beach back when life was simple. The game was called Don't Step on Otis Redding; we treaded water as long as we could, wiggling wildly, too

afraid to touch the sandy bottom out of fear that we might recover Otis's unfound body. That was our urban legend.

THE actual show at the Wagon Wheel is a blur because my
stage fright has not diminished, meaning every performance is executed in an altered state akin to a blackout. Co and I
and the guys in Poopshovel can't get over the fact that we're all
actually in bands and playing together and that people are here
to see us. Bill, Poopshovel's singer, keeps walking around with
a stoned grin, saying, "Man, this is so cool and weird, you
guys." A portable platform is erected in the middle of the room
to serve as a stage. My mom, her boyfriend Jack, my dad, his
wife, Co's dad and step-mom, and a smattering of our siblings
are all in the audience. Though my dad and his wife leave before we're done, my mom seems mildly impressed that there
are a lot of young people present who appear to like and understand our need to make ranting, clanging music. She does,
however, give me that look with a sigh that says, "You used to
be such a pretty girl." It's most disconcerting trying to rock in
front of your puzzled family the first time. You must avoid eye
contact while on stage to prevent an identity crisis.

Having survived our first out-of-town show without sucking
too badly, we retire to friends Dan and Anita's house for a
small party. Dan and Anita are our only married, grown-up
friends; Dan drums for the band Killdozer and Anita is an at-
torney for the state. They actually own their house—I can't
imagine how that works. Vicki, claiming fatigue, immediately
retreats to their guest room (guest room!). Co and I stay up till
all hours laughing, talking, smoking, drinking, and eating. We
find Vicki's desire to be alone odd, but she's always been different from us.

"Where's Vicki?" Anita asks.

"Oh, she went to sleep."

"Doesn't she like us?" wonder Dan and Anita.

"She's a bit of a loner," Co and I reason.

"Weird."

"Ya, and I'm a bit of a stoner; when's that Pizza Pit delivery going to get here—I have total munchies."

Co and I sleep on the hardwood floor covered in spare blankets while their pug Nelson snuffles and snorts in our midst. The next morning, a little worse for the wear, we ramble off to Smart Studios with our pooled four hundred dollars. An older guy I used to know from the Chris/Butch years greets us at the door. Everyone used to call him Spy Dog and he looks like Tom Selleck.

"I'm sorry, guys [meaning girls]," he begins wearily with a sad sigh, "Butch is sick, he's been on the road and he's absolutely exhausted. He won't be in today." Spy Dog's performance is about the worst acting job I've seen in my life. Not only that, he acts like he's never seen me in his life. I doubt Butch is sick. Maybe not interested. Maybe even at this late date I'm still viewed as the injured dumpee, someone to be avoided. Or perhaps he caught our set last night.

Fortunately, the dear man who gave me my guitar, Steve, is Butch's partner and by default he will produce and engineer our recording. Always quiet, Steve does not verbalize, offer suggestions, or give directions. We have no idea what we're doing, what we want, what we're after. Perhaps Steve is experiencing audio shock due to our extreme amateurism; he appears embarrassed. Worse yet, he acts all irritated when I mention anything about our common past when we were nicknamed Mr. and Mrs. Sex. We never had sex. I always really liked him, though. And Vicki doesn't say a word. To compensate for everyone's discomfort, Co and I babble incessantly, saying nothing. We blindly feel our way through three songs that don't get finished in our allotted time slot. We'll need to return some other time when the studio is available again, when we can coordinate days off from work.

We drive back to Minneapolis on the pissy side of a mood

swing, blaring Rolling Stones cassettes and staring out the windows at the stretch of 94 West between Madison and Minneapolis. I gaze at the land that separates my old life from my new life; I leave multiple sclerosis and my confusing family back in Madison and watch bumpy hills and glacier-sculpted bluffs smooth out and flatten into expansive prairie as we enter Minnesota, my new life. In my new life I am well and entirely reinvented. On the open flat land, uncomplicated by dips and dives, the possibilities are endless.

9: The Dawning of a New Era

I DON'T want my picture in the paper. I quit."

Tears are gathering in the corners of Vicki's eyes before they drop onto her wide cheeks. I thought it was just another afternoon of band practice in my damp, moldy basement. But our drummer just quit. She just bought a new drum kit; this makes no sense. Coleen slumps at my kitchen table in the living room of my ugly brown house. Co's face is red and looks about to explode; she's appropriately sad to my smoldering chill. It's an unseasonably hot day in May, and I pace around the too-quiet dusty room in my shorts and sneakers. My yellowing second-hand furniture is covered in festive vintage tablecloths to hide other people's stains.

Zuzu's Petals' dark, barely discernible picture appeared in the Minneapolis *Star Tribune* today in the Now Hear This music column. This is a first and it feels huge, of major importance. To me, anyway. And obviously to Vicki, as well. Today I walked around campus feeling like I landed that all-important job-after-college. My band is in the big-city newspaper. Granted, nobody probably saw or read this small piece buried in the back of the Arts and Entertainment section. Nobody probably linked me, the oldest girl in English class, to this poorly lit, blurry photo. But all day I knew it was there. I'm Somebody! Never mind the fact that we're described as being drunk and sloppy. It's true, even intentional. Isn't everybody?

"Fine. Quit. See ya. We don't need you." I'm such a hard ass when I don't want to process or feel something important that's going on. I handle Vicki's dilemma as unfeeling as Spock (though let me go on record as stating that I hate, with a passion, everything *Star Trek*). The way I see it, if Vicki's rejecting the band, then she's rejecting me (I will pass Logic 101 this semester on my fourth attempt). I'm too revved up by today's tasty press, my head dancing with scenes from my upcoming stardom; my imagination's been spinning off its axis all day. Oh, the interviews I've been conducting on the tour bus in my mind. Vicki's announcement is a total buzz kill.

Here we are again, Co and I, losing another band member. Is it us? Maybe, though we've heard drummers are an incredibly fickle, unreliable breed—a good drummer is hard to find; it makes the good ones fey infidels. I take Vicki's decision to live a life of obscurity as her problem. Why would anyone want that? I take her rejection of my dream, of Zuzu's Petals, with anger because that's preferable to wondering if there's something about us and the way we do things that is off-putting. I'm getting used to loss.

Besides, it doesn't matter. I already know what to do. We'll ask Linda, the new counter jockey at the café (though we no longer work there, we're still in the neighborhood and know all of the café gossip). Linda's an actual drummer who's asked to join us on congas in the past, just for fun, just because she loves to drum. Linda attends our gigs voluntarily and enthusiastically. She's drummed for a slew of bands; she's more socially adept than Vicki, and very va-va-voom pretty. We want our picture in the paper, damn it. That's the whole point. We're dying for recognition.

Damn it again, we're supposed to finish recording next week in Madison; we have a single to release. We've already arranged to provide transportation for Dave and Danny from Soul Asylum and their soundman—they have an acoustic show at the Memorial Union and they're between vans. The fee for the free ride is a little studio assistance; we clearly need a translator. Co and I will just have to honor our commitments without Vicki and pray the drum tracks are good enough to use. Vicki who?

❧

H EH-HEY Butch, nice to see you!" Co and I sing. When we bring our rock star friend Dave in to assist us, Butch finds the time to pop in to fiddle with a couple of knobs. We're doing something called mixing that I don't understand. It's really tedious, like aurally editing a film syllable by syllable, not a recommended profession for those of us with short attention spans. I wouldn't dream of saying anything out loud about Butch finding the energy to make an appearance when we bring along a guest star. That would seem bitter, and Lord knows, bitterness in a lady is such an unlikable quality. So I just notice. So does Co.

L INDA shows up at our practice space and plops herself down all casual and cool at Vicki's newly purchased, deserted drum kit. She looks like a femmy tomboy, popping her gum, wearing a leather motorcycle cap, jeans, and Doc Martens. Linda has long sleek chestnut hair; her brown eyes are direct and bright. She's a music head; she has her own show on listener-sponsored radio. She knows everyone. Everyone likes her. She's genuinely, naturally superfriendly. Linda appears to like people a lot. Co and I are prone to snottiness. Linda adds a new, much-needed element to our band and she hasn't hit a drum yet. The only problem I can foresee is that Linda's already committed to another band, the Wahinis, a sixties-style surf band.

"This song's called 'Shipwrecked,'" I say, then Co and I play the same eight-note riff in unison.

"Oh, I've heard you play that one." Linda snaps the snare drum and holds a steady beat on the kick drum. She hits the drums really hard.

Co and I cannot believe the difference that Linda makes. Instead of an interesting independent rhythm, an added texture to our churning songs, there's a consistent beat holding it all together. Playing is easier with this luxury. Co and I stare at each other, our eyes locked in disbelief. We're both thinking the same thing: OhmyGod, this is amazing.

"We want you," I blurt. Linda assumes we'll be trying out a variety of drummers, which is hilarious as she's the only person we've considered.

"We need a commitment," Co and I take turns explaining our stance, "this is an exclusive, full-time gig."

"We're going for it . . . tours, records, pictures in the paper."

"Give me a little time to tie up loose ends with my other bands," Linda says with a flirtatious smile while drawing on a Camel Light, "but count me in."

THERE'S something else about Linda. She, too, has suffered at the icy hands of a chronic degenerative autoimmune disease at a criminally young age. Linda has rheumatoid arthritis and is no stranger to incapacity, having recently recovered from a debilitating bout with the disease. She's familiar with shots and specialists and steroid medication. She knows what it's like to have arms and legs that can't do what they're supposed to do. She, too, doesn't want to talk about it and chooses to go forward while trying not to think about it. We have something unspeakably heavy that binds us.

"Ten more years!" my entire family shouts from the balcony at the Northrup Auditorium. I'm walking across the stage after butting in line, lying that I had "a plane to catch," so I can shake Walter Mondale's hand and collect my college diploma. I have somehow managed to earn a Bachelor of Arts degree, but I need to hustle out of the ceremony—there's a party to throw. Rog and his pals are early guests, and my family is clearly not over him, gushing, giggling, and patting him on the back while they glare at me in disbelief. Presenting me with an acoustic guitar, my family members leave in the early evening to drive

home to Madison. Much later Sven shows up with his creepy
friends who I don't trust.

Now a college graduate and owner of a Chevy conversion
van, it's time for an apartment of my own. Zuzu's Petals can finally afford to rent a studio space—a locked room at a roofing
company that can only be utilized after business hours—that
we'll share with the bands the Contras and Arcwelder. I rent
the nearby top floor—okay, attic—of a house close to the Mississippi River for three hundred dollars a month. When I move
in, there is no lock on the door leading into my one-room
dwelling with peaked ceilings. To get in, I must walk up a
wheelchair ramp to the back door (which has a lock, but is
never closed) and climb the back staircase. My downstairs
neighbor is paralyzed from his nose down with Lou Gehrig's
disease, or ALS, a chronic degenerative autoimmune disease.
He has twenty-four-hour nursing care and he breathes through
a respirator. I learn via a typed welcome note left at my door
that he communicates with the only part of his body that he
can control, his eyes. D. painstakingly spells out words onto a
letter board by making eye contact with each desired letter. I
see him laid out on a hospital bed in his living room through
the blinds every time I come and go. I think about him constantly. I don't worry about my unlocked door, assuming that
viewing D. in his condition will divert wrongdoers. Besides, my
apartment is nothing more than my crash pad/business head-
quarters between everything Zuzu's Petals and my shifts at the
diner; I don't require much from my home base.

There have been a couple of scary episodes with overdrinking. My overdrinking. One night I passed out in the parking lot
of the Uptown bar after a performance. I drank way too much
scotch; the soundman said it was like a switch turned me off
and I became blurry and sloppy on stage. Someone else drove
the van and Sven carried me into my apartment and tucked me
in. No good. That can't happen again.

"Please don't drink so much," Sven pleads, "it's bad for

your disease." He has a point, but who's he to talk? He spends more time at the hobo camp than at my apartment, and he's obsessed with digging scrap metal for money. "You really need to stretch," he urges while pushing one of my legs into a hamstring stretch, "I think it's the key to your health."

Another night, someone has hash in our practice space after a gig. The combination of smoking hash after a night of drinking sends me up to the railroad tracks behind our rehearsal space, where I fall to my knees and throw up onto the tracks. I heave so hard that I also urinate. Removing my underwear underneath my dress, I drop them on the tracks and gingerly step away from the scene. Unfortunately a coworker, Tony, who's a non-scary friend of Sven's, witnesses this unladylike display and returns to the Hi-Lo with a funny story that he never tires of telling. Tony and Sven find this hilarious, probably because it's so gross, and I'm usually so controlling.

"I want you out." I should have said this to Sven a year ago, but I'm finally saying it. I've watched him become one of them, a railyard man, a bum. At times I've been interested and concerned, but mostly freaked-out or too consumed with the band. Sven's crossed the line, the line between having a job and a place to live, and oblivion, the line between the edge and over the ledge. It can happen quickly, and I can no longer be Sven's only connection to the real world, to an apartment, to life as most of us know it. Sven prefers spending his evenings scrounging for copper, gutting the old railroads and mills, unearthing a dead past. And now he's taken to hopping trains. He's riding the rails, and I don't want him in my apartment.

Most of us are handicapped in some way, either on the inside or outside. Many of us have some thing, some trait or condition, that creates lifelong obstacles; family alcoholism, crippling shyness, emotional immaturity, mental illness, color blindness. I consider myself damaged goods because of the MS; that, to me, is an outwardly noticeable handicap whether people can see it or not, and it's my cross to bear. At least I have

some knowledge of the load I'm lugging and that's a tiny bit
empowering. Sven is damaged goods in another way. Maybe I
think I can only be with someone who is somehow handicapped because I know that I am. But I'm tired of thinking and
living that way.

Our first gig with Linda is an outdoor "spring fling" festival
at the University of Minnesota. Getting her first taste of what a
weirdo I am before a performance, Linda looks put off; hopefully she can accept this infringement. Performing with Linda is
a breeze, and Co and I are overjoyed until out of the corner of
my eye I spot Sven. He's spreading rose petals around the front
of the stage as we play. He looks like a deranged male flower
girl. The petals are, no doubt, salvaged from a Dumpster behind a flower shop. I'm embarrassed to know him.

PART TWO

WE'RE AN
AMERICAN BAND

10: Ay-Oh, Let's Go

Zuzu's Petals is playing at the 400 Bar. This is the first time Linda's joined us inside our hangout as a member of the band. There are three bands on the bill and we're in the middle; we're moving on up. Slightly. It's a Tuesday night, not a big night for a show, and none of the bands on the bill draws large crowds. It's just your average crapshoot night for the bar, like maybe they can sell enough booze to pay their bartender and flip the bands a few coins.

"Hey, do you have a copy of the set list?" Linda inquires before we begin.

Co and Linda have been mingling with the crowd, chatting and laughing. I'm sort of standing around, unable to really speak, busying myself with chain-smoking, applying the Think System, trying to concentrate on becoming someone confident, sassy, and accomplished.

"Whatever," I frantically hiss, not registering her request or its relationship to me.

"Whoa," Linda says, eyeing me suspiciously. "Okay."

Put off, Linda walks away and finds Co. I light another cigarette and drift back into the zone.

When it's time to step onto the world's smallest stage, a stage we've graced a handful of times now, the vibe is different because Linda's behind the kit, chewing gum, wearing her leather motorcycle cap, fiddling with her stash of drumsticks, and smiling like she's happy to be here. She exudes joyfulness and confidence. She is so appealing. Linda and Co go over the game plan while I tune my guitar.

I have no idea what I'm like on stage, I suspect I'm slightly dorky, nervous-seeming, and sarcastic. I pray I'm semicool at least some of the time, singing in tune most of the time, and somewhat amusing part of the time. I like to dance to the groove and shake my ample butt or stand dead still (a habit acquired back when our microphone cords were hung from the ceiling) and expel my lyrics and melodies behind an icy stare, followed by closing my eyes and letting my upper body and head move in waves with the music. Behind my right shoulder Linda is hitting her drums with power and authority, the gum she chews in a flirty, sexy secretary way keeping time. She lifts her eyebrows to people in the crowd and makes eye contact, laughing, pointing a drumstick at that inevitable moron who yells "Freebird" from the crowd. Co slinks and slithers, gyrates and screams with a Mick Jagger pout, and does hopscotch dances while she rolls her head in time with her bass. Her voice can be Marilyn Monroe sexy or Nina Hagen authoritative. I'm in awe of my bandmates; they're so fucking cool.

After the show Co pulls me aside in all seriousness and says, "You really freaked Linda out."

"How?" I'm stunned.

"Blowing her off and ignoring her when she was trying to figure out what was going on before the show."

"Shit."

"I told her you're a freak before shows and to ignore you, but she wasn't wild about the idea."

"Crap."

FOR Co, Linda, and me, it's full speed ahead; anyone unable to keep up with us might as well jump off now (not that anyone's really jumped on).

Our first single has two songs, a pro-choice rap by Co entitled "Babblin' Mules" ("Hey, hey, if you had your way/Wouldn't be where I am today/I'd be barefoot and cookin' your food"), and the cowritten "Shipwrecked" ("Are you still drinkin'?/

Well, so am I/But not like you are")—because clearly we have a
handle on our alcoholic tendencies. This is how we cowrite:

Laurie: "I have a chunk that goes like this." I play a few
notes or chords or a melody with a few words I've been chewing on.

Co: "I have a bit that goes like this." She plays a melody on
her bass with words to accompany.

We mix them together, my part the verses, Co's part the chorus, and voilà, a Zuzu's Petals song. And now we have Linda,
who also plays guitar and fiddles with riffs.

Linda has not played a note on our single yet she is completely immersed in our business; she even draws a car-
toonesque slack-jawed donkey for the cover art. Between the
three of us and John at Susstones, we send our single absolutely everywhere. A couple of recipients say a word or two
about it in their fanzine or newspaper, some give it a spin on
their college radio show, some even like it.

The next thing we need is an official press photo that has
our contact information printed on the bottom to send along
with the single and our scanty press clippings. We are itching
to go on tour. A professional photographer takes a stunning
picture of Co. Linda and I look pleasant enough, though
Linda's luscious hair blends in with her jacket and I look like
I have a tiny penis because my shorts are bunched up—but
not to worry, the wooly caterpillars over my eyes and the
grown-out perm are easy distracters. This photo is all about
Co in a polka-dot shift and low-top tennies, her long hair
carved out and framing her I-have-a-secret face, her curves
apparent.

We stuff padded envelopes with our single, press clippings
(blown up in size at Kinkos to appear larger and more substan-
tial), an eight-by-ten glossy, and then we mail them to every
nightclub from Minneapolis to Portland, Maine. Our first stab
at booking a tour will be on the East Coast because Linda's sister lives in New York and Co's dad has recently moved to

Boston; meaning we'll have above-average accommodations in two key cities.

"Hi, this is Coleen from Zuzu's Petals. I'm calling to see if you've received our press kit and single?"

Thank the Lord Co can cold-call strangers and sound both sexy and professional.

"Me? I'm the one in the polka-dot dress. Mmm-hmm. I play bass."

She rolls her eyes. "We're planning on being in your area in March; are there any vacancies on your March roster?"

"Great! Um, how much?" *Fifty dollars,* she mouths to us while we silently cheer and give her the thumbs-up.

"Okay. I'll call you back closer to the date for confirmation and directions to the club . . . are there any local newspapers, weeklies, or radio stations we should send our stuff to?" Co's degree in Mass Communications is hard at work here.

"Ya, I look forward to partying with you, too [big boy]," she purrs. Linda and I mime sticking our fingers down our throats. Not all calls are this successful. We do manage to cobble together some semblance of a tour; it's titled Spread the Myth '91 because we feel more important when we attach titles, names, and handles to our projects. Eric, Soul Asylum's soundman, offers his services on this tour because he's clearly without work for a month and a dear friend, and he probably has a huge crush on Linda—which I notice everyone has. Uncomfortable with visions of us making our first cross-country voyage alone, and concerned for our safety because of our intense naïveté, Eric will work for essentially no money. We are grateful to have this tall hulking Viking with long thinning hair, a handsome Swedish face, and a great big heart. This is a charity gig offered by a concerned big brother who happens to know how to operate and repair musical, sound, and automotive equipment. Eric prides himself on his ability to drive long stretches of the American highway with little or no sleep. He pretty much knows his way around every city in the country and is in no way a weirdo, which is unheard of in his line of work.

Okay, so we weren't able to secure a whole lot of shows with one single on an unheard-of label and paltry press, but enough to almost justify the drive. Thank goodness for that cute photo of Co. Our first show is in Madison at O'Kayz Corral opening, once again, for Poopshovel. From the stage I see my mom standing on top of a table, flashing away on her Instamatic camera. Then my entire cheerleading squad from another lifetime, another world, another me altogether, shuffles in looking scared as hell. O'Kayz is not your Meatloaf-on-the-jukebox softball bar—it is a punk rock club where the people inside don't shampoo ever and find suntans unfortunate. My identity starts to break up on stage and I have a private meltdown, my inner voices fighting over whether I'm a LaFollette cheerleader playing air guitar to Aerosmith after a couple of brews or a semivalid musician who happens to be on stage at the moment. I'm so nervous and confused that I can't play my guitar worth a lick; my hands shake and tremble, my brain scrambles. I break strings. I fear the sound of my own voice— never a good thing if you're standing at a microphone.

WHEN I was a cheerleader in high school, my squad attended cheerleading camp on a college campus in northern Wisconsin. We stayed in dorms and were supposed to follow a busy daily schedule filled with learning new cheers, followed by showcasing our talents in nightly competitions with a variety of squads from all over the state. Because Madison was pretty much the universally accepted coolest city in the state, we felt urban and copped "above it all" attitudes to these small-town girls who took their cheerleading way too seriously.

Bored, some of us drifted from our required activities. Carol and I wound up riding on a country road with two townie boys we met at Hardee's. The car might've been a GTO and

Aerosmith was definitely on the eight-track when we parked. The cute blond boy I was assigned to broke away from kissing and starting sucking hard on my neck, and I must say, it felt good at first. They dropped us off in front of our dorms after dark and we scrambled into our rooms.

"Oh my God!" exclaimed one of the prissier members of my squad, "look at your neck!"

I walked over to the mirror on the wall. Covering the right side of my neck was a black purple welt the size of a baseball for all to see. Fortunately we would be returning home the next morning. Unfortunately my family planned to leave on vacation to a lake in Michigan for a week immediately following my return.

I wore a bandanna every day with my cutoff overalls and tube top.

"Take that thing off, it looks ridiculous," my mom finally commanded after a couple of days.

"I can't."

"Why?"

"Because," I started, "we had an accident at camp when I was on the bottom of a mount and we all collapsed and Marie kicked me hard in the neck."

"So?" she said impatiently.

"The girls all teased me and said my bruise looked like a hickey."

"Let me see."

I sheepishly unknotted my blue bandanna and peeled it away from my injury.

My mom shook her head without amusement and said, "I know what a hickey looks like, and believe me, *that* is no hickey."

Though my mom may've been clueless about the need to protect me from big bad neck-sucking wolves, cheerleading saved my life in a way. It got me away from the Mean Girls in middle school who I was too scared to walk away from even

though they tormented me mercilessly (the Larson twins did
not make cheerleading). Cheerleaders wore an invisible protective shield because they were school property and served an
age-old social function. We were wholesome symbols of enthusiasm and community spirit.

WE have four days off to recover from our crappy Madison show, during which we need to drive to Boston
for show two, opening for my friend Chris's band Come, a
dark moody rock quartet with a big buzz. Geographically I
know this doesn't make a lot of sense, but it's the best we could
do. We bide our time in Columbus, Ohio, because Eric's familiar with the town and we'll be playing there in a couple of
weeks, and we don't have anywhere to stay until we get to
Boston. Eric parks our van in parking lots and we try to sleep,
two in front, two in back, with sleeping bags and pillows scattered around our chilly, fully clothed, filthy bodies. We don't
have any money to speak of—just whatever we saved at home
after rent and bills and the pennies we received from our gig in
Madison. My Texaco credit card pays for gas, and my AAA
card protects us from catastrophe. My tip jar, an old coffee can
full of change, pays for tolls.

On the road, my experiences are reduced to sensory flickers
and crystallized blurs. We're in a new dimension that doesn't
adhere to clocks, or dates, or borders. Highway life attracts a
different breed of cat; truck drivers, traveling salespeople, families, drifters, people with secrets, people running, people hiding. Then there's your garden variety of fugitives, retirees, and
entertainers. Zuzu's Petals fits into more than one of these categories. We, the people of the road, pass in and out of truck
stops, gas stations, and Denny's at all hours of the day and
night. Rarely looking too long, rarely speaking, just moving.
Driving. Hoping the next bathroom doesn't stink to high
heaven. "Watch your gag [reflex]," I say to Co as she enters the

single-stall truck stop toilet that I can't get out of fast enough with my nose buried in my sleeve. Other people's waste is hideous. She looks saddened by my report. We are developing strong, taut thigh muscles from never touching down on toilet seats that may be contaminated with God knows what.

As Co, Linda, and I try to adjust to how the road thing works, we each try very hard not to seem needy or capricious:

"I know we just stopped like a half hour ago but I really have to pee," Co whispers with a wince.

I lean over my green velour captain's seat in an attempt to get closer to her green velour captain's seat. "I don't have to go yet," I say, "but if you say you have to, I'll second that motion."

Eric doesn't like to stop more than necessary because he takes great pride in the length of stretches he's able to drive without a break. No piss stops until two or more people have to go.

I come from a long line of cross-country drivers. My family thought nothing of ten-hour round-trip drives every weekend from Madison to the Upper Peninsula where Wisconsin connects, briefly, with Michigan. Crammed to the ceiling in a station wagon, my family of six drove till we hit ocean whenever possible. Neither of my parents begrudged long drives; in fact, we all grew to love them. My maternal grandmother, a single mom, drove her two young daughters from Illinois to Miami to upstate New York alone and often. I like nothing more than having the excuse of not being able to do anything because you're in a moving vehicle. All you can do is look, think, talk, and sing along; things I could do forever.

D RIVING and staring at the drizzly highway, I don't want to spend too much time absorbing the suck value of our Madison performance. Instead my thoughts rest on another thing that once happened to me at O'Kayz:

My last year in Madison, while Phyll and Co were already in Chicago, I had a roommate named Helen who was a red-haired vixen from Minneapolis. She and Tommy from the Replacements were pals; they either dated or hung out or attended a prom or something, I'm not sure which. When the Replacements were scheduled to play at O'Kayz Corral for two nights, I accompanied Helen to soundcheck because she wanted to pop in and say hello and possibly get on the guest list.

My initial thoughts on the Replacements were cynical: Butch had their first album *Sorry Ma, Forgot to Take Out the Trash* and always claimed that they were going to amount to something because their singer and songwriter, Paul, was extraordinarily gifted. All I heard was boy-centric punk rock. My guy friends got soooo bent out of shape whenever the Replacements came to town. They'd spend the entire day getting fucked up and trashing their apartments; I felt extremely excluded and couldn't understand what they were all so psyched about. When their second album, *Hootenanny*, came out, I began to comprehend the furor; this collection of songs—some wild, some funny, some dead serious and insightful, all profoundly poetic in the good way, and all over the map in style—managed to summarize me and my friends: "getting nowhere as fast as we can," and not wanting to "die before our time cuz" we'd "already used eight of our lives." Or so we liked to think.

The Replacements' O'Kayz gigs were their first out-of-town shows marking the release of their upcoming album, irreverently titled *Let It Be*. Helen and I walked the two blocks from our rented first floor of a run-down house on a subzero February afternoon to O'Kayz. The empty bar looked homely and dingy brown in the light of day. The promoter was talking to the soundman and the band was loitering around the bar sipping drinks. Making eye contact with their singer Paul, I had that make-you-want-to-puke jolt of recognition, that rare unexplained sense of familiarity with a stranger, that "don't I know you from another life?" freakout.

I said to Helen as I eyed the darkly good-looking guy who was clearly a man and not a boy, a rarity among our constellation of males, "I want to meet him."

She looked annoyed and said, "Don't you know who that is?"

And I said, "Ya, I know who that is."

I sauntered up to him and asked if the band had been given dinner and he asked me if I'd like to make him dinner. Charmed I'm sure, but I did not. Though I was more than happy to sit around and drink Heineken and smoke cigarettes with him. He asked my age (twenty-three) and wondered if I had a boyfriend (I said "yes," though technically my troublesome boyfriend and I had broken up, though we still slept together on occasion). All the while I was surging with butterflies, completely sunk by the sound of his low gravelly voice. I knew him somehow, and not from his records or because he was the cream of the crop in our musical world. It was more like a déjà vu or something as weird as that.

I was wearing a white T-shirt that belonged to my other roommate Bill that said "Love" in hippie psychedelic letters, no bra. I had on Lisa's Levi's 501s from eighth grade; every inch of the original jeans material had been replaced with patches. On my feet were my trusty black old man's oxfords. My hair was a bleachy grown-out perm, and I must've recently suffered a bout of discord because my bangs were cut way too short. I remember what I was wearing because there was an aura around this chance meeting and I knew that I was going to overanalyze it for the rest of my life.

We both smoked Marlboro Reds and agreed on the superior quality of a lot of country and pop songs that most deemed uncool, like "Galveston." But he didn't seem to want to talk music. Paul told me he liked my shoes and he liked to dip his grilled cheese sandwiches in ketchup and wondered if I did the same. I did not, but I found his very human desire to connect on a basic level incredibly stirring. We wound up making out in the basement of O'Kayz before he went on stage. And then they probably drove to Chicago for their next gig. After *Let It Be* took hold of the public imagination and became the quintessential voice for our generation, the Replacements whirled out of our constellation and into the big time. Since then I've held a torch in my heart that I know is completely unrealistic. I constantly tell myself to get over it.

R EADING in the van makes us all carsick. We all have nicknames: Co and I remain Betty, Bettel, or Betty Lynn; Linda is Spaz or Lynn; and Eric is Girly (as in girly man).

Pulling into Boston, the most confusing city in the country, during morning rush hour, the car stereo drops out of the dashboard and onto my right foot, which at the time is operating a gas pedal. Co's dad lives somewhere to the right of the big red Citgo sign, the only landmark in the city that helps me with my bearings. When we show up at the club, the Middle East, we are served baba ghanoush and that, or something we all had earlier in the day, causes gastrointestinal distress that might be food poisoning, but the show must go on.

When in a new city, I highly recommend opening for friends who are in very popular bands like we just did in Boston; you get a built-in crowd and you feel like an insider because you personally know the objects of the crowd's adoration. I met Chris from Come on Martha's Vineyard during the Carly Simon summer and we drank tequila shots and hitchhiked together. He was a long, lean guitar-playing boy from Westchester County with floppy reddish brown hair and a cute slightly upturned nose. He was trying to have a wholesome Cape Cod summer away from drugs. We could've been fooling around the whole time but instead, we became close friends and continued to keep in touch, writing long letters about our musical progress and confusing relationships.

I still have horrendous stage fright of the visibly trembling type. The girls graciously endure my personality defect and allow it to coexist with our musical ambitions. I've gotten used to expecting the three or four hours before showtime to be filled with panic and anxiety. I'm losing a lot of weight. Stage fright must be a lot like sniffing glue or inhaling nitrous oxide—I feel like my head's going to pop in a seeing-stars/total rush kind of way. Then the gig happens, someone else goes up there with my body, and my memory is wiped out until after the show.

But don't get me wrong; we're having a blast.

THE headlining band in Portland, Maine, Otis Coyote, might have to cancel our show because their bass player unexpectedly quit. Eric claims he's up for the job if they are up for an extended rehearsal before the gig. Eric, a jack-of-all-trades, pulls this off without a hitch. I can't imagine being so proficient and comfortable with an instrument. Tipsy and elated, Co, Linda, and I storm the stage and join in on Otis Coyote's stomach-churning finale, a sloppy rendition of Steve Miller's "Take the Money and Run." I am fixated on Steve Miller's gall to rhyme "Texas" and "facts is" and repeat those lines over and over, forgetting the rest of the lyrics that are involuntarily etched in my memory through overexposure to FM radio.

After the show we are invited to stay with Otis Coyote's guitarist, Curtis, and we all take a small flatbed ferry to a tiny residential island. Curtis lives in a little A-frame lodge with his girlfriend and their setup is ultracozy and warm and grown-up. It's only fitting that a steamy stew is waiting for us on the stove when we arrive. I am charmed and slightly depressed by my surroundings, wondering why, exactly, I'm envying them.

Ψ

SOMETHING'S happening: Playing several nights a week, living by the seat of our pants, applying nail polish to the tips of our sore fingers for protection, being constantly together, laughing, smoking, drinking, eating, rarely showering. Reader, we rock.

BACK home I have a freshly minted new boyfriend named Ang. Ang is a drummer with long, black, curly-in-ringlets hair and pale blue eyes. He's one of Eric's best friends and he works in a guitar shop where he makes, repairs, and collects excellent guitars and amps that he shares with friends and rents to acquaintances. Thanks to Ang I now play a '63 Gibson SG with double Humbuckers (whatever that means) through a Marshall tube amp that's fortified by an electric green Ibanez Tube Screamer effect pedal. Technically speaking, I play through top-of-the-line vintage collectible gear that would make a gearhead drool and turn chartreuse with envy—which I kind of enjoy because I don't understand any of it or appreciate its value. Ang is like my gear tailor and I love, love, love the wall of sound it produces.

Ang and I met in the rehearsal space we share with his band the Contras and he's often hired by local bands to work as a guitar tech. We'd been eyeing each other for a while. I always smiled and waved at him while he was teching for my friends on the side of the stage during shows, and I could feel his eyes on me while I was up front rocking out. He seemed shy with women and reserved—always superbusy collecting and distributing gear, and working, and practicing, but always friendly. One night he drove me home from a party and I invited him to crash on my couch. My loveseat-size couch and the mattress on the floor I call "bed" are in the same room, but Ang is a gentleman. His legs pathetically dangled off the top of my half-couch and he looked like a giant tangled up in the beige afghan knitted by my mother.

I'm not big on making the first move, but this was ridiculous. "Hey, would you rather join me over here?"

He did. Things evolved from there. Ang will do absolutely anything for me because he says I've added a new dimension to his life; I turned him on to my favorite restaurants and will cook for him on occasion. He just works and drums and meets up with me in between commitments. This is a good arrangement because we're both completely absorbed in the demands of the music world. We're like the poor artistic version of yuppies in the sense that our work is our obsession, but it's nice to have someone to eat dinner with and curl up next to.

Ang is one of those genuinely kind people with a strong sense of right and wrong, and I feel honored to be in his company. He thinks I'm hot, which makes me feel grand.

WHEN you're in a traveling band, the club is supposed to be responsible for providing a hot meal. The quality of our days is often determined by the quality of this meal. In Providence, Rhode Island, we're taken to a deli that serves delicious jalapeño corn chowder. The headlining band, Senator Flux, is from Washington, D.C., and its members are really smart and well educated (as in master's degrees), something that is revelatory for me. Usually rockers tend to be college dropouts or at least real-world dropouts. Senator Flux does well with the Brown University crowd. I've always envied Ivy Leaguers and their pseudo-hippie-intellectual-preppie air of self-assuredness. For some unexplained reason, the promoter licks Co's sweaty, smelly, unshaven armpit in a show of affection. I would never do that; I don't care how cute she looks in that photo.

IN New York we drive from Linda's sister's condo in Bronxville to the Bowery to play at legendary dump CBGB's. Eric offers a loitering man ten dollars to keep an eye on our van while we walk in and out of CBGB's unloading our equipment. There are no doors on the stalls in the bathroom. The whole place is dark and dirty and unfriendly. And empty, except for a woman from Minneapolis who's recently moved to New York, and Linda's sister, and a couple of Japanese tourists. Our tiny audience is receptive and we put on one hell of a show. This place gives me the creeps and I promise myself as God is my witness, I'll never play CBGB's again; it's decades past its heyday when Blondie, the Ramones, and the New York Dolls ruled its roster.

After we're done I can't wait to get back to Bronxville for a shower and TV, but a man at the bar says, "Hi, I'm Albert. I put out Poopshovel's records and they told me about you," he says, talking very fast. "I liked your show, how'd you like to put out a single on my label, Community 3."

"Sure," we say, dumbfounded.

THIS is good for us somehow.

IN Albany, New York, we are scheduled to play before hardcore punk band Helios Creed and a fancy folk/pop group called the Blood Oranges. Oftentimes attention is not paid to the musical compatibility of bands that are scheduled to play together from night to night. We are, well, us. When a shoe cascades by my head from the audience and a drunken guy heckles us, Co screams, "Fuck you, jarhead." I then announce the next band, calling them "the Bloody Oranges" because I'm riled and I feel like insulting everyone within earshot who is not with Zuzu's Petals. As we finish our last song, Linda lobs a well-aimed drumstick at our heckler, hitting him soundly on the forehead.

Co and I loll around the bar after our show while Linda flirts.

"Ever seen a grown woman naked?" Co says to me because Linda's talking to a cute young thang. We snicker to ourselves while remaining dreadfully boring and monogamous.

A nervous, nondescript woman asks me if I know Paul from the Replacements because we're from Minneapolis.

"Ya, I know him," I say, feeling protective and defensive.

"Tell him Tanya from Albany says 'hi'; we write letters," she says.

I don't know why, but this bugs me.

We hate it here and want to leave. We don't get paid as promised. Linda is nowhere in sight. The bar is closing, the bartenders want to leave, but Linda is missing. Pathetically drunk, Co and I imagine Linda maimed, raped, and murdered. We move onto the street and into the van and sit, waiting for Linda, hoping we don't have to report her as missing to the police while we're so drunk.

"Hey," she says, hopping into the backseat like nothing's up.

"Where were you?"

"Oh, I went to some guy's apartment to look at his record collection." Which she probably did.

Linda is a few years younger than Co and I, and she's the youngest of four children in her family. Co and I are both the eldest of four. This is unfortunate for Linda.

WE'VE made no new friends in Philadelphia therefore we have nowhere to stay after our gig. It's 1:00 A.M. With less than one hundred dollars between us and no major credit cards, we drive out of the city until we're too exhausted to go any farther. While creeping through some skanky New Jersey town called Cherry Hill, a neon swatch of rundown strip joints, we pull into the parking lot of a rent-by-the-hour hooker hotel. All agree to endure the affront since it only costs thirty dollars. Eric refers to it as a "fuck dump." Inside, our eyes first rest on the Vaseline finger smears all over the walls. And there are bloodstains on the bathroom floor and pubic hairs on the bedspread. Lord knows what lurks in the shag carpeting. I advise everyone to sleep on top of the beds fully clothed to avoid STDs. In the next room a loud, violent-sounding domestic brawl ensues. On HBO we watch a show called *The Making of Silence of the Lambs*, which is something we should not be watching.

"If someone breaks in the room to rape and kill us," I advise Linda, my bunkmate for the night, "roll off the bed and under it." Co and Eric are on top of the bed closest to the door. I figure Linda and I have a chance to escape unseen while our friends are being murdered.

This is considered paying your dues.

I WAS eleven and babysitting my three siblings on a hot August night. I don't remember where my parents were, but I hated babysitting. I was known as "the meanest babysitter in the world." Fights erupted, there was screaming and yelling, and a lot of "you're not the boss of me's." It wasn't pretty.

Regularly paralyzed with fear at night by being the oldest and only one awake in our house, I was more than certain that Bad Men were going to break in and murder us. One time while babysitting, a car peeled up our steep driveway while drag racing around the neighborhood—I was sure it was the end. To my parents I acted like I was grown up enough to handle the responsibility of babysitting, and I must've known where my parents were, someone's house in the neighborhood, or at a restaurant. But on that August night, the tornado sirens went off.

I've had a "tornado problem" since my first viewing of *The Wizard of Oz* on TV at my Gogi's house when I was four. When the movie tornado headed toward the Gale farm in

Kansas, I hid behind a brocade upholstered chair, refusing to come out from behind it, afraid the TV tornado was in the room, or just outside. And for whatever the reason, every time the sirens went off, I was blinded with panic. They go off a lot in southcentral Wisconsin over the course of a summer, as it's part of "tornado alley."

My mom is a storm lover, one of those go-outside-and-take-a-look types. She had little patience for my tornado anxiety. That night when my parents returned home from wherever they were, they couldn't find us and started searching every room in the house. We were asleep in sleeping bags in the southern corner of the basement on the concrete floor next to laundry piles. My folks found this amusing.

THIS is something that all of us like to do in the van: sing along to rock songs on the radio using great big ballsy Ethel Merman voices. Songs like AC/DC's "Back in Black" and Black Sabbath's "Crazy Train" are especially effective, but Dylan's "Lay Lady Lay" also works because there's no people like show people—which we now are. Sort of.

"Arggggh, Clapton," Co, Linda, and I cry in unison when "Layla" comes on the radio. Clapton is our kryptonite.

It is within the confines of the van that we get to know one another better than we probably want to: Co can make one of her nostrils close completely, visibly collapse, simply by inhaling through her nose. I can lay my lower lip across my horribly crooked bottom teeth and make it look like I have only one tooth. We call the tooth "Billy," and I secretly flash him when you'd least expect it, but never by request. Linda can do a frighteningly accurate imitation of the cartoon character Droopy. Eric's a little too reserved or shy to share any of his hidden talents.

Regardless of who occupies which seat, the driver is always "Dad," and the copilot is always "Mom." "The kids" are the whiny troublemakers in the back who are always hungry and having to pee. On a Sunday morning driving through the mountains of Pennsylvania, Dad (Eric) flips in a cassette of *Jesus Christ Superstar* (original Broadway cast). I am Mom and the kids are asleep in the back.

To my surprise and delight, Eric knows every song, lyric, utterance, and dynamic to the entire soundtrack. Like me. We sing without stopping for two solid hours; sometimes Eric is Judas and I'm Mary Magdalene, sometimes I'm Jesus and he's Pontius Pilate, sometimes we're both King Herod. Outside, sun streams through the Poconos. I have never felt so happy, alive, and free in my entire life. The kids, for once, don't complain.

O N our return visit to Columbus, Ohio, for an actual gig, the manager at the club, Stashes, says, "Congratulations, your picture is on the cover of a magazine!" We rush down the block to a record store and scan the piles of free press resting in a variety of metal magazine racks. Gasping in unison, there we are on the cover of *Rock Around the World*, a schedule and guide fanzine that tells about every band on tour at the moment. I sent *Rock Around the World* one of those padded envelopes containing our "promotional package." Grabbing several copies, we run to the van with our spoils. This type of press will help a lot, since it's an international publication. There it is, my teeny-tiny penis for all the world to see.

T HE last show of our first tour is in Ann Arbor, Michigan. We're opening for Babes in Toyland and Tad (a popular punk band out of Seattle that makes records for Sub Pop, a cool Seattle-based record label that won't give us the time of day). Bands out of Seattle are starting to Mean Something in the underground music world, but I don't know a thing about them. I do know that this is considered a tasty gig for fledglings like us. It's safe to say that we have nothing musically in common with these two bands.

Our drive is a short one, Columbus, Ohio, to Ann Arbor, no more than three or four hours on a drizzly afternoon. I'm Mom dozing in the front passenger's seat, the kids are napping. When Eric mutters, "Shit, fuck, damn," I snap to attention. A siren is wailing and we're the vehicle that's being pulled over. The kids stir.

"Girly, have you been speeding again," they scold.

A young officer who looks like Rolf the Nazi in *The Sound of Music* is standing at the driver's side window asking for Eric's license. As the owner of the van, I pass Eric the vehicle registration and insurance information, and the officer grabs the documents and goose steps back to the cruiser.

"Were you speeding?" I ask.

"I really don't think so," Eric whispers.

Rolf returns with another officer, who looks like Mr. C from *Happy Days.*

"This vehicle is registered as being maroon; when and why did you paint it?" inquires the officer.

"Um, this is the color it was when I bought it, sir," I say, leaning forward so he can see me in the passenger seat. Maroon. Would Barbie drive a maroon Dream Van?

"Everyone out of the vehicle with identification. Leave all of your belongings inside," Rolf barks.

Huh? We're all being corralled into the police car and they lock all four of us inside the cruiser. Helplessly we watch them return to our van. In slow-motion horror our instruments spill, drop, and tumble onto the pavement. The drizzle turns to rain. The claustrophobia of being locked in the backseat sandwiched between my two friends is building into a full-on panic attack. I have to check out to prevent myself from freaking out. Can they do this to us? We haven't done anything wrong. I hope our instruments aren't too badly damaged because of their rough handling. I don't know what they think they're going to find.

Rolf returns to our detention holding a red purse and a briefcase.

"Whose purse is this, whose briefcase?" The owners claim their possessions and are promptly handcuffed. The other two step out of the cruiser to ask questions.

"What's going on?"

"Drug possession."

"Huh?"

"Marijuana and paraphernalia. Where is the rest stashed? Tell us or we'll call in the dogs. We'll find it, so you might as well save us a few hours and tell us right now."

"Marijuana and paraphernalia" means a speck or two in a pipe and a teensy-weensy roach and some rolling papers that Eric uses to roll his own cigarettes.

"Sir, we're just a small-time rock band on our way to play in Ann Arbor at a campus nightclub. We really need the money from this show to pay for gas in order to drive home to Minnesota. We're not druggies or dealers or criminals of any kind."

"You might as well just tell us where it is," Rolf persists, licking his chops at the prospect of bringing down a drug ring, "We'll find it."

"I swear to God, sir, you've found all there is to find."

"We're taking them in and booking them for possession."

"Will we make our show?"

"That's not our problem; you should've thought about that before you decided to break the law."

Two of us drive the van in silence, following the police car into the Maumee Police station. The other two sit in back of the police car dying of fright. At the station, the two in cuffs are shown to a holding pen, a purgatory before going behind bars. Rolf is still gung ho about making a bust, while Mr. C clearly sees the folly in all of this and seems irritated by the paperwork. The woman sitting behind a desk in the office tells the two who are not under arrest that we should never smoke pot in the van, they can smell it every time. A lot of pot has probably been smoked in that van, probably even before I bought it judging from its decor; with the shag carpet and velour, it's a stoner's paradise.

The two not arrested are free to make unlimited phone calls; first they call the club to tell them of our status, claiming that they'll clear up this matter in no time and make it to the show. The folks at the club are not so sure; they tell us the Ohio/Michigan border is notorious for drug busts. Evidently huge amounts of drugs are funneled into Detroit. Who knew? One of us calls her mom in search of bail money, but the mom is also without a major credit card at the moment and adds, "If you've been smoking pot, I'll kill you"; not in a literal way, more of an "I'd die of embarrassment" way. "Where's *she* been," wonders the daughter with amusement.

The two arrestees are allowed back into the office for their obligatory phone calls. Bail must be raised for their release. A member from the band Arcwelder is called because we share a rehearsal space with them and know that they are engineers by day; he probably has major credit cards. He does. We race to Ann Arbor in stunned silence.

Zuzu's Petals have been detained in Ohio on drug charges and will not be appearing tonight," a guy announces over the loud speaker at the Blind Pig in Ann Arbor. The crowd jeers and boos and yells stuff like, "Fuckin' pigs." My dad, recently divorced for the second time and residing in a northern suburb of Detroit, is in the audience, accompanied by business associates.

We run in breathless, hours late, and the manager yells, "Get up there! You have ten minutes before Babes in Toyland."

Co and I are carrying our guitar cases and we plug into the Babes' amps while Linda adjusts Lori's drums. We rip through two or three songs at breakneck speed, still wearing our jackets, surging with the aftereffects of our harrowing experience with the law, for the first time ever feeling tough and street-wise, for the first time, truly punk rock. We are grateful for the release performing provides.

Except now I have to face my dad.

"Tell me what happened. Are you all right?" he asks, crushing me with a bear hug. I tell him. My dad, a fast driver, has no great love for state troopers. He doesn't play the stern disciplinarian, or the disappointed and injured parent. He might be a tad embarrassed that his guests feel sorry for him because poor Lance clearly has a troubled, wayward daughter. But that's about it.

G ROWING up in my house with young parents, each kid had a different role with my dad. Any passion of our dad's that our mom found uninteresting, one of us filled. My brother was Dad's hockey buddy, Megan was his fellow super-friendly sporty buddy, Hillary was the princess waif in the basement who was often alone and ignored as the third girl preceding the birth of the heir—her role was tentative, but we didn't worry about her too much because she was beautiful, and beautiful people are treated kindly by the world. I was Dad's rock 'n' roll pal. For Christmas I never received the Donny Osmond and DeFranco Family records I requested on a carefully itemized list. Instead my dad gave me records by Badfinger, the Allman Brothers, and Don McLean. The very first record he bought me was *Different Drum* by Linda Ronstadt and the Stone Ponies. I was in kindergarten and he was trying to break me of my Monkees habit—I doubt he knew that the quiet, hat-wearing Monkee Michael Nesmith wrote "Different Drum."

A low point in our musical outings was the annual John Denver concert once I became too old to be seen at a John Denver concert (though I secretly always liked them). The highlight was seeing *Jesus Christ Superstar* on Broadway. My family went to New York for Thanksgiving the year I was in sixth grade, and my dad and I bustled down Broadway to catch a matinee featuring Ben Vereen as Judas. Like the Beatles' *Sgt. Pepper's Lonely Hearts Club Band*, the Who's *Tommy* was one of my dad's favorite Saturday-morning housecleaning motivational albums. When the movie came out, naturally I would attend with my dad. *Tommy* was not the most apropos film to take a twelve-year-old with a wild imagination to; it scared me shitless when Tina Turner entered that sarcophagus filled with wall-to-wall needles. The summer before I started high school, my dad, remembering my first girlhood obsession, took me to a small nightclub to see two of the original Monkees on a low-rent tour. While in college, he'd meet me downtown at Headliners and we'd take in Leon Redbone or George Thorogood together. I wonder if my dad can trace the link between our one connection and my career choice.

L EAVING the Blind Pig in Ann Arbor before Tad's set, we drive through the night, heading straight home. Eric takes the night shift; Co, Linda, and I take turns behind the wheel after daybreak. While passing through Lyndon Station, Co turns to Linda and says, "Ever hear about the time we drove through a fire?" Co relates our harrowing adventure, pointing out the charred sticks piercing the landscape where there were once majestic pines.

11: Our Lady of the Highway, Pray for Us

R EENTRY is difficult. After unloading our gear at the rehearsal space and dropping everyone off at their respective dwellings, I trudge into my dusty apartment. Only now what? Laundry? Nap? Houseclean? Open bills? I feel lost. We've just been through something together, and as sort of sick of one another as we are, I find it hard to cut the cord, burst the bubble, return to, *gulp*, reality.

After two hours at home, we meet at the CC Club for drinks. It's hard to break the cycle of drive, eat, go to a bar for sound check, hang out, play. It's easier to stay on the road once you return home, to pretend you're still on tour. Only there is no gig tonight and it leaves a gal feeling empty, without a purpose. We drink beer and share our war stories only to be usurped by all of the other guys in the bar who are able to one-up every harrowing tale we try to share with their own lurid hijinks: "One night in Memphis I was held hostage by a psycho girl at gun point." "Oh ya, the entire band was strip-searched by a German lady border guard." All of their stories have slightly sexual undertones. I sigh and look around. This whole bar is full of people, mostly male, who are still on the road at home.

The next morning I schedule studio time at Six Feet Under studios so we can record our new single. It should come as no surprise that Eric can also operate recording equipment with aplomb. For this recording, Eric, along with his friend Tim, who runs the studio out of his basement, will engineer and produce. Ang makes sure everyone has great-sounding gear and beams at me with pride, constantly reminding me that I rock.

With Linda on board in the studio for the first time, this session goes smoothly. Because it's Eric at the helm, we're all completely at ease with one another. Aside from his familiarity with all of our tics and foibles, he knows our songs inside and out, offers minor alterations, helps me find the guitar solo for my new song "Johanne," and patiently helps us find our voices while encouraging us to rock really hard and play really loud. Laughs dominate the raucous party atmosphere in this dark, dreary basement, and the session goes well. Because of this, our second single reflects this joy.

The recording begins with a sonic three-chord blast we now call "Jackals." I wrote the music, Co wrote the bass riff and the lyrics: "I like Laurie and Linda, I like people who say what they mean, I even like geeks, but lately I only know freaks." Eric torked up the sound in the studio doing a bunch of tricks with effects and machinery that I don't understand. "Jackals" sounds heavy and menacing; the multiple layers of guitars and feedback coupled with Co's authoritative voice deliver a powerful punch. Side one ends with "Categories," a social rant penned by Co. This time she's protesting the tendency to pigeonhole and label artists: "Describe yourself in just one word," she challenges. At song's end Co flips off the media, saying, "I know . . . you're a chick band," that I top off with a sarcasm-drenched "right."

I've written a long, slow ballad called "Johanne" that is about as melancholy of a song as I have in me. I wrote it after a musician came up to my apartment for sex. This encounter confused me because I sort of assumed there would be a relationship attached. The one useful morsel I got from this lowly tryst was the chords that would turn into "Johanne." It is by far the best unrequited love song I've written to date; I'm not sure if it's because I asked my phantom lover to show me a new chord pattern, or because I was so stunned by the unfortunate outcome of our exchange: "All these things I do because, because I'll never fall in love with you," I lament. I'm excited about giving this song a vague, puzzling name so I choose the German spelling of the name John. Or so I think. Co says, "It's spelled J-o-h-a-n-n." Her name is spelled C-o-l-e-e-n making her "Co" with a hard O and not Colleen by any stretch—I'm suspicious of her authority on the subject. I insist that it's spelled with an "e" on the end, which is wrong. So now every-one will think that I'm singing about a girl named Joanne; it might make us popular with the young lesbian set, which is ab-solutely fine with me.

The recording process gets better each time we do it. I think I've found my true singing voice; it's not very loud or powerful, but it's mine and I'm comfortable with it, as comfortable as I am with anything. Which is not at all. But at least I'm no longer trying to sound like someone I'm not, like the impossi-ble mixture of Hank Williams and Wendy O. Williams. Gone are the days of screeching and yelling. Which depends on the song and the blood-alcohol level, of course, but I've settled on gathering strength from the lyrics and by staying in tune.

We choose artwork from a black-and-white deco-era art photo entitled "Independence Day." It's a picture of a flapper joyously riding a phallic rocket up to the grinning moon. We issue a handwritten warning on the back cover, "The name's ours, suckers" because there are, all of a sudden, a profusion of bands all over North America calling themselves Zuzu's Petals, which is absolutely unacceptable. I have real reasons why we're called Zuzu's Petals; we're not trying to be cutesy or kitsch.

SOMEONE has found an old prayer card, probably in the folds of a rummage sale purse, and it has a picture of the Virgin Mary in prayer on it. Not only that, Mary is lovingly looking over the world with protective grace. Mary on the card is ten times larger than the world she stands on top of with an aura of illumination; a ring of mist encircles the globe, the ring is drawn to be a highway with ant-size cars driving around the global thoroughfare. The prayer card asks, "Our Lady of the Highway, Pray for Us." We can't afford a soundman/driver for our next East Coast tour; we're going it alone. Making copies of this prayer card on postcard-size-cardboard, it announces the dates and locations of the shows on our second self-booked tour.

S T. LOUIS is an eleven-hour drive from Minneapolis. My family lived in St. Louis for a year when I was two. I have no memory of this time, but still it's somehow significant to me. St. Louis, I decide, is in my blood (like grease paint, alcohol, and nicotine). Given the time, and I have a lot of it staring out the window of a moving vehicle all day, I can attach unnecessary importance to just about anything. And the thing of it is, these subconscious pep talks work, because everything in St. Louis is fabulous—the club, the other band, Small Ball Paul, the people there for the show, who actually have our first and second singles. It makes our drive that began at the crack of dawn worthwhile.

Our second show is in Louisville, Kentucky, the following day, a 264-mile drive. Not having any appealing options for overnight accommodations (it seems many of our new friends still live with their parents), we begin our drive after the show, hoping to find somewhere decent to park before daybreak. Coleen and I cannot see in the dark worth a damn, so it's up to Linda. It's only polite to stay awake and keep Linda company and to allow her to choose the music she'll drive to. The problem is, Linda is so much more highly evolved musically than Co and me that she listens to rare, obscure music favored by music snobs; stuff like Nick Drake and Kevin Ayers, who are miles away from Foghat and Head East. This music makes those of us not driving very sleepy. Once she clears East St. Louis, unable to safely drive another mile without nodding off, Linda pulls into an all-night truck stop. At 4:00 A.M. it's teeming with activity; this is a culture unto itself. Sex and drugs, coffee, eggs, and country music permeate the air. When we stroll through with our messy hair and crazy thrift store dresses that are all starting to tear at the armholes because of the rigors of our profession, we could easily be mistaken for pavement princesses (truck stop whores). We scowl and give dirty looks to anyone who's leering or jeering, and hurry in and out with a potty stop and a big sweet Coke before attempting sleep. Very tired, and feeling a little unsafe, we imagine things like being abducted, raped, murdered, or worse, sold into white slavery. But maybe that's not a "we" thought, maybe that's just me. Regardless, all of the windows are rolled up, all of the doors are locked, and it's well over eighty degrees and muggy. The air in the van is stale and thick but we need a couple of hours of sleep. But it's not exactly sleep, your eyes are closed and your brain is demanding unconsciousness, but your survival instincts insist that your ears stay open. Every twenty minutes or so you find yourself lifting your head and peering out the window looking for the source of the guttural laughter or honking horn. You wake up confused and drenched in sweat.

IN high school Linda was a varsity diver. Upon entering college, Co was granted sixteen free credits (an entire semester) for testing out of German. In grade school I purposely misspelled "read" as "raed" because one of the Larson twins had just been eliminated and I didn't want her to be mad at me for outspelling her.

IN Louisville we're booked into an old dark bar called Uncle Pleasant's that sounds pedophilic to us. A dozen pool tables decorate this joint, never a good sign. There's not much to do once you pull into the club except play video games and shoot pool. Two things I hate to do: shoot pool and play video games.

To earn our very large two-hundred-dollar guarantee, we're supposed to play three sets' worth of material. We don't know three sets' worth of material, not even close, though we dredge up everything we've ever half learned or discarded. On a break between the second and third set I plea with the bartender/manager, "You know, nobody's really paying attention anymore, can't we just call it a night?" He stands committed to the terms of our agreement, which were not crystal clear to us when we booked the show (or maybe we just blocked out the three-set stipulation, overly wowed by the two hundred clams). There are actually people here watching us (because the cute press photo made its way into the local entertainment weekly), but by the third set most patrons are playing pool because that's either what they came in to do originally, or they're bored because we're in the midst of repeating our first set.

It really bugs me that I'm not slick enough on the guitar to be able to spontaneously pluck out new material on the spot. It's just occurring to me that when other bands play horrendously sloppy in front of their audiences under the guise of material, that they're choosing not to play well, choosing not to try, consciously aware that they're punishing their audiences. I wish that were an option for us. We pretend like it is.

THERE'S no air-conditioning in the Dream Van, and sometimes I remember that I have MS because of the stifling heat. When overheated and overtired, I can feel—meaning not feel because it's numb—all of the damage done to the left side of my body. I rationalize my career choice by pointing out that I spend half the day flopping around in the van chugging water, which has got to be better for me than hustling around that stuffy diner taxing my body and brain. The Coca-Cola, beer, and chain-smoking that fill the night doesn't really count. And it's a really good thing that Linda has prescription Motrin at eight hundred milligrams a pop.

Linda and I don't complain much or call attention to our health problems. There's almost a superstition surrounding our diseases, like if we bring them into the forefront, it's an open invitation for them to invade our bodies and act up. I'm beginning to think there are probably millions of people out there going about their lives with closeted autoimmune diseases.

FOR the last decade it has been sort of a punk rock thing to harbor at least a small degree of hostility toward your audience—to snarl at, spit upon, flip off—in other words, to bite the hand that feeds you. Right now it's in vogue to be really boring and introverted on stage, to ignore the audience while lost in the windmills of your brilliance. I want to put on a show like it's a backyard play on top of a picnic table with a little Ziegfield Follies mixed in.

Sometimes Zuzu's Petals gets into trances of sound and vibration while on stage; our bloody fingers are hitting metal strings or pounding drums so hard the sticks and strings break, and it becomes a night of primal scream therapy. Other times our bodies gyrate and sway, our feet unconsciously tap-dance, play hopscotch, and fall into ballet positions at the mike. Our hands are dirty, calloused, and banged up. The ridges of our fingernails swell and bleed. We're covered in mysterious bruises, probably from hauling heavy cumbersome equipment in and out of clubs every night. A helping hand is never refused. We can do it ourselves, but we appreciate the help.

"We're a bunch of gay men," Co decides out of left field one afternoon in the van. We chuckle. "No, really, think about it," she continues, "we're campy and into clothes, we shop whenever we can, and we love scruffy pretty boys hell-bent on breaking our hearts."

"Oh, man, you're right."

"Gay men with vaginas."

"But a lot of my gay friends are in better relationships than

we are, and they're much better groomed," Linda argues, shuf-
fling through the shoe box filled with cassettes. "Hey, has anyone seen that Bee Gees tape?"

"So if we're not gay men, what are we?" I ask, adding, "I
last saw it under Queen."

"Nope, that's Abba."

"Fine."

"Bitch."

"Who you calling 'bitch,' fag?"

"Loser."

Not that we defy stereotype. The next day all three of us get
our periods.

THE drive from Louisville to Charlotte, North Carolina, is
464 miles; we've driven approximately 1,349 miles in
three days. In Charlotte we pull up to a cinder block building
aptly called the Fallout Shelter. A guy with a menacing mo-
hawk approaches us and out of his mouth spills, "You all have
a pleasant trip?" in a syrupy-sweet drawl. We smile and nod
with our lips pulled tight so as not to laugh. I like how gracious
and polite people are in the South; midwesterners can be so up-
tighty.

Every night we meet other bands from the town in which
we're playing, and they're usually very congenial. Each and
every one of us wants the same thing—superstardom; those
claiming to only be doing it for the "love of music" are lying. I
wonder if any of us will make it; the odds against that are staggering. On occasion a bitter guitar-playing guy will scoff at me,
noting aloud my irreverence toward my instrument and my
lack of virtuosity. Lighten up, dude, it's just a prop, a writing
tool, something fun to bang on. I doubt these bitter naysayers
spend half the time I do on lyrics, on getting the right words together in a line. We're assumed to have a leg up on these local
bands from other cities because we're actually on tour. Most of

the musicians are younger than us. Most of the musicians are male.

It's over ninety degrees in Charlotte in September, so when the young, attractive techie offers us lodging in the unoccupied, air-conditioned home in which he's house-sitting, we're more than happy to oblige. The only hitch is that the manager who was kind enough to give us the show is the young, attractive techie's girlfriend and employer. And, for some reason, she cannot know that we will be spending the night with her boyfriend. Which is so dumb because we only want the air-conditioning and a night away from the puking members of a party house.

Regardless, we park our van several blocks away from this promising house to ensure the girlfriend does not know that we're inside. Two of us promptly crash on top of a cat piss-atomized bedspread, too exhausted to complain or move elsewhere. One of us stays up with the techie and ends up doing the wild thing as the girlfriend rings the phone off the hook and circles the house in her Volkswagen. The following morning we eat at our first Waffle House, feeling low-down and trashy. Within a week, one of us has a burning crotch and some awful infection.

You know that rock 'n' roll lifestyle and all of those fringe benefits we've been hoping for? They are not there for the asking, readily available, at our beck and call. I don't know why. Rock guys always have girls dripping off them, even skanky rock guys. We're not even skanky—well, sometimes—but not as a governing principle. Apparently males aren't socialized to be fawning self-sacrificing fools. When one of us has an opportunity, it's almost like an obligation to act upon it. The one time one of us does, though, there are consequences.

WE'LL do anything for a laugh, like order things in restaurants we don't really want, like peach wine coolers, or just because the entree has a name like "Moons Over My Hammy."

ACCORDING to our atlas there's a large stretch of beachfront that is a national park and campground in Virginia Beach, Virginia. We have three days off so we decide to take a mini vacation. I am no camper—ask Rog—but sleeping bags in the open air and out of the stale stench of the van is manageable. There is no one else camping within seeing distance. Skinny-dipping backlit by the moon, and frolicking on white sand running up and down the beach, chasing schools of dolphins like little girls—these may possibly be those incomparable perfect moments that I'll embellish and romanticize ad nauseum as I age. While crashed in a sleeping bag on the sand, I fix my gaze on a single star in the sky, mesmerized as it moves like a line in an Etch A Sketch. We are our own bosses, completely free and fending for ourselves. Dependent on no one. When it's the three of us alone, I feel like we could conquer any obstacle. Though I've never been naturey, it's nice to be in it for a change; it sort of wipes the gritty, stale slate clean.

I have one credit card; it's a low-rent card for Spiegel catalogue. It offers something called Travel Plus. With Travel Plus and my AAA card, we are sometimes able to stay in a halfway decent inn at Motel 6 prices. On our final night off in Virginia Beach we book ourselves into a La Quinta courtesy of Travel Plus because we need to clean up before heading north to the big cities.

While in constant company of ravishing brunettes, I realize that I don't know how to "do" my hair. I have hair the color of dirty truck-stop toilet water that's a thin, frizzy glop stuck to my skull. Co and Linda have blow-drying skills and strategies. I look like trailer trash every morning in Denny's because I have to wear those awful pink foam rollers to tame my hair. Not only that, I've had acne since I was twelve and it doesn't seem to be going away as I inch closer and closer to thirty. Co and Linda have an occasional zit, so infrequent that they call attention to them. Linda washes her face with a Buf-Puf every night. I'm often too tired to bother. If we were the Brady girls, I'd be Jan surrounded by two Marcias.

It might come as a surprise that it is considered punishment to have to share a bed with Linda. She is a diagonal-sleeping, flip-flopping kicker. In autumn before the first hard freeze, it is punishment to sleep with Co on account of her snuffling, gurgling allergies. It is punishment to hang out with me all day when I'm in a bitchy mood but easy to sleep with me; I'm so afraid of offending anyone that I usually lie flat and still and stay awake most of the night. Linda can be spacey, chronically late, or take too long ignoring the fact that she has equipment to load after a show, meaning that someone else will do it for her. Co can be a know-it-all; quick to point out what others are doing wrong and sometimes when she drinks too much she becomes "Drunkenstein," a real monster. I can be a mean drunk. Linda can be not as smart as she usually is after a few too many and she's prone to embellishment and/or exaggeration. There's usually a good chance that we're amusing drunks, at least we like to think so. The guys who work at First Avenue in Minneapolis call us the Slur Girls. You probably have an idea of the many flaws I possess on any given day: I love smoking and think it's glamorous, am prone to negativity, I sometimes bolster myself at the expense of others, I resort to the old silent treatment when things are not going my way, and my humor can cross over into the land of cruelty when I'm feeling low.

Linda has been spending a great deal of time on the phone talking to a booking agent in England; they seem to have hit if off. She gives him blow-by-blow descriptions of our antics. This guy wants us to tour England in the near future. Our second single is evidently hot over there.

"Oh, Co and Laurie are sitting under the sink for no reason

after drinking several vodka and cranberries," we hear her disclose.

"Co and Laurie are racing down the hallway on a luggage carrier. Oops, they just crashed."

"Co just yelled at us for smoking in the room first thing in the morning."

We're not terribly outrageous no matter how you slice it.

IN Richmond, Virginia, we are on a bill with another band calling themselves Zuzu's Petals.

"We have two records out," I warn in front of the club as we unload our van.

"We're going to England," we hiss (though nothing's been confirmed).

I don't find the humor in this booking, though I probably should. ZZP-Richmond is a female-fronted pop band that sounds like 10,000 Maniacs (which is not uncommon these days). There's nothing objectionable about their music—they're extremely proficient—except they're a little on the boring side. I'm determined to be the last Zuzu's Petals standing at the end of this name war.

THE things we have going for us is that we've managed to cobble together some interesting and occasionally catchy tunes. We have chemistry, and sometimes charisma. Co and Linda have exquisite stage presence; Co is alternately sexy and aloof or tough and fierce. Linda is flirty and smiley yet powerful. Co and I harmonize nicely, our voices blend well like unpolished Indigo Girls or something. Sometimes we are fresh, and/or exciting and/or rocking. Sometimes people will say to us, "You guys really rock for girls." Which, I assume, is intended to be a compliment. We write ballads and country-tinged tunes, but there are also rockers of the head-shaking, bend-at-the-waist variety. We have amassed some incredible costuming at the nation's thrift stores; suede fringed vests, skintight satin cocktail dresses, leather coats, Victorian velvet minidresses. On occasion we catch ourselves thinking that we're kind of cool because we are.

But on any given night we could suck. Linda calls our particular brand of sucking "sucking hard." Because that's what it is. A bad sound system, a broken string, an off night, can throw us over the edge and into the land of sucking hard. I struggle nightly with my guitar, especially when it comes to nailing solos. I love the streamlined melodic single-note guitar solos favored by George Harrison. Unfortunately that clean and simple style is probably the most difficult to pull off. There's not much you can do when your ship is going down except drink too much and pretend that is the reason you suck so hard.

I have a particularly bad habit that infuriates my bandmates: after a song littered with mistakes, things I'm sure are glaringly obvious to the audience, I call attention to them on mike by saying, "Oops" or "Sorry about that." Nobody probably notices these gaffs until I call attention to them, but I assume that everyone in the club is a better musician than me, and therefore I must note my many fuckups. My compulsion to apologize is like a reflex I have no control over.

A ND we'd better be rested because in the next seven nights we're playing Philadelphia, Providence, Hoboken, New York, Brooklyn, New Haven, Boston, and Portland. We seem to be on the same tour as Nirvana, a band out of Seattle who used to be on Sub Pop but are now on a major label—they just released a record called *Nevermind* that was produced by Butch.

Duct tape will repair absolutely anything. We tape our bra straps and dress sleeves to our skin, tape our cords onto our guitars so they don't slip out during a set. We wind duct tape around our cuticles if they're too sore or bloody from strumming or drumming.

In New Haven we share the bill with a covenant of black-clad, black-haired, white-faced ghouls, a Goth band who fills the air with such extreme seriousness that all we can do is giggle. They carry a mascot, a stone gargoyle, to the stage with silent reverence. "Be careful," whispers the Morticia Addams look-alike, "don't drop him."

"Aren't you cute with your Aveda products," purrs an Elvira wannabe while Co and I do our hair and makeup in the bathroom mirror.

Stumbling out of the ladies' room while releasing guffaws, we're accosted by a smiling, balding man wearing black horn-rimmed glasses. "I know who you are!" he sings like he's the rock 'n' roll Mr. Rogers.

He holds up both of our singles proudly. This has never happened to us, and because it's a guy who would not look out of place with a pocket protector instead of say, Joe Perry from Aerosmith, we're mildly disappointed.

By night's end we accept the invitation to stay at the apartment of our first fan, deciding he's either harmless or he's a sociopath. We're banking on the former. We could become human sacrifices if we stayed with the Goth kids, so Mr. Rogers seems like our best bet. We follow him in our van to a prefab apartment building and enter his bachelor lair filled with doilies and frills; it's a place a grandmother would feel at home in. He pulls from his fake wood wall shelves mountains of photo albums containing prints of all of the thousands of rock shows he's attended around the world. The only food in his house is Entenmanns's cherry coffee cake, something I hate.

Co and I feign fatigue and our host insists we sleep in his lacy canopy bed.

"Oh, you simply must; you're my guests," he implores. Burying our faces in our sleeves to muffle our giggles, we leave Linda to ooh and aah over his library of photos.

I'm not making fun of this guy. He's an extreme fan. I don't understand his obsession, but thank goodness people like him exist, people who support musicians in the earliest phases of their careers. Who knows, maybe someday we'll be Somebody and he'll have the satisfaction of claiming to have seen us when there were only six people in the audience like there were the first time he saw R.E.M., like there were the first time I saw R.E.M.

BECAUSE we are purse-totin' mamas, we need to carry our handbags on stage and place them at the bottom of the microphone stand or next to the drum stool so that no one rips us off while we're working. This becomes our trademark, and we buy a lot of fine vintage purses in our spare time while loitering around the nation's small and large cities. Because I now play through a Marshall amp with tubes, I've torn off the two Ls at the end of "Marshall" so it's now named Marsha.

From night to night we never know what to expect. All we can hope for is that someone shows up and likes our music (or our drummer's good looks), and that they'll tell their friends about us so that the next time we visit, there will be more people in the audience. We are new music evangelists, our movement as grassroots as it gets. Over fifty in the audience while we're playing is considered stupendous. Of course I have no idea who's out there on account of my out-of-body hysterical state. To an observer I might look like a psycho or a bitch as I sit alone at a table in my trance of self-calming, not hearing what others are saying, not receiving them with warmth (this is why they invented dressing rooms). I'm not a prima donna—

really—just a complete basket case burning up with white-hot panic.

We get ready for our shows in friends' or relatives' apartments, public restrooms, or in the van:

"She puts on more makeup . . ." Co croons from the backseat, able to perfectly apply liquid eyeliner on a bumpy road, to the melody of Clapton's reviled "You Look Wonderful Tonight."

"More and more makeup," Linda adds while also applying liquid eyeliner.

I can't do liquid eyeliner because my left hand shakes too much.

"And then I ask her, 'Do I look all right?'" I chime in.

Co and Linda respond, "My darling, you need more makeup . . . tonight."

Each member of the band attracts a different demographic: Linda has the most males between eighteen and thirty-five; Co draws most females between eighteen and thirty-five; and I get quiet introverts, pseudo-intellectuals, and the undiagnosed, untreated mentally ill.

It's important to ingratiate ourselves to the person in charge of booking the shows in each city; if this person likes you, the next time you blow through he or she might give you a better show on a weekend night playing before a band guaranteed to draw a large crowd. We can forget about returning to Charlotte after that cute techie debacle.

We're still paying our dues.

I WISH I could provide a picturesque account of the American countryside, or a glimpse at the uniqueness of its cities, but all we're seeing are interstates and dark bars. You've seen one Goodwill, you've seen them all—though each one promises a long-forgotten treasure that we're dying to unearth. Daily thrift shopping preserves our sanity on a budget.

When Zelda Fitzgerald was my age, she became absorbed in ballet. Okay, obsessed. It turns out she was pretty good—talented enough to be invited to join a highly regarded European ballet troupe. The fact that she was in her late twenties, married to a celebrity author, and a mother, made her ballet jones raise eyebrows. It was the 1920s after all. Zelda was perceived as far too old to be entertaining grandiose thoughts of ballerina superstardom, even though maybe it just felt really good to express herself through this rigid, physically demanding art form. Because of her alarming hyperfocus on ballet, Zelda was deemed unstable—okay, insane—and thus headed toward incarceration inside mental facilities for the rest of her life, until her sanitarium burned to the ground with her in it. In Portland, Maine, I turn twenty-eight. Or am I twenty-nine? Thank goodness the times have changed.

WE now make sure that we have a gig booked in Minneapolis for the night we return home to avoid culture shock before returning to our day jobs. The left side of my neck down to the bottom of my shoulder blade is a mass of sore, gnarled muscles from the weight of my guitar. I can cut away about six layers of calloused skin on the tips of my left fingers, go in deep with a nail clipper, and not draw blood. My cuticles on my right hand are infected and swollen because I constantly drop my guitar pick while playing and end up using the fronts of my fingers as a pick.

HELLO?"
"Hi . . . is this you?"
Hello, it's me. There's no mistaking the voice on the other end of the line. It's Paul. The gifted guy from the Replacements. I saw him at a Soul Asylum show and bounced up to him with a big "hello" because he's never out and about making the

scene. He asked for my phone number and I pulled a pen out of my alligator purse and shakily scrawled my number on a matchbook cover. I assumed he'd lose it and never call. But here he is.

"I was wondering if you'd like to have dinner with me," he says.

Dinner with Paul. Boyfriend named Ang. Maybe Paul and I are just friends.

"Sure!" I say. He gives me his address—I ask for directions—and I pick him up in the Dream Van the following night. Neither of us wants to be seen by anyone we might know on this might-be contraband dinner date, so he guides me to a Chi-Chi's way out of what I consider "town."

"I like the armrests on your passengers' seats," he notes, settling in a captain's chair, looking like no stranger to the inside of a van. "I have sensitive elbows from the guitar and can't rest them on hard surfaces."

"Thanks!" I respond with way too much enthusiasm and wanting to blurt to him that I'm blind in one eye, but I stop myself. Christ, tone down the Tigger effect, I say to myself. I'm painfully aware that Paul is much cooler than I am.

Paul crumples an empty blue packet of True cigarettes that he's pulled from his jacket pocket. "Hey, got a square?" he asks.

"I've got a roundie," I respond because I've never understood why cigarette slang calls them squares instead of roundies.

"Roundie." He chuckles. I can feel him looking at me hard.

I guess we look different from normal people. His almost-black hair sticks out everywhere; his striped button-down shirt is a little too loud in a good way and it doesn't match his piped slacks. I'm dressed like a secretary from the late forties, in a wool pencil skirt and a silk button-up-the-back blouse with a princess collar. I suppose my Doc Martens boots disrupt the effect. Our waiter recognizes Paul immediately, not in a direct "aren't you?" kind of way, but in a nervous, shaky-hands kind of way that is unnerving. Paul slunks down in his padded chair on wheels, looking like he'd like to disappear. This makes me stage-fright-caliber nervous. I have no idea if we manage to order meals or carry on a conversation until Paul leans forward in his seat, chin almost on the table.

"Are you okay?" I inquire.

"I have a pain in my chest," he whispers. His sad, beautiful chocolate-drop eyes look at me searching for something; he is truly a brown-eyed handsome man.

"Maybe it's a gas bubble," I suggest, always eager to manage a medical emergency not my own, "lift your arms over your head."

He does. The pain does not subside. He asks for the bill and pulls a roll of Turns from his jacket pocket.

The pain disappears once in the van, and we joke about our classy first formal date.

"Would you like to come in for a minute?" he asks when I pull into his driveway.

As I enter his two-bedroom bungalow, he awkwardly bends forward to kiss me. His mouth is gorgeous, with puffy curved lips, and I'm ready for action, but he stops. It's so nice to be with someone as nervous and skittish as I am; it fills me with a sense of relief, makes me want to kiss him for a long time.

Paul pulls away from me, extracting himself from the leg I've wrapped around his thigh.

"I want to start this out the right way. Let's go slow."

"Okay," I say dumbly, and drive away elated, confused, certain he'll never call again because I've dorked out so badly, not passed the cool test, have too much padding on my hips.

The next day Ang accompanies me to Madison for Thanksgiving.

12: London Calling

WHEN not out of town, I'm working eight-hour shifts at the Hi-Lo to support my rock habit.

"Laurie! Telephone!" Rose calls out in her soft singsongy voice, relieved, no doubt, to step away from a sink filled with greasy, yolky dishes.

"Hey, Boom-Boom, answer da phone," my boss growls, "it's your parole officer."

I'm more than happy to step away from the picky breakfast people whom I'm doing the great favor of serving.

"Hello?"

"Hello, Laurie, Everett True here from *Melody Maker*," says a man with an English accent on the other end of the line.

"Oh. H-h-hi," I manage, my voice cracking while I frantically fumble for a cigarette in my patent-leather purse that rests upon an industrial-size bag of potatoes. I totally forgot about my interview with London. It's impossible to remember all of the things you're supposed to do in a day when you leave for work at 5:30 A.M. It's really hard to think of anything charming or witty to say. Quick, out of snarly waitress mode and into girl rock star. I don't transition easily; I'm not well practiced in giving good interview.

Here I am, covered in a thin layer of grease, smelling of sour dairy, yet my band has been honored with Single of the Week in one of London's top music publications. It reads:

Three girls from Minneapolis make a merry hell with splintery guitars, relentless rumbles, and a fine disregard for behaving politely . . . a cross between the Breeders and the Raincoats, which

means that ET [the man interviewing me on the phone at the
moment] is going to have to get behind me in the queue when
the marriage proposals get chucked around. Love them madly.

THE single we recorded with Eric, released by Albert in
Brooklyn, is being embraced. How can these two situa-
tions—top honors in an international publication and waitressing—occur simultaneously? I know, I know; it happens all the
time.

The Hi-Lo is so loud that I have a hard time understanding
Everett. He's telling me about how much he likes my slow ballad about unrequited love, "Johanne." Naturally this makes
me like him and his quiet intelligence tremendously. My workmates find things to do close to the back door I'm huddled inside, trying to stretch the phone cord as far away from earshot
as possible. In the five minutes we speak, I hear myself talking
about my traveling salesman father taking me to *Jesus Christ
Superstar*. Good God, why would I tell such a silly thing to all
of England? All of my imaginary interviews elude me and I
hear myself mutter, "I dunno" to one of his questions.

We're going to England next week. That English promoter
that Linda talks to all the time on the phone has convinced us
that it is imperative to play England while they're enjoying our
three-song 45. England "gets" us. Linda's parents loan me
money for a plane ticket; my parents are still financially wiped
out from their divorce. Babes in Toyland are superstars in England. The things we have in common with Babes (number of
breasts in the band, home base) is contributing to our initial attention. We still sound nothing like Babes and their primal, gui-
tar-driven, big, big sound and big, ferocious voice. England will
soon figure this out.

OH. Hmmm. You're much cuter in your photos." This is
how we're welcomed at London's Heathrow Airport by

the booking agent who has enticed us into transatlantic travel.

It's nine in the morning, making it 3:00 A.M. on our clocks. It's my first trip overseas. It's my first time on a flight where drinking and smoking are permitted, therefore I did both to excess. Here I stand with a cheap wine hangover, horrid breath, bloodshot eyes caked with yesterday's black makeup, and a rat's nest of hair. I'm in a rock 'n' roll band. You can't possibly expect cuteness under these circumstances. My bandmates look like they're with me, only dirty long dark hair looks better than dirty not-long not-short, not-straight not-curly, not-naturally-blonde-anymore hair.

Co and I exchange furtive glances; our agent, I'll call him Jimmy Bullseye, is not a handsome man by any stretch. With an enormous beaklike nose and emotionless black, beady eyes, with hair so drab it's colorless, who's he to judge cuteness? Zuzu's Petals cold callers are always referred to Linda because she is very friendly and likes people. A phone flirtation evolved into hot and heavy because you can get carried away long distance. Co and I are thinking, Poor Lynn, he's really gross, how's she gonna give him the slip?

Jimmy Bullseye is without the vehicle and driver we were told would greet us at the airport. This means we must maneuver sixty-pound anvil guitar cases, drum hardware, cymbals, assorted technical gear, and luggage from Heathrow to the Scotland Yard neighborhood on the tube during Monday-morning rush hour. Dragging our load to transfer trains, I moan and insist we take a cab. We haven't seen a wink of London. We board a big black gangsterish expensive cab. We, of course, have little to no money until we perform and get paid. Hey, London is sunny! We pass rows of joined white houses that appear to be straight out of *Oliver!*. London is also clean. There's the river Thames. Westminster Abbey. Scotland Yard. A pub.

According to Jimmy Bullseye, we'll be staying in some nice vacant rooms above this pub called Griffin's. "Incidentally," he says in a hushed reverent tone, "Peter Sellers used to live in the same room that you'll occupy." As if that will impress anyone but my dad. I'm dying to shower and sleep, to peel off my holey black leggings and Doc Martens boots. It's lunchtime in the pub when we step through its doors. Lugging everything inside to the farthest out-of-the-way corner so as not to disturb the patrons who appear to be office workers on lunch break, we slump at a table next to our load. From the looks of it, English men are no strangers to the liquid lunch. The few women inside are drinking soft drinks and not beer. The bar is long and made of a polished dark wood, a red brick wall behind the bar gives it a rustic look; tables and chairs are sprinkled about, and a gray-meat meal rests on a steam table at the end of the bar that makes high school hot lunch look heavenly. Starving, we order French fries, only fries are chips, and chips are crisps, and we have to say "without gravy" or be very sorry.

Our new home for the next three weeks will be an empty room upstairs. Only we can't go up there because the manager, Tom, could lose his job if his employees caught wind of our presence in the building, and Tom supports a wife and infant son and there are no jobs at home in Ireland. According to Bullseye no one associated with the bar, meaning not only employees, but also patrons and neighborhood shopkeepers, can know that foreign strangers are occupying an empty room in the building under Tom's charge. So we sit in the pub all day and into the night. I'm not exactly sure when we decide to order pints, but it's early on.

I HAVE never heard the ugliest word I know, the word "cunt," bandied about so casually and with such frequency. The men call each other cunts, and us, too. I'm not sure what shocks me more, hearing "cunt" constantly, which feels like a blow to my stomach every time my ears try to digest it, or the way we're being treated. I can't tell if it's because we're American, or drinking pints, or in a rock band, but we're being treated like Nancy in *Oliver!*. Nancy was a common whore, a murdered common whore. "Fat," "spotty," and "ugly" are a few of the other words that are being slung in our direction. We're not even fat, just not skinny. I feel myself involuntarily toughening again.

Tom eyes us sympathetically. He speaks gruffly to his help and kindly to his customers. As the night wears on, it is becoming apparent that Jimmy has never asked Tom permission to allow us to occupy an empty room upstairs. Jimmy has gambled on Tom's kind heart. We have deposited ourselves in the center of London, we've been up for twenty-four hours, we're drunk, tired, and a little scared, and we have no place to stay.

Around closing time, Tom starts drinking heavily. He and Co exchange verbal insults, things like, "Who are you calling 'fat,' fat ass." At first this jokey exchange about lack of sex appeal is funny. But out of nowhere Tom lunges for Co's throat; I'm guessing that this was intended to be playful, but it's way too rough. Co struggles, coughs, cries. The three of us march to the bathroom for an emergency band meeting. While we make our exit, Tom and Jimmy argue heatedly off to the side by a stone fireplace in the back of the pub. We save our arguing for the ladies' room, where there really is a water closet on the wall above the toilet; you yank a chain to flush.

Co and I can't contain ourselves any longer: "I thought we had a place to stay."

"Where is our driver and van?"

"Do we even have any gigs?"

"He's a fucking liar, Linda."

Linda says, "Relax, Jimmy's taking care of everything, there's been a misunderstanding, everything will be ironed out."

As we adjourn and step out of the women's bathroom, my eyes rest on a grizzled old man with the fingers cut off his gloves; his fly is down, he's sporting a Vince Lombardi winter hat, and he's feeding leftover sausages that an employee is handing him to his poxy-looking wiener dog.

Tom whispers, "Okay, there's a spare room upstairs, but I could lose my job if anyone caught wind of this," lamenting, "I can't throw you out into the streets." He looks like a young Rod Steiger and his thick Irish brogue is indecipherable after a few drinks. Tom is two years younger than me though he looks ten years older.

To make it look good, like we have somewhere else to stay, we stage a departure, hitting the streets with our suitcases. Tom makes a show of allowing us to store our band equipment in the back of Griffins. Thankfully the pubs in London close early on weeknights. Walking the quiet misty streets of London is like a dream, not at all the circumstances one imagines for a first evening stroll through the city. It's empty, everyone's gone home save a pair of tipsy stragglers in nightclub clothes, a boa, and top hat, and us, tired American rock girls with greasy hair and greasy leather jackets.

Once around the block and we have our bearings: our landmarks are a Pizza Hut and a department store with mannequins in the window wearing drab polyester skirts and blouses circa 1975. Clearly we are nowhere near whichever section of town constitutes "swinging London." It's hard to believe that one of the biggest cities in the world is asleep before 11:00 P.M.

Knock, knock. Tom peeps through the front door and says that the coast is clear. Co and I are led to a bedroom that is decorated with two rolled-up mattresses on rickety fold-up frames that are possibly haunted by the ghost of comics past. Linda casually announces that she's going back downstairs to have a drink with Jimmy and Tom. Co and I lock eyes in disbelief for the second time today, too tired to discuss. We collapse onto our cots and are awakened in what feels like five minutes by the sound of breaking glass. The wind-up travel alarm clock given to me by my mom as an early Christmas present claims that it's 5:00 A.M.; they recycle early in London, and pubs have a lot of glass in need of breaking at this hour. This is not the London morning street vendor wake-up call from *Oliver!*. There are no pale maidens singing, "Who will buy my sweet red roses." Linda is not in our room.

FOR the next five days, the number of days that must pass before we have a gig, Co and I wander the streets of London together. Because we are sullen and bitchy, Linda hangs out primarily with Jimmy, which I think she wants to do anyway. Much has been made of English cuisine, or the lack thereof. The dairy is sour and clotty, the meat is based on internal organs, and there's no evidence of produce anywhere in our wanderings. There are no "ripe strawberries, ripe" being offered by singing turn-of-the-century farm girls in crisply ironed aprons. My internalizing of musicals-as-reality has dealt me another staggering blow; this is nothing like *Mary Poppins*, either. We draw nourishment from bottled water, too-strong beer, and Cadbury's Fruit 'n' Nut chocolate bars, rationalizing that all food groups are being represented.

Poverty makes the sights, the museums, and even public transportation out of our realm. Because we are next to Scotland Yard, we watch the changing of the guard several times and listen for Big Ben's toll, but he's broken. We walk through the free part of Westminster Abbey, and stroll along the banks of the dirty old river. It's wet and chilly, which feels worse when you're sad and tired.

It's Christmastime; there are shoppers, decorations, and merrymaking everywhere you look. There's feasting in restaurants behind steamed-up windows and lavish bakery displays in storefront windows. Co and I are like paupers peering into windows, longingly salivating for food, glorious food. "They're probably eating kidney pie," Co reminds me.

In the pub, we witness on a daily basis vicious barroom

brawls that feature head butts, shoves, grabbed lapels, and blind swings. I'm no stranger to day drinking in a bar, but I've never witnessed casual flesh-on-flesh physical violence. I blame the strength of the beer. Everyone around us acts like these fights are boring daily occurrences; no one seems rankled by these incidents except Co and me.

We take to hanging out in our barren room, writing letters and postcards, sneaking in and out. I feel like Anne Frank without the serious life-threatening horror. I identify on the level of being holed up in a room, being extraquiet, fearful that the spooky bar employee from Transylvania (I kid you not) will catch us, which in turn will force Tom and his family into involuntary immigration and a life of poverty.

Back home I, unofficially, have two boyfriends—which is something I highly recommend at least once in a lifetime. If you saw my hideous passport photo that my bandmates request to look at when they need a laugh, you would find it shocking that I had any sort of human companionship. In this photo, taken at Kinkos directly following a shift at the diner, I look like an unattractive large-headed male whose only discernible features are his nose and eyebrows.

Ang is perhaps the nicest, best-liked guy in town; Paul is a much-loved songwriter. Ang is generous, principled, kind, and innately good. And he has hair like Slash. Paul is recently divorced, has an out-of-town girlfriend, and what appears to be several others on the phone and in the mail. I don't see any danger of this turning into anything much. It's just that he's so fun and funny, and interesting, and thrilling, and sexy, and talented.

I call Ang on the phone and tell him each harrowing detail, worrying him sick. I call for support and sympathy. I write cheeky letters to Paul, making light of our squalor and cracking jokes about our unfortunate situation. Ang doesn't deserve this. I don't deserve Ang, carrying on the way I do.

❧

AFTER five penniless days, we ride the tube to our first show, lugging hundreds of pounds of equipment on a Saturday night, dressed in velvet and taffeta and heavy boots. My hair is a nest, my mates look messy and lovely. According to my nemesis Jimmy Bullseye, our rental gear, namely amps and drums, will be waiting for us at the venue, Euston Rails.

And what do you know? They are delivered—only the speaker cabinets are empty, there are no speakers inside (a much-needed element to produce any type of sound). Jimmy, trying to save a penny, has rented cosmetic cabinets used for video shoots (no one actually plays their instruments during video shoots, they play along to the record). I'm stunned silent. Everything Jimmy Bullseye has promised thus far has fallen through. I may implode.

Enter Mitch. He is wearing the most outrageous plastic, lace-up-the-side neon green pants and a warm enchanting smile; he's a black man with rainbow dreadlocks—today's Artful Dodger. Mitch works for the Mekons, a popular band out of Leeds with Minneapolis ties; our Eric has worked with Mitch, which is how he heard about us. Coming to our first show to welcome us, he quickly assesses our situation and goes right to work introducing himself to the other band on the bill, asking them if we might borrow some of their equipment. "Relax," he says, "enjoy yourselves; I'll take care of everything." Mitch sees clearly what we do not. We're in trouble. We need help. He tells Jimmy he'll work for us for the remainder of the tour for next to nothing, enough pocket change for food, beer, and cigarettes.

I haven't a clue how to operate a foreign amp; the circuitry, knobs, and wattage are written in German. Our first show in London sucks extrahard; we can't hear one another, my guitar sounds like a flügelhorn, I scream at the top of my lungs because I'm pissed as in mad, and pissed as in drunk.

"John Peel [legendary BBC music guru] was here," Jimmy Bullseye tells us after our show, "he thinks you were brilliant."

How can I believe a word coming from this man's mouth? Besides, I know our show was an amateurish display of howls and wrong notes; we played below average even for us. I've noticed over the course of a week that the English toss off "brilliant" like we would "okay . . . I guess."

The following morning Mitch appears at the pub donned in somber Sunday morning black leather pants. The few men in the pub enjoying a morning ale become silent when Mitch strolls in; some wear amused smiles, and something hangs heavy in the air, and it smells like racism. Mitch is either wary, used to it, or above it, because he ignores these geezers and remains focused on the business at hand.

"I think it's high time you ladies had a proper English breakfast," he says with a smile. Mitch escorts Co and me to a small diner around the corner where we eat our first English breakfast; barely fried eggs, thick raw bacon, Wonder bread fried in Oleo, stewed tomatoes, and baked beans. Within two weeks I will find myself craving this unthinkable meal.

OUR next show is at a university in Southampton. The occasion is a prewinter break hoopla. Jimmy B., clever publicist that he is, has requested condoms on our rider instead of the usual modest pleas for bottled water, Coca-Cola (that I suspect is the surplus supply of the failed "new Coke" from years back), and beer. Condoms are all part of Jimmy's master plan to hype us as nymphomaniac alcoholics.

"You know, Jimmy, we really don't like this false hype; the drunk bimbo thing really sucks," I say in an effort to be assertive.

"Sod off, cunt," he snaps. "You don't know a thing about getting the proper attention you need to make it in the UK. If I were you I'd concentrate on my guitar playing."

One of the other bands on the bill calls themselves Mad Cows' Disease; the disease must be explained to us and we doubt its likelihood—it sounds like another twisted example of British humor. Back stage, a lunchroom, there is a Christmas tree decorated with condoms waiting for us.

We're just happy to be out of our depressing room above the depressing pub and faced with an opportunity to perform. It feels great to play in front of these happy students. Because there have been two features written about us in *Melody Maker*, and a handful of mentions in the *New Musical Express*, the students in the crowd take us seriously, like we're a legitimate band. It does wonders for my desire to put on a show.

At night's end a girl asks us if we'd like to stay at her house and her name is Pip. Pip is a student with a handful of roommates; it's your standard college setup in a falling-down house. Pip likes our band and is excited to have us over. I no longer have the desire or fortitude to provide wild, exciting nights for college students now that I'm on the far back end of my twenties. I'm trusting that Linda does a good job because Co and I excuse ourselves and retire on a mattress on the floor in a drafty room still clad in our show clothes. Central heating has not been in the picture thus far. December in England is not akin to December in Minneapolis, but it is that damp, bone-chilling Brontë-esque cold nonetheless. You get sweaty on stage, then the sweat dries and your clothes stick to you, your bra smells sour, your skin has an added layer of dirt, sweat, grease, and smoke. You're itchy and go through life with this added ambiance until the next shower.

We are paid four hundred pounds for this show, which Jimmy pockets, claiming that it won't even scratch the surface of our mountain of expenses. I'm pretty sure four hundred pounds (almost eight hundred American dollars) can more than cover our modest needs.

I N Bourne we stay with a Polytech student (whatever that is) named Justin. He finds it perfectly fine to trash us to our faces: "You look old." Or, "You're not that cute." He might be teasing in that nervous, seventh grade courtship kind of way, but I just know guys in bands don't have to put up with this shit. I fall asleep on the floor, where we all squish side by side, mass-grave style, while *The Life of Brian* plays on the VCR. I hate Monty Python.

What about our music? Every time we play, which is far less than we were told, we're relieved. On stage we are in a familiar place, our place, and the release of pent-up frustration performing provides is lifesaving. The difference in electricity and equipment makes it harder to sound right. The increased strength of English beer makes it hard to sound good. The intense tension caused by Linda's affair with a pathological liar who is screwing us over makes it harder to play well together. We are on stage less than one hour of the twenty-four that constitute a day. It's the time off stage where life is lived; on stage your life belongs to others.

Jimmy Bullseye travels with us, but thankfully so does Mitch. Oh ya, and we have a driver, a Scottish fellow I'll call Blotch; he drives our rented minivan and only allows Cream on the car stereo, which is in violation of our no-Clapton policy. Maybe he thinks he can subliminally turn us into a proper power trio with the required guitar virtuoso with his Cream record. Jimmy B. pockets all of our money after each show, claiming that our expenses are exorbitant. On occasion we are thrown a pound or two for food or cigarettes. Mitch's largest responsibility has become making sure Blotch isn't too drunk to drive after our shows. Blotch drinks all our free beer while we're working and is oftentimes in no condition to drive when it's his turn to work. I love Mitch, but there's one thing about him that's hard to ignore; he has a ripe odor to him. I know that b.o. is natural and that Americans are overly obsessed with masquerading and washing away their odors, but all the same, it bugs me. Young women crashing on strangers' floors in sour bras should not call attention to delicate nostrils.

I don't have an opinion of the English per se except that their average street person is more articulate, informed, and better read than most Americans. With the exception of Pip and a woman in the band the Zimmer Frames, we haven't spoken to any women. More like, women haven't spoken to us. Maybe it's that press in the morning tabloid announcing our alleged deranged booze-drenched sex addictions: "Girls, watch your boyfriends . . . " was the opening line announcing our arrival. There are definitely some people over here who come to see us in the same manner they would go to look at the Dionne Quintuplets in their little human zoo, or Lobster Boy at the state fair. We're a curiosity. Freaks of nature. American chicks on stage playing rock 'n' roll. C'mon, we didn't exactly invent it.

It is to our advantage that there's a revolt against high-maintenance beauty in these earliest 1990s. Our unkempt appearance is all the rage. Besides jeans patched to oblivion that we've owned and worn since middle school, we mix and match outdated symbols of femininity—always with irony—the thrift shop prom dress, the fifties housewife dress, the sixties paisley and lace, always topped with flannel or mohair and torn stockings.

We're having a public identity crisis, trying to straddle all of our options. We're trying to have it all and be it all while at the same time mocking the stereotypes. It's absolutely exhausting, and no one's really picking up on it.

IN Newport, Wales, we are taken to the bar owner's home for dinner. I feel like Alice in Wonderland, a big giant blonde falling into this miniature cottage where everything seems of a smaller gauge—tiny table, tiny rooms, tiny doilies, itty-bitty tea roses on the wallpaper. Our host looks like a shorter, older

Tom Jones, and I have no idea why a grown man with a family would have the likes of us home for dinner. But it's instantly apparent that he's a kind, happy person; his wife is loud and friendly, calling attention to the "knickers" hanging out under our skirts with cackles of amusement.

In the kitchen the radio is tuned to the BBC and the couple discusses in Welsh their outrage at the horrible situation in Eastern Europe. Then it occurs to me that this is all happening in close proximity to where we are, that it can't be ignored because a stone's throw away there is genocide going on for no reason. Bosnia is probably closer to us in Wales than New York is to Minneapolis.

This home in Wales is filled with love and good feelings and it's infectious. The host family is teasing and laughing and hugging and kissing, and asking lots of questions. It's interrupting my snippy gloom. The meal is barely edible and involves large slices of lopped-off iceberg lettuce with Thousand Island dressing, but it doesn't matter. These genuinely happy people catch me off guard. They're not poor, but they're far from wealthy, and I'll bet it's not something they spend a lot of time thinking about. Imagine that, friendly joyous people, for no particular reason except that they are. It's their pleasure and duty to give us a meal in their home simply because we're American kids seeking our fortunes. To me they've just defined the real meaning of "home."

At the club, TJ's, a young man who's a dead ringer for Tom Jones in his twenties says to me, "You're American, you're rich; give me a fag!" I silently pass him a cigarette.

BATH is pronounced Bawhth. In Bath it finally sinks in. Nirvana is changing the landscape of music. I love them. The English love them to rabid obsession. Their new album *Nevermind* is the only music we hear in clubs. Music history is being changed before our very eyes.

Just last fall on our East Coast tour, Nirvana was a couple of days behind us in all of the same clubs. We saw their posters everywhere, with the naked swimming baby, announcing their appearances. Now three months later, *Nevermind* has soared up the charts, embraced by alienated youth and adults world-wide. It's a bestseller, huge. A fusion of punk rock and pop and slickly produced by Butch, it's a great record, a masterpiece. Nirvana will no longer be playing in the same venues as Zuzu's Petals. Finally, a rough three-piece band on top of the charts striking a note deep in the vein of the main stream. I dub it the Winter of Nevermind.

AN American man is a regular at our home base, Griffin's pub in London. He owns a business next door and has been watching our drama unfold for nearly three weeks. I think his name is Greg.

I hesitate to address this blatantly because I know that Linda in particular is not fond of being singled out during this phase of our collective life, but it has to be said; a romance between Linda and Jimmy Bullseye has flourished in this unfertile set-ting much to the chagrin of the other two Petals. Co and I are so pissed off at Bullseye's lying, creepy ways, for being rude and disrespectful and appalled at our nerve to question our sit-uation, and the countless bad decisions he's made without con-sulting us. We're angry with Linda by association, and rightfully so. Shows in Scotland and a New Years' Eve show in Munich were promised, and then taken away. They probably never existed. Once again, birth order becomes unfortunate for Linda because now she has to deal with the two bossy oldest sisters.

Over pints (which we discovered English ladies don't drink), Greg tells Co and I about Bullseye and his past at the pub with another all-woman band from New York that he lured over to England last October. Bullseye proposed marriage to one of the band members. Things didn't work out for them. He's also popped the question to Linda. We're not getting paid for the paltry handful of shows we've played because, according to Bullseye, the expenses are astronomical, and he's doing all of this hard work out of love for the band, and why aren't we grateful?

"Do you wanna get out of here?" asks Greg. He offers us a change of scenery, a different pub down the block. Co and I have no money. His treat, he insists. The new pub is fully decorated for Christmas; it's larger and homier than Griffin's, furnished with couches and carpeting, with holly and pine boughs lining the bar. This makes me acutely homesick. The jukebox is playing "Somebody to Love" by Queen. My eyes fill with tears and my throat tightens. Not because I don't have somebody to love, hardly, but because Queen's singer, Freddie Mercury, has died recently from AIDS. I've loved Queen and their flair for musical drama since middle school. As I look around the pub, many patrons are shedding tears.

"A shame," says a man while wiping his eyes with a handkerchief.

"We've lost a great talent," laments a woman sitting alone at the bar, drinking a half-pint.

"We'll miss you, Freddie," says another.

"We love you, Freddie," a burly man in tweed announces as glasses are raised to the air in a toast.

Freddie Mercury is a national treasure in England, and his death is being openly, publicly mourned. A room full of straight-laced-looking pubgoers is singing along, openly hurting together, and paying their respects. This is not an American behavior, though I wish it were.

As Christmas inches toward us, more shows are canceled and we're expected to hole up in the pub through the holidays. Shows are supposed to resume following Boxing Day (the day after Christmas, when everything in England closes). Fuck that. I'm not spending Christmas socked away in that creepy annex above the pub. Co and I want to go home. We've snapped; we're totally freaking out with the new insight on Jimmy Bullseye. We spend the night of December 23rd at Greg's apartment, which overlooks the Tower of London and its underground torture chambers. Greg checks his computer for possible ways that Co and I can fly home.

Early the next morning, Christmas Eve, we hustle our belongings out of the pub while Linda and Bullseye sleep. It feels like we're fleeing in the middle of a war, though, of course, no one is shooting at us or threatening our lives. We sprint to the United ticket counter, hoping to beg our way onto a flight to Minneapolis with our nonnegotiable group-rate tickets.

Greg speaks to the man at the counter first. "I noticed that this flight isn't full. These girls are in a bad situation here and need to get home for Christmas."

I step forward with my useless ticket and burst into tears for the first time all trip: "I just really, really want to go home, please . . . if there's any way."

Co stands next to me, blinded by tears. Shockingly enough, this rare ticket counter employee is no Scrooge because he lets us board. God bless us every one. Grateful and relieved, we collapse together in our seats, still crying. We'll never see Greg again. We wonder if we'll see Linda again.

I spend Christmas Day with Ang at his parents' house. Paul calls me on New Year's Day. I'm just a girl who cain't say no.

13: When No One's Looking

Co and I have compiled a detailed account of every underhanded deed, every bold lie, every gesture of disrespect that Jimmy Bullseye committed during our time in London. When Linda returns to Minneapolis a couple of weeks later, she calls Co like nothing's happened. Co instructs her to meet us at the practice space.

Following us out of England was more favorable press; we were Picked to Click in '92 and a live review of our last show at the Mean Fiddler in London with a large photo was featured in *Melody Maker*:

Zuzu's Petals are my kind of girls. Nice girls with all the equivocalness that implies. They're amiable, pretty, self-effacing, and chatty. They're so disarmingly sincere they teeter on the brink of sarcasm. They're so amenable, you suspect they might be plotting something. In their bumbling, shoulder-shrugging, friendly way they make themselves powerful. It's inspiring.

The difference between Zuzu's Petals and, say Hole, or Babes, is that you're not absolutely sure what drives the Zuzu's. They're not transparently obvious. You have to work out what's going on behind their smiles. This is why what they do is far more dangerous than putting on a show. When people are up there, and they aren't pretending to be anything other than themselves, it's like indecent exposure. . . . [She then goes on for a couple more paragraphs, describing the show] See them next time they're over, fall in love with them, and offer them your firstborn.

Linda knows us well enough to realize that all she needs to do is show proper remorse to win our hearts back. She does. Learning the hard way that a grifter was scamming not only us, but also her, is hard. We feel sorry for her. It's a drag when you realize that you've, once again, fallen for someone who is Not Well.

Whew, with that out of the way, there's business to attend to; Twintone is finally prepared to offer us that recording contract we've been groveling for all these years (now that most of their roster has moved on to major labels). The tasty English press wore them down. We did everything they told us to do. Not scouted and recruited like their other bands, we badgered them into reluctant acquiescence. Their offer felt more like, "Here's your damn contract, and we're still not convinced that you don't suck." Making a gorgeous first album will be our revenge.

PAUL, my sort-of new boyfriend, is so incredibly healthy. This surprises me in an utterly sweep-me-off-my-feet kind of way. Get this: He drinks his coffee with half of the caffeine taken out. He eats fresh fruit every day. He retires around 10:00 P.M. and wakes up bright and early to either walk or bike around nearby Lake Calhoun. He works out on a Nordic-Track. He writes and records music at home all day with an unswerving work ethic and unbelievable self-discipline. He grocery shops and cooks. He takes long, candlelit baths and reads Swami books. He meditates and reads. He quit drinking and drugging yet is still fun. So many newly sober people seem like a part of them died once they quit their addictions. Not this guy. He still smokes, which makes him human to me.

Here's the kicker: he wears a robe, pajamas, and slippers in the evening. I've been in a T-shirt and underwear for at least a decade. The normalcy of wearing bedtime attire is powerfully seductive. And he has a big bed off the ground, on a frame with a box spring and everything! He is quite happy and at peace. By loving himself in all the right ways, mentally, physically and spiritually, he, in turn, has so much love to offer me. He is also a rock star.

Oh, and he's self-educated and he Reads. Real Books. I used to Read, but it interfered with . . . what? My party schedule? Books were my first love, my comfort zone. Our dates often wind up at the library (the library!). I'm in trouble. I've got it bad. I'm hooked. In L-U-V. Love.

And not that I've mustered the nerve to break ties with Ang because I'm not confident about the viability of having a rock star boyfriend for long, and I really do love Ang; he accepts me and my neuroses unconditionally. I've been honest about this "side project" and he's patiently waiting it out, prepared to pick up the pieces, but not for much longer.

Paul says to me, "The last thing I need is to be with a party girl in a rock band; I've been warned that you're bad news."

"That's *so* untrue," I protest, folding my arms for effect.

I say to Paul, "I'm falling in love with you, but, you know, you have a terrible reputation as a serial philanderer; I can't set myself up like this."

"I am living proof that people can change," he says to me. "I've changed." Well, look at his sobriety. *Ay caramba,* I surrender. This might be my crossroads where I make a deal with the devil, but who cares—there are thousands of girls out there who would love to have such a dilemma.

The guy is a fucking rock star. Is this going to be a problem? I knew his art, his music, before I knew the man. I love his art and all, but I prefer the man. And. We're in the same line of work and he's been dubbed by *Spin* magazine "the Soul of Rock and Roll," the voice of my generation, our Bob Dylan. Paul, until recently, fronted the Replacements. Paul has Respect and Integrity coming out of his ears. People love him in an almost creepy, worshipful way. He's intensely private; I have no secrets. He is a bottomless well of talent. He's of-another-era charming, a quality that will get you every time. And that low, gravelly voice, that strong, skinny frame, that crazy darkest brown hair . . . you can't blame me for going under. I'm not starstruck—for some weird reason I consider us a logical pairing. We're like the rock 'n' roll Nick and Nora Charles, only we're probably the only two people I know who actually watch the *Thin Man* movies and I'll never be as cute or thin as Myrna Loy.

"Hey, Roundie." He now calls me "Roundie" and I don't call him anything because he's not "Paul" to me like he is to everyone else, but I can't think of a fitting nickname.

"Hey!" I say, trying not to sound overeager.

"Wanna come over and *stay in*?"

"Oh, yaaa," I twang, trying to sound like a good Scandinavian Minnesotan.

Staying in. What a concept. I haven't stayed in, or not gone out, in years, probably since I turned eighteen and was old enough to go out. I thought going out is what grown-ups did. Staying in means cooking dinner. Paul makes barbeque ribs with a homemade salad he calls Parthenon salad because there's feta cheese crumbled on top of it. Staying in means watching American Movie Classics or *Biography*, or reading, or playing Scrabble. Staying in never occurred to me. Now that my job entails being in a club every night surrounded by bands, the last thing in the world I feel like doing is going out to watch a band.

I don't bother fussing over what it means to couple myself with a rock 'n' roll legend because he's just this healthy guy who wants to stay in with me. This romance is a separate entity from my band. I know that Zuzu's Petals hasn't earned beans in the respectability department. I'm a girl in an all-girl garage band; some people think we're horrid. To pair me with this songwriting saint is like a sacrilege. I couldn't look more different from the actress who publicly lusts after him and sends him gifts in the mail. I only tell my bandmates (and my suffering nice boyfriend) about this fleeting affair, this fling. If this whatever-it-is gets around, it would mean more fodder for our critics. I would be accused of coattailing. All of our hard work would be discounted. That would suck royally. It bothers me that I'm actually worrying about what others will think when I'm so happy.

Paul lives in a neighborhood so good I didn't know it existed until I was invited over to his rented cottage situated between two lakes. The lens through which I view the world is sharply changing its focus. What's happening? Whatever it is, it's more fun than I've had in a long time—he'll even watch musicals with me—and I'm going to let it happen. Hopefully it won't trash my career before it's even launched. I'm going for it; this feels once in a lifetime, like the big one. I want to throw myself in his embrace of health and normalcy. I can keep everything going at once and keep it all separate. Not a problem. He's someone I want to be around, someone I want to be like. Having received letters from me, he says, "You're a writer, you should write." I'm toning down my partying out of respect and admiration of the example he's setting for me. We buy "artwork" at Goodwill to decorate his cottage. The first night I spend the whole night at his house instead of cutting out after dinner and a movie, because I still sort of have this other boyfriend on the line, we wake up in the morning holding hands. I'm in Trouble.

And did I mention that he's a rock star? I've had two rock star boyfriend dreams in which Tom Petty is my boyfriend and he's a nice boyfriend. This is a step up from earlier dreams in which Neil Young was my boyfriend (thankfully there were no sex scenes). Paul is intervening with my "I don't want to be with a guy in a band" stance, but I've been breaking that rule for, like, forever—the difference is, this one is light-years beyond me in career trajectory.

❦

FOR the first half of 1992, Zuzu's Petals tour the East Coast two more times, in June and in August. I think. It's all starting to blur together. I know that we play at the New Music Seminar in New York with a bunch of Minneapolis bands, and that everybody has equipment stolen. Co hooks up with her new boyfriend in New York, Linda meets her future boyfriend in Hoboken, and I spend my final night with my nice boyfriend with the hair like Slash. We're asked to record a single for a label out of New York called Shimmy Disc, and when not performing or on the road, we record as much as we can, wherever we can. I'm too busy to think. We're not complete unknowns and yet there's no big hype around us. A mild buzz perhaps. I am almost too worried about our future and about the competition to notice what a fun place this is to be. When you come down to it, though, we're brazen hussies when we're feeling good. And we're feeling pretty dang good.

I'm also newly in love, an all-consuming and terminally confusing place for me. I look for answers in the music of Joni Mitchell; she drives everyone in the van nuts with her soprano warbling. Having survived love affairs with Graham Nash and James Taylor, I assume Joni can help me with my current state of affairs. She says, "You can't hold the hand of a rock 'n' roll man for very long."

As a new songwriter I find my greatest inspiration studying those who came before me, namely Rodgers and Hammerstein and Bob Dylan. The women I originally looked to without realizing that they were supposed to be role models were Joni, Carly, Chrissie, and Patti, but also Christine McVie in Fleetwood Mac, and the sisters in Heart, and, as a girl, Karen Carpenter. Nowadays there are more music-making women out there than ever: Babes in Toyland, the Breeders, Sonic Youth, Hole, L7, Scrawl, Calamity Jane, the Friggs, Come, the Poster Children, Antietam, the Lunachicks, Brenda Kahn, Throwing Muses, Shawn Colvin, Victoria Williams, to name just a few. Or maybe I'm just more aware of them now that I'm in the

thick of things. Like L7 may have modeled some of their material on Ramones songs, we've drawn most of our inspiration
from the Minneapolis boy bands from the late eighties. Because
there's a movement labeled "foxcore" to describe hardcore hot
babes making rock music, and their most noticeable fashion
statement is the naughty little Lolita look—a fashion phenomenon described simply as "kinderwhore"—I've switched over to
old-time movie star dresses and curled hair in an effort to purposely look like a woman, not that I'm really plotting or thinking too much about it. It's just where my attention has settled
for now. You do have to somewhat call into play your sexual-
ity—whatever it is—because it should be celebrated when
you're young, and free, and on fire. And now there's something
out there called "riot grrrls," that seems to consist of a bunch
of girl power complainers—get it: *grrr,* like growling—but who
has time to pay attention to trends? Especially when it involves
looking like lady lumberjacks; that's so five years ago for us.

When asked if we're riot grrrls, Co answers, "We're not riot
grrrls, we're a riot."

ON a two-day break in Boston, I suggest a day trip to
Martha's Vineyard because it seems criminal to be that
close and not visit. There's something about that island, that
parcel of land that is so deep inside of me, that it's almost like a
geographical parent; I need to check in, touch base, before I
can continue gallivanting. I need to refuel and breathe its salty,
musty air because I feel safe there.

We park the van in Woods Hole and take the ferry across.
While wandering down Summer Street, passing its pristine-
white colonial homes to hitchhike to the beach, the three of us,
true ragamuffins after a couple of weeks in the twilight zone,
pass a tall, lean young man who was once my summer love and
several years' pen pal. I see him. He does not look at us. We
pass each other. I say nothing.

Two blocks later I whisper to Co, "That guy we passed back there was Joe Drake."

"The letter writer?"

"Ya."

"Why didn't you say something to him?" she wonders.

"I dunno." Maybe because he has a number after his name like Thurston Howell and we're such dirtballs. Maybe because I know he has a master's degree from an Ivy League school and I'm in a chick band. Maybe because when we were in high school we engaged in heavy petting in lawn chairs and when we wrote letters I thought we were in love. He always signed his letters with the pen name Quentin Crisp. I now know who Quentin Crisp is.

Zuzu's Petals hires a lawyer, a tall Iowan known to work with musicians when not defending the public; he looks over our Twintone contract. We have no management—though I think a couple of people have called me and inquired and I never followed up or understood our need for representation— so our new lawyer offers to field calls and inquiries for the time being. Dan is nice and honest and he knows a producer out in Boston who might be interested in our project.

When our lawyer Dan refers our demo tapes to his friend Lou in Boston who has just completed producing albums by Bob Mould and the Goo Goo Dolls (who are not yet, but are about to become, huge stars), Lou claims to like our demos and agrees to produce our first album. Fort Apache in Boston is Lou's studio of choice; Zuzu's Petals loves the idea of heading into Boston for two weeks to record. But Twintone can't afford to pay for our room and board for two weeks, plus studio and production fees. Lou agrees to come to Minneapolis; he'll occupy my apartment and I'll stay at Paul's.

Lou is horribly allergic to cats, and I always have a cat. Lou finds accommodations with friends in Minneapolis. How em-

barrassing. How awkward. Can't anyone give this guy a decent
hotel? We've just landed on the record label of our dreams and
I'm already complaining. Fortunately, Lou is a good sport as
well as an MIT-educated engineer, meaning he's smart. He used
to do sound for Hüsker Dü back in the day. He has friends
here and is excited to eat spicy Thai food at Kindu.

Our first album. Sigh. A coherent body of songs that make
sense together. A collection that follows a theme, an emotion, a
sound, a style. A collection that is expected to have at least one
radio-friendly tune, called a single, on it. When Lou arrives, a
quiet-spoken man with curly dark hair, we rehearse with him
and Dave from Soul Asylum. They help us understand the importance of getting the most out of our arrangements, rhythm,
and phrasing. Dave has always been generous with his time
and gifts with other musicians. Co, Linda, and I—babes in the
woods—accept all suggestions given by others because we're
greenhorns and they're experts.

"I can't believe the condition of this equipment," Lou mutters in disgust upon entering the studio booked by our record
company. He spends the entire first day of our session quietly
cursing in his Boston accent, his black curls the only part visi-
ble as he disappears into the bowels of tape recorders and mixing boards.

Part one of recording is basic rhythm tracks, the foundation
or spinal cord, bass and drums. After Co and Linda nail their
tracks, they return to their day jobs and check in at the studio
after work to do any vocal or rhythm overdubs. My workday
at the Hi-Lo ends as early as 10:00 A.M. on half days. Lou and
I spend a great deal of time in the studio alone together. I'm
struggling mightily with my guitar tracks, horribly embarrassed
by my lack of finesse or knowledge of music theory. It's taking
us a long time to layer several tracks of minimally flawed performances to fill out our sparse sound.

Lou does not look confident about the way things are going.
Most of the records he's made are instrumentally driven.

"Don't worry, Lou," I assure him. "I promise that once we get the vocals on top of this soup, we'll be fine."

In a fit of frustration, of feeling worthless on the guitar, I call Paul and ask him to come down to help me with my guitar solos. I feel awful about asking him while at the same time wondering why he's never offered assistance or acted terribly interested in our project. I brush it off as "he's been doing this for years, why would he want to go into another studio with another band?" Somewhat reluctantly he rides his bike to the studio and listens and reworks my guitar solos on two songs. He rewrites them in a way so that they both sound good and can actually be played by me. I finally play every note after several takes. These improved solos make a tremendous difference.

This all seems natural; the asking of my boyfriend, who is also a musician, to lend his ears and talents because I'm struggling. I've certainly offered lines of lyric in exchange. It doesn't occur to me that this might be perceived as cunning. Isn't that just what happens organically when you're in the same business and in love? I see no fault in this act; he didn't play a note, or write any of the songs. He did, however, help me get closer to what I wanted.

And while I'm on the subject of ethics/nepotism, let it be known that I'm a chord whore. "Give me three chords," I've said to a variety of musicians, including Paul. It's like a writing exercise, an icebreaker, a warm-up to spark my creativity. If there are no musicians in proximity when I sit down to compose, I pull out my trusty music book, *Cash Box Hits of the 60's and 70's*—my parents bought it for me when I was starved to learn the Carpenters' "Close to You" on the piano. This book contains a gold mine of chord combinations. I write many a song using mixed-up versions of Blood, Sweat, and Tears' "Spinning Wheel," Henry Mancini's "Moon River," the Seekers' "Georgy Girl," and Tommy Roe's "Dizzy." Sometimes I'm haunted by overheard riffs being played in other rehearsal rooms in our practice space and I copy what I hear and make changes according to my ear's liking. I have no idea who I'm borrowing from.

"I wish I may, I wish I might/Find what I'm looking for/ The cold wind blows through my sheets at night/My cupboards are bare," I sing. "God calls on the telephone/She has a temper/My life grows with the rain and snow/She hangs on the wall/This is what the faithful call divine intervention," I confess.

"Take a look at my hand/See where I stand/It's one thing you really won't understand." I challenge anyone listening carefully to my lyrics to uncover my neurological secret. "If you could see through two eyes what I see through one," I say in another song, "You'd see you could have it all/But choose to have none." My lyrics leave a trail of clues about the disease I claim to be doing such a fine job of ignoring: "Take a look at me/This is my dream/It's one thing you never can take from me. Once I was a lonely, bewildered, strange señorita/Men offered me diamonds and rubies/I said, 'No thanks, I want your guitar.'"

"Drinking while intoxicated/The cause of death was dying," I muse.

"If I said to you the things that you say to me/You'd be heading for the hills/Well, I'm swinging from a tree," I point out.

I've had my whole life, or at least six years, to write and rewrite this collection of songs. I am offering up my lyrical diary and suddenly Lou is not quite as nervous. Co has written some songs, we've cowritten a couple, but on this collection I've penned the majority. Lou and I have spent a lot of time alone working on this record and I feel comfortable asserting myself and making decisions away from the watchful eyes of the group without having to compromise or seek permission. I don't consider whether or not this will impact the band, I'm enjoying the work and the learning process. We'll call the record *When No One's Looking*, a line from my song "Johanne."

An independent record company in Los Angeles, Restless, has just bought Twintone. Eager to own the first records by the Replacements, Soul Asylum, the Jayhawks, and Babes in Toyland, who are all now on major labels, Restless is not overly interested in what's going on with Twintone today. Fortunately, they are intrigued by our British attention and approve of the results of our recording session with Lou. This means that some of their promotional time and budget will be allotted to us. The local painter Kate Van Cleve paints a picture of Co, Linda, and me as girls on a playground, her stick-figure paper dolls colored in heavy shades of red and purple—this will be used for our front cover. For the inner sleeve of the CD and other publicity photos, the photographer with whom we've had luck in the past stands atop a ladder and shoots us having a mock tea party clad in party dresses. Usually someone gets the shaft when trying to settle on a photo where all three Petals look great, but these photos turn out okay for all of us.

Restless approves a video budget and a proposal sent to them by a production company in Chicago. We're making a video for my new best unrequited love song, "Cinderella's Daydream." The video's storyboard has the three of us as washerwomen mopping floors in an industrial space. Exhausted from mopping, we take a break while *It's a Wonderful Life* airs on a television in a workplace break room. This sparks a collective daydream sequence featuring footage of us performing in a dance hall in front of a mirror ball and dancing couples in vintage formal wear. The look and feel is 1940s; Rosie the Riveter goes to the ball. I wear an inky blue sequined taffeta dress with razor-sharp pleats jutting out from the full skirt. I bought the dress on Martha's Vineyard years ago and I've never been able to zip up the back, on account of my "wide rib cage." (I get the zipper up half-way and realize that I'm only being shot from the front.)

When Co, Linda, and I are together in any sort of professional capacity we are always "on." Co is wry and funny, as is Linda, as am I (I hope). We're happy and cynical and goofy and fun, sort of like the Beatles in *A Hard Day's Night* if they'd been ten years older, female, and not nearly as prolific or brilliant. This initial surge of attention and excitement feels great. It's very easy to be engaged and friendly and charming.

Twintone hosts a record release party at the Uptown. It's safe to say that Zuzu's Petals has not been embraced by Minneapolis—we usually have to travel a few hundred miles to find devoted fans. I've always been warned that becoming hometown heroes was the kiss of death and that it's better to get out in the world to make your mark. Maybe it's because we sucked so hard around town for a matter of years before getting our act together. Or maybe it's because we have the audacity to hang out with our peers who are higher up on the showbiz food chain. Or maybe because we're difficult to pinpoint and categorize. Or because I'm not a great guitarist. It's hard to say. Regardless, this show is the first and only time we will sell out a local venue. And even though I act like it doesn't matter, I really wish Minneapolis audiences would love us.

OUR first official *When No One's Looking* tour is in England (as much as we've tried to avoid it). Aware of my paranoia about going back to the scene of a year ago, our lawyer makes sure that we have hotel rooms booked in advance of our arrival; we'll stay at the Dalmacia Hotel in Hammersmith, a low-fare inn that regularly takes in bands. The Dalmatia consists of an assortment of rooms, three floors up (no elevator) and one floor down. It's situated in a painted white brick house; the breakfast room is the common room where all the guests gather for the "breakfast included." It's attached to homes and shops on a quiet block of Shepherd's Bush Road.

The room we're to occupy is tiny by American standards.

Even the crappiest Motel 6 room, say by the airport in St. Louis, has enough room to swing a cat in. We're used to having space so that we can avoid one another and our anger, passion, pain, foibles, and odors. Too-close quarters implies unsought-after intimacy. I'm speaking for a large body of people, maybe Americans, maybe my family, and not the band. Well, maybe the band, too. At first our English room is cute, like a teeny-tiny summer camp room. Three miniature twin beds are arranged in an L against the walls of our rectangular room. We have our own bathroom instead of a shared potty down the hall. Every time we come and go, the room seems to be shrinking, the long ends of the rectangle gradually narrowing.

The only way I know what's going on with the band is through the eyes of the media. I take the term "the power of the press" literally. If someone in the press likes us, we're doing great. If someone hates us, we suck. If someone who used to like us goes sour on us, I worry. It's possible that now that we're here again, our two minutes in England might be up, and there's not much we can do about it.

Our first show is in a neighborhood in London called Hampstead at a place called the White Horse. Mitch is our road manager. The White Horse, a basement, is packed to the rafters when we walk in after our interview with Sally from *Melody Maker* at the coffee shop next door. The larger the venue and the more people in the audience, the more comfortable I am on stage. Don't ask me why. Everett, our once-devoted graying-around-the-temples journalist friend, is in the audience with his new girlfriend, an eighteen-year-old dead ringer for Courtney Love. We dedicate our faux jazz instrumental tune, "Dork Magnet," to him. Everett is not wild about our first album, according to his review of it in *Melody Maker*, but he likes what we are or what we symbolize:

> When I think of Zuzu's Petals, I think: Jägermeister [something
> we introduced him to the last time we were in England], three

girls all muffled up chucking snowballs at the sports fans, an empty bar with a few loners at one end, sweating sleepless nights at six a.m.; life. When I think about Zuzu's Petals, I stop fractionally and a smile forms itself around my lips. Zuzu's Petals shamble and hurt like the rest of us, but ultimately, they're hopeful about what life might turn out to be.

Our show at the White Horse is a blur, a rush, and then it's over. We're called back on stage for an encore, a first, which we do with our jackets on because we're readying ourselves to leave the building.

The thing of it is, I'm flattened by love; it takes precedent over everything else that's going on around me. On this strange clock, I sneak into the hallway of our hotel in the middle of the night to write gushing love letters to Paul, part *Penthouse Forum*, part sociological travelogue. In the next room a guy farts loudly and constantly as he snores while a soccer game blasts on his television.

We have a new European record label, Roadrunner, thanks to our new record company in L.A., Restless, who bought Twintone. Roadrunner specializes in heavy metal. They have pressed vinyl albums of our record because many people in the UK still listen to music printed on vinyl and not to CDs. The album format makes it finally seem real to me: the artwork looks better, and it reminds me of lying on my stomach as a little girl, poring over album covers, trying to decode their cryptic messages. Roadrunner has no idea what to make of us; their top act is a guitar virtuoso.

The tiny TV in our little summer camp room is a luxury. There is even some sort of abbreviated form of cable, meaning we get more than two channels. On a night off we watch *Thelma and Louise* in silent tears while eating chicken kabobs. I wonder to myself if it's worth dying to make a point.

❦

Drawer willy!" a snaggletoothed Brit is bellowing in our faces after a show.

"Huh?" Many of the English we encounter are difficult to understand when they're drunk. We're told we sound Canadian.

He slows down, imploring, "Drawer a willy."

His red face is inches from ours as we try to shake him and roam around the club in Reading, though it's not really a club, more like a converted high school lunchroom.

"I don't get it," I snap impatiently.

"A willy! A willy! Drawer a willy," he moans as he opens an autograph book filled with signatures and renderings of penises.

Oh, a willy. He wants us to draw a willy. Okay. We assign Linda willy duty, but he insists we each draw one.

The Willy Guy excitedly pantomimes his story to us, involving hopping a train from another town and running from car to car to avoid the ticket collector because he only had enough money to pay for a ticket to see his beloved Zuzu's Petals. His eyes don't look in the same direction, which is par for the course when it comes to our fan base. Demographically speaking, he's a "Laurie guy." I affectionately refer to our few fans as the Land of Misfit Toys.

When the headlining act, a musical legend from Minneapolis, is on stage, our Willy Guy hollers, "Get the fat bastard off the stage—bring back Zuzu's Petals. I want Zuzu's Petals!"

His voice cracks pathetically as he reenacts torture at having to listen to the punk rock royalty in front of him. I'm sure this goes down well with the guy from home we will be opening for the next eight nights. I go across the street to Bennigan's and order a Pink Squirrel.

On a Saturday morning we're shuttled to Camden market, a fabulous flea market—finally the London of my *Oliver!*

fixation. A journalist and photographer follow us around for a feature. I buy a pair of gold lamé bermuda shorts simply because they exist, because someone thought it was a good idea to make this garish pair of shorts. Shopping can really cheer a girl up, and it is one of our favorite things to do. I'm concerned that we're not being outrageous enough for the journalist. We buy some cool stuff and stop in a pub for a morning pint and play the Stranglers on the jukebox. My stomach can't hack beer for breakfast and I order a Coke, but English Coke is just no damn good, especially without ice. Why don't people over here use ice? Hopefully Linda is making up zany stories and Co is preaching because I'm in my head writing love letters home.

We are playing well-attended gigs nightly; we're handling ourselves like pros; we have rides to every show; this is pretty cool and fun for the most part. Spending an afternoon in a photography studio, we play dress up with the provided wardrobe and decide on flannel pajamas. Our American friend Valerie is the photographer; she just finished a job shooting the Cranberries and shows us her proofs. Their lead singer is a gorgeous platinum blonde pixie; I could never look like that, and I let it worry me. That night we play somewhere.

ON a Sunday morning we have a Mark Goodier session at the BBC studios. It's Sunday morning and no one is around the massive compound, the site that's been visited by Petula Clark, Dusty Springfield, the Kinks, the Beatles, and David Bowie. The producer and engineer gossip about a festival they've recently worked, complaining loud and bitterly about Linda McCartney, bragging about turning off her mike in the middle of a performance because she was singing flat. From an outsider's perspective, Paul McCartney is one of the few mega rock stars that has his head screwed on properly. Why are people so down on rock wives? That night we play somewhere else.

W HEN we return to TJ's in Newport, Wales, and dine in
the miniature house of the jolly Tom Jones look-alike,
the mood is heavy. Somber. Unbearable. The carefree, cackling
wife has died of cancer since our last visit. After our show, our
host slaps a cigarette out of my hand in desperation.

"Smoking killed my wife," he wails, on the verge of tears.
I hold off until we're off the premises.

In a year's time, the family that unknowingly defined
"home" for me has been ravaged. Things can change forever,
for the worst, in the blink of an eye. I guess if you avoid intimacy and family life you don't have to experience horrific
painful loss, but then again, you don't get to experience the joy
I witnessed the first time this family opened their home to us.
I'm beginning to think it's worth the risk.

O UR last show of this short tour is in Rotterdam, Holland,
and we have a day of interviews scheduled in Amsterdam.
These interviews are to precede our extensive European tour
that will take place in two months. The Rotterdam gig was
arranged by Roadrunner, which has offices all over Europe,
and they want to inflame the European press with our magic.
A handsome blond guy who speaks English with a Colonel
Klink accent, an employee of Roadrunner Amsterdam, will be
our handler.

"So . . . would you like to go to the red light district?" he
asks with a straight face.

"Um . . . no," we say with half chuckles and mild sneers.
"How about the Anne Frank House or the Van Gogh Museum?"

He looks utterly baffled. He's used to working with heavy
metal bands.

Linda's parents, temporarily living in Brussels for her dad's business, are in Amsterdam to spend time with their daughter. I'm embarrassed to see them because I've never paid them back from my first English plane ticket, which I think Linda should pay for because of all the grief she caused us, but without that grief we wouldn't have had all of that terrific press, hence no record deal. . . . *Anyway*, no one can afford to pay them back. Co and I excuse ourselves from our too-serious Dutch host and Linda's family, claiming to want to explore, but we're itching to find the first coffee shop that sells bong hits. Strolling down the canal it becomes apparent that every Dutch man, woman, and child is tall, beautiful, and striking.

"Um, you guys?" an American college student, a long-haired girl of maybe nineteen, sputters with a shaky voice. "You guys? I can't feel my hands or lips."

"Uh-oh, someone's smoking their first pot," Co and I sing while sucking on the bong handed to us over the counter.

The freaking-out girl's friends try to quiet her, but she persists. "You guys, I'm scared. Ohmygod, you guys . . ."

I feel sorry for her and embarrassed for her as she begins to hyperventilate and is escorted out the door by her friends. I think about the night in Chicago when I couldn't feel my leg and wonder if Co ever thinks about that night. We never talk about it. Since I fell in love with someone who doesn't hang out with us like our other boyfriends, we don't talk about much except for business. I'm paranoid that when my songwriting is singled out, it causes a rift in our twelve-year friendship. Her songs are praised, too, but statistically speaking, I've penned more so the odds are in my favor.

Back in the offices of Roadrunner Amsterdam with two phones in front of us, Co and I aren't in much better shape than the American student. Being seasoned cannabis veterans, we're not freaking out, but we've got the giggles in the most delightful way. We're supposed to press whichever button is glowing red and there will be an interviewer on the other end of the line.

"In your song 'God Cries,' God is a woman," observes a male German journalist with a sharp, strong accent. "Are you a lesbian?"

I put him on hold and do the Sprockets dance from *Saturday Night Live*. This scenario—a foreign office building, seated in front of telephones with waiting journalists while super-stoned—is too foreign and funny, Co and I can't stop laughing long enough to answer any questions. But we try our very hardest to appear presentable when Linda's parents drop off their youngest daughter after their day together. Once again, we're the stoned babysitters. It feels really good to be having fun with Co in the old way we used to have fun while being in this unreal situation together.

Driving from Amsterdam to Rotterdam, I notice for the first time the scars on the landscape caused by World War II. There are no old buildings, just a lot of concrete that came after the destruction. I wonder how that would change your outlook, the knowing that it happened on your soil not too terribly long ago; it's so far from our everyday American reality. The club in Rotterdam is like the inside of a candlelit castle, and though I have a horrific bronchial hack—maybe I shouldn't have brought that carton of Export A Canadian cigarettes—I sing better than I ever had in my life. I don't know if it's because I'm trying harder because I'm a little sick, or because Co and I had a fun day together, or if the sound system is top-notch and I can clearly hear myself and the band, or if it's by chance, but it's so nice when it happens.

14: Ant Music

Unscathed by our abbreviated English tour, we're gearing up for a tour of the United States, followed by a tour of Europe in support of *When No One's Looking*.

Paul is about to release his first solo record, *14 Songs*. I love the collection of songs on this record; I can trace the earliest days of our courtship through these songs. That, I think, is what people do when they strongly connect with someone's songs—they plug them into their own lives and feel spoken to by the songwriter. Many critics don't care for this record; they're bristling over the breakup of the Replacements and missing the good old days, or they don't like the slick production (which sounds no different than the last two Replacements records), or they prefer Paul as a fucked-up basket case. Naturally, I do not; happy, healthy Paul inspires me. It's his life, after all. His songs belong to the world, but he doesn't. I sang backup vocals on one of his tunes, "Dice Behind Your Shades," because I happened to be around on the day they were overdubbing. It's a song that could be about him and me, or about the biography of Bob Dylan he just read, or about Carson McCullers, or about something or someone else. One thing I now understand about songwriting—a song is usually about several things; it's about whatever fits or flows the best. Serving the song is chosen over a faithful or truthful storyline. Singing background was a thrill and all, but I'm more concerned with our conflicting schedules and the fact that we're both going to be out of town and away from each other for months at a time, right in the middle of these tingly, early phases of love.

To remedy this situation, Paul flies me to Los Angeles for a couple of days before I begin my next tour. He's there shooting a video before he heads out on a tour of his own. The two days in Los Angeles will be the first time either of us has been in the same city for more than a day in almost three months. It's also the first time I've ever been to California. And Restless is in L.A.; I think it's a good idea to visit the office and meet their staff with the hopes of inspiring them to work on promoting *When No One's Looking*. Restless' offices are situated inside a little house plopped among warehouses and parking lots in West Hollywood. The fact that Restless is inside a little house appeals to me; it's an artifact in a town where I've noticed nothing is old.

A tall, skinny, extremely energetic woman around my age is in charge of publicity and she walks me through the Restless house, popping me in and out of each office. Some of the business guys at Restless, the money men, clearly don't "get it" when it comes to Zuzu's Petals and they say things to me like, "I'm an old-fashioned Jackson Browne kind of guy." What they do see, however, is an opportunity to cash in on a trend—all women, a novelty, reasonably attractive though it would be nice, in their minds, if we were all skinny all of the time (we seem to take turns and fluctuate), we're receiving favorable reviews, and we've shown a willingness to tour and court the press. Our record will not be like pulling teeth to promote. We've done a lot of the legwork before landing on this unlikely doorstep in Hollywood. Restless will, for now, invest their limited time and money on the promotion of *When No One's Looking*.

The fact of the matter is I like all of the attention I'm getting as an individual rather than as a group member. We, the Petals, are constantly, subconsciously competing for attention. If you were paging Dr. Freud, Co, Linda, and I could be seen as sisters competing for Dad's (the public's) approval. I'm starved for positive attention for whatever deep-seated reason that I'm oblivious to; I crave affirmation and support. When it

comes to showbiz, any attention, positive or negative, is supposedly good. Rock 'n' rollers have no business being picky
about what type of recognition they receive. Oftentimes the
negative attention propels rockers into stardom. Just like Co
would like to be noticed for her creative contributions rather
than her stunning God-given breasts, I want people to recognize my lyrics. But even though you present yourself to the
public as a complete package, so to speak, you don't get to
pick what others will latch on to. You don't get to pick what
others will notice about you.

When the publicity woman, Patty, shows me into her office,
I freeze at the doorway, hesitant to enter. On the wall in her office, facing me is a wall-size painting. Not a scenic painting.
Not a rock poster. Covering the entire wall in front of her desk,
instead of a window, hangs a canvas painting of Paul. This is
disconcerting, to say the least, and I feel a suit of armor start to
build itself around me. I realize that to Restless, my relationship with Paul is probably more interesting than any record I
have to promote; the Replacements' back catalogue is their
cash cow. Paul is clearly Patty's idol or something. How weird
is that?

"I don't want my love life used as bait for the press, on or
off the record," I say.

I know this is an impossible request. We're public domain. I
hope that this is not what people will notice about me.

Patty takes me to the offices of *Billboard* magazine. It's important to have a face with the record they're trying to promote; they have mountains of records hoping to be reviewed.
The writer I meet at *Billboard* used to work as a deejay in
Madison. We quickly find common ground in the joy of
drinking at the 602 Club. Patty takes me out to lunch in a
sparse metallic restaurant where the portions are way too
small and she isn't eating and I'm hungry. Everyone around
me is gorgeous and slight; they all appear to be doing very
important business while nibbling on plain arugula leaves.

Thank goodness I'm in a skinny phase. Skinny for me, not for L.A.

After lunch, Patty deposits me in a chair in front of the desk of the president of Restless. The president, I'll call him Rob, is amiable and red-haired. We sniff each other out making small talk.

"I have a friend who's managing Adam Ant." Rob chuckles. "Remember him?"

"Adam Ant? I love Adam Ant." And I do.

"He's about to do a comeback tour," Rob says, leaning back in his chair with a smirk.

WHEN Adam Ant played at the Dane County Coliseum in Madison in 1981, I was a second-year sophomore in college, and I had to go. Large-arena shows were unacceptable to my club-going crowd. Adam Ant was playing in this big crazy venue because he had a smash hit, "Goody Two Shoes." Smash hits implied selling out, but I'd loved Adam ever since he made the scene during England's punk explosion under the tutelage of Sex Pistols manager/star maker Malcolm McLaren. Adam was Roman statue beautiful and his first minor hit, "Ant Music," was a perfect collision of pop and rock. It was absolute candy to my ears and I couldn't get enough of it, like the Go-Go's "Our Lips Are Sealed" or Rick Springfield's "Jessie's Girl." "Ant Music" was one of those catchy cool songs that got stuck in my brain and drove me crazy. My roommate Lisa agreed to go to the stadium show because I bought her a ticket and she was not immune to Adam's beauty.

The crowd in the coliseum was female and pubescent. There were only three or four us old enough to enter the beer garden, Lisa and me being two of them (the drinking age was still eighteen). During the warm-up band, an unheard-of Australian new wave group called INXS, the guys from Adam's crew circulated in the crowd, inviting young girls to a party across the street at the Sheraton Hotel after the show. Lisa and I watched these exchanges but were not invited, even though I wore black vinyl pants and a 1930s silk camisole.

On stage Adam was more than a pretty face with those dark good looks I'm so fond of; he was a showman. He bumped, grinded, crooned, and flirted in a swirl of energy and hijinks. He fancied himself a swashbuckler. I developed a strong performer crush on him. After the show Lisa and I returned to our attic apartment atop a brick house on East Johnson Street.

Everyone but Lisa and me was still in school studying to become something or other. Not me, not Lisa. My lame excuse was that I was "studying life" while desperately trying to discover myself. Lisa flunked out as much as I did, but we never told anyone when we were on forced hiatus; we showed up every morning at the Memorial Union for coffee, went to work for a few hours while pretending to go to class, and returned to the union in the late afternoon for beer. We hung in a fringe population of idle poor—we acted, dressed, and partied like aristocrats while barely subsisting on meager food services incomes. Surrounded by wealthy transplants from major metropolises that acted out pauper fantasies, stealing toilet paper from the library while pocketing Daddy's American Express gold card, we all blended together in a punk-hippie-bohemian college town melting pot. Our furnishings came from junk heaps, but our apartments in chopped-up falling-down houses near campus were artistic feats. Lisa made a wall-size brick fireplace, complete with mantel, out of construction paper and crayons. She mounted a stuffed swordfish she found at a garage sale above the mock mantel.

R EALLY?" asks Restless President Rob. This is our first meeting and he's studying my face, uncertain as to whether or not I'm being sarcastic or sincere about loving Adam Ant.

"No, really. I love him." I have an idea. "Can you ask your friend if Adam Ant has an opening act for his comeback tour?"

"Really?" Now I see Rob's wheels spinning.

"Well," he says, "you would get to play in front of a lot of people and reach a totally new audience. Tell you what, I'll call him and check things out."

"Oh, thank you," I utter breathlessly.

Paul's staying at the Mondrian Hotel and I can't wait to go back and call the girls with this amazing news.

I call Co first. "Betty! I met Rob at Restless and you'll never believe this!"

"What?" Funny, she doesn't sound excited. Maybe it bugs her that I'm in L.A. doing Petal business without the other Petals. I'm purposely not telling her that I'm staying in a hotel room, a suite, that will make the Comfort Inn unbearable from this day on. The suite Paul and I occupy is ten times larger and ten times finer than my apartment.

"Rob knows Adam Ant's manager," I go on, "and he's going to see if he can get us on a tour opening for him! Isn't that incredible?"

"Wow." This "wow" is flat, bordering on sarcasm, but too bored to be snotty.

I call Linda next. She's an Anglophile; she'll be ecstatic. But I get the same monotone reaction from her. Go figure.

That night Paul and I stay in and order room service. With my first forkful of organic mixed greens, I'm sacrificing my future tolerance of salads from Denny's. Paul and I watch the disappointing final episode of *Cheers* flat on our bellies on the plushly covered floor, and suddenly feel the rumblings of a small earthquake. I'll take tornados and blizzards any day over the angry earth splitting open at the seams. Paul and I only leave the hotel room for business or to go to the Pink Dot convenience store across the street for cigarettes.

⚡

"GOOD news!" says Rob at Restless the next day when I drop by to sign posters. "The Ant people like your CD, and if we kick in ten grand for tour support, it's a go." (The ten thousand dollars will be deducted from our future earnings.)

"Great!" I say.

Being paraded around Restless, with people in the office seeming to get it and like what we've done while lapping up all of this attention, it's like many drugs: It feels so good going in that you ignore what you know deep down to be true. That it's toxic—poison. I'm proud of our record. This personal appearance of mine has helped the group as a whole, I've given our "product" a face. I don't mind being that face when things seem to be going so well. I don't suppose my bandmates wish to have my face alone traipsing around L.A. I rationalize my high by reminding myself of the high stakes I've been playing— the loans, the van, etc. My ambition is blind; I'm driving but not seeing the road ahead. If Co or Linda were in L.A. right now and didn't visit the record company, I'd be upset. But I'd also chafe a little if one of them called me from a four-star hotel the minute I walked in the house after my shift at the Hi-Lo.

"The tour starts next week," Rob continues. "It lasts one month, covering the entire U.S. The first show is in San Juan Capistrano."

I'm too embarrassed to say, "Where?" Later that day Paul tells me that it's in Orange County and that it's standard procedure to try out your show at the Stage House in San Juan Capistrano before breaking into the major market of L.A. Oh. Shit. I need to fly home immediately to get in the van and drive back to Southern California. We are supposed to be on a different tour and I don't know if it ruffles feathers or not to cancel our preexisting tour to take on this tastier gig. I don't care if it does. A whole month with Adam Ant. Imagine. My new wave heart goes pitter-patter.

For the entire month of March 1993, we will precede Adam

Ant in big glitzy venues. I know, I know; we're supposed to be opening for New York buzz band Madder Rose and we're supposed to play at the South by Southwest music festival in Austin, Texas. And South by Southwest is a very important gig; most of the quality music industry people attend, the press swarms the event, and a lot of undiscovered bands sign major-label recording contracts after a successful showing at South by Southwest. It's an Integrity gig. But I want my thirty nights of "Ant Music"; I don't hesitate to consider whether or not this is a wise career move. Besides, our record company, for the first time, seems really invested in Zuzu's Petals.

I T ' S a very long drive from Minneapolis to San Juan Capistrano, California. Insanely long. Fortunately, we have a driver/soundman and between the four of us we should be able to drive straight through. Look, an all-you-can-eat steak buffet called the Toot Toot Lounge. Never break a "no-buffet" rule. Hey, there's Wall Drug, we must be in South Dakota; it's an extralarge truck stop filled with self-promoting merchandise. Our driver/soundman, I'll call him James, has mounted an old-fashioned tin hotel bell that dings when you push the button on top of its mushroom shape. He dings it every time we cross a state line. I'm not into this ritual. Shit, there's a blizzard in the New Mexico Rockies and the highway is closed. We're from Minnesota, damn it; a March snowstorm is child's play. We all lean forward, watching James's white knuckles on the steering wheel; snow's not falling down, it's falling sideways. Feeling close to death, I pronounce, "I feel alive!" We act like we're in a covered wagon and not a heated conversion van. Not a big deal, Co and I have driven through a fire.

For the duration of this longest drive ever I have head-to-toe grand mal anxiety. I'm nervous, excited, and worried. What if we flop? What if we get booted off the tour for being imposters? I can't sleep at all. Forced to spend a night in a motel until the highway reopens in the mountains, we miss the first show of two in San Juan Capistrano. Somehow we make it to the Coach House a little worse for the wear. A young woman from Restless is awaiting us with flowers.

Acutely aware that we are not in Kansas anymore, I am out of body to the nth degree before hitting the stage. The Coach House must seat at least one thousand; this is clearly Show Business we're dealing with. All three of us are conscious of this fact and we all upgrade our wardrobe, wearing fishnets under our Doc Martens. Co and Linda increase eye makeup and hair glossing while clad in black A-line vintage dresses or jeweled, sequined sleeveless tops. Our first show sucks hard. I remember nothing. Sometimes you just have to go up there and get through it, knowing that after the initial aftershock wears off, you'll be in better shape for the next round.

I will never forget Adam, though. The largest-we've-ever-played-in club is packed with enthusiastic fans, the air is crackling with energy. The legendary guitarist/songwriter and longtime Adam collaborator Marco is playing with Adam on this tour. Marco is one of my favorite guitar players; he favors clean rockabilly chops and fuzzy power chords. Adam whirls onto the stage clad in a luscious white flowing man shirt with black leather pants and black boots, a total rock 'n' roll Errol Flynn.

At some point I hear him say, "Let's hear it for our charming opening act, Zuzu's Petals," in that adorable English accent. "Their new record is fantastic." That plug is our record company's ten thousand dollar kick-in hard at work.

Late into his show, Adam rips into a song while running full speed throughout the club with a cordless mike. We're watching this from a private viewing room upstairs set aside for VIPs; the room is full of stereotypical California boob jobs with gold chain-wearing dates. Suddenly Adam bursts through the door of our annex, microphone in hand, and jumps atop the counter we're leaning upon to get a good look at the stage.

Adam proceeds to smack his face, full on and hard, on the Plexiglas window that divides our private viewing area from the rest of the club. I recall seeing him wearing glasses during sound check. Clearly this hurt like hell, but adrenaline can masquerade this for a while. This dorky gaff sends Zuzu's Petals into hysterical laughter.

The next three nights are slated for the Fonda Theater in L.A. It's kind of boring to be in the same town for three days with little money. We spend our time waiting to play by lolling around the Restless house, ordering burgers at the Sunset Grill, eating at the rock 'n' roll Denny's, and buying the cheapest pretty underwear on the sales rack at Frederick's of Hollywood. Generally speaking, theaters are gorgeous facilities and the Fonda is no exception. From the darkened stage the audience stretches into infinity. I could get used to this type of venue with bright lights and a large stage. The lights obscure your ability to see anyone in the audience, though the people out there think you're looking at them. All three shows are sold out. The Ant crew, bored when not hard at work, pal around with us (Linda). They clean and repair our equipment, marvel at our low-rent transportation and lack of "proper" accommodations. They wonder how we can survive sexually, all sharing the same room every night. We all wonder about this, too.

It's opening night in the Fonda Theater, and I fall on my ass while squatting down to take an authentic rocker guitar solo. Never wear heels on stage. After the show a member of the Bangles pops her head into our dressing room to say hi because she's married to Adam's tour manager. Prince wrote "Manic Monday" for her group. With knit brows and an understanding smile, she seems to say, "Good luck, you're gonna need it." A rumor swirls backstage that Richard Dawson, emcee for game show *Family Feud*, is Adam's father—though this is never verified.

Adam's backup singer, Annabella, is the only other woman

on the tour, so she spends a great deal of time hanging out with us. She's bummed out because she was told to "tone it down." We are allowed a photograph with Adam backstage. We might be superstoned. In the photo I gaze at Adam in unabashed adoration. A skinny platinum blonde with an orange tan gives us her card in case we want a sponsorship from Adidas, should we become famous anytime soon. There are a lot of heavily madeup, big-haired, hot-bodied women in tight short-short outfits backstage. It is rumored that Adam favors anonymous kinky sex with groupies. This rumor is never confirmed but I do notice that a lot of his material is about S&M. There are flocks of women with stunning bodies and homely faces waiting outside the stage door for Adam.

After each show at the Fonda Theater we drive out to Van Nuys to stay at a Motel 6. An eight-month pregnant teenage hooker solicits herself in front of our room.

H ERE we are, ladies!" James exclaims while pulling over the van.

I drag myself out of a backseat nap, irritated at the interruption, disoriented.

"The Hoover Dam!" James announces with glee.

"I'll wait in the van," I mutter, while everyone piles out to look.

I hate sightseeing. The only touristy feature of interest I've seen was a billboard announcing San Simeon, William Randolph Hearst's decadent mansion where he entertained Hollywood's A-list and kept Marion Davies. When trying to sway a vote into touring San Simeon, no one bites. "You know, Hearst was the guy and San Simeon was the place modeled for *Citizen Kane*."

"No, let's just get to San Francisco in time for sound check."

WE have interviews on the phone or in person every day for small publications, a smattering of nationally distributed magazines, and radio stations. *When No One's Looking* seems to be doing well out there. It's so strange having a record out; it's like sending your children to school and hoping they don't fuck up too badly. The odd thing about giving interviews is that after a few days you wind up with a repertoire of stock answers and anecdotes that don't change much from day to day.

They ask, "What's it like being a woman in a rock band?"

We say, "It's pretty cool," or, "I've never been a man in a rock band, so . . ."

Or they ask, "What's it like being in a Minneapolis band?"

"It gets pretty cold," we might say.

Every day we're asked, "Who are your influences?"

It's hard to be quick with groovy-sounding answers even though you've had all day to invent sharp, snappy quips to the questions you know you're going to be asked, but you hear yourself saying, "Oh, a lot of the Minneapolis bands, the Replacements, Soul Asylum, the Jayhawks."

So many of these questions are not very creative, inspired, or inspiring.

"What women have influenced you?" is a very broad question that we are asked every day.

We yawn the usual: "Patti Smith, Chrissie Hynde, Deborah Harry, and Exene," when I should say, "Louisa May Alcott, Julie Andrews, and Carly Simon."

WE are sitting around Tijuana, Mexico, waiting to play in this giant toilet called the Iguana. This is a rock club meant for college kids at UC–San Diego. They can walk across the border and drink underage. The Iguana is made of concrete and chicken wire; it's a big black empty space containing a bar and a stage. Inside reeks of stale beer and urine, not exactly a new odor for the traveling rock musician. There are large grated drains on the cement floor and the custodian is hosing the place down when we enter.

There are hours to kill before sound check. We anticipated trouble with customs and drove down way too early. We were waived through with no fanfare after vacuuming every inch of our van in a self-serve car wash in case there was an encrusted pot seed in the shag that would result in us spending the rest of our lives in an unfriendly Mexican jail. We're still paranoid after that Ohio debacle. There is nothing in Tijuana but touristy trinket shops, the Iguana, and a restaurant calling itself Señor Toad's. Everything else is dry scrubby desert.

With so much time to kill, we park ourselves in a booth at Señor Toads. The specialty of the house is tequila shots served by a man dressed like the Frito Bandito, only the holster criss-crossed across his chest holds shot glasses instead of bullets. This man's job is to pour tequila shots, put the shot drinker into a head lock, tip her head back, toss the shot down her throat, and clamp her jaw down tightly while gently shaking her while still in a headlock. He finishes her off by shoving a wedge of lemon between her lips, upon which she bites down hard to prevent gagging or puking all over the table. The novelty of this abuse does not wear off for Zuzu's Petals and their soundman James.

In a matter of minutes we're reduced to shaking invisible maracas and slurring "*chica, chica*" to one another, which we find gut-busting. Losing track of the fact that we have to work that night, we get crawl-on-our-hands-and-knees hammered before sound check. The sight of three extremely boisterous, sloppy, inebriated rock girls trying to Helen Keller their way through a sound check for some reason warms the cockles of the hearts of our employers, the Ant camp. Thank goodness, because in my more lucid moments I'm thoroughly braced for being fired from the tour, defrocked as frauds.

After our performance, a blur, we overhear a drunk guy tell

his buddy, "The opening band was the fucking worst band I've ever seen in my life." He's probably right.

During Adam's set a woman approaches us, wearing a necklace in the shape of a necktie that is made entirely of fake pearls: the knot and tongue of the tie consists of rows upon rows of pearls. In our collective state of mind, this accessory is mesmerizing.

"I'm supposed to interview you. I borrowed a friend's car and drove it to the border," she explains, though she's easily as drunk as we are, "and I don't have a driver's license."

We worry about her, and her story makes no sense to us, and I'm not sure if an interview is ever accomplished. Upon her exit, she presents Co with her necklace, a souvenir of her appreciation. (This pearl necktie necklace sees lots of action in the years to come.)

My final image of Tijuana involves crawling on my hands and knees through Adam's dressing room in search of a toilet in which to puke. Pebbles and broken glass are encrusted in my palms and kneecaps.

P ACK your bags, kids! We're going to spend Thanksgiving in Puerto Vallarta, Mexico!" my dad announced one black November evening after work.

"Yay! Fun Daddy!" we all sang around his large frame, overjoyed at the prospect of a week on the beach versus Thanksgiving in Madison—it looked like the surface of the moon outside with all the brown lawns and bare trees.

I was a senior in high school and relished the idea of an off-season tan. My mom scowled in silence off to the side.

For a week I lolled on a beach in a string bikini, sipping on sangria and piña coladas while reading *Hamlet* for English class. My siblings frolicked, my mother read, and my dad relaxed. Our villa had its own swimming pool that was refreshed every morning with fresh gardenia and hibiscus blooms.

My mother rarely spoke the entire week. When we got home, she said, "That trip could have put all four of you through four years of college."

My parents paid for my first year of college, but that was it. The money had run out. My siblings either skipped college or went deeply into debt. I did both.

S OMETIMES Adam's tech crew takes one bus and drives directly to the next city to get a head start and the band follows the next morning in the other bus after sleeping in a hotel. Sometimes both buses head to the next destination directly following the show and the band members each have private bunks to sleep in during the overnight drive. Sometimes we have to leave directly after a show, too, and drive to the next town, only we don't get to sleep except for oddly and in abbreviated shifts. Adam, we've learned, has an extremely nice wardrobe lady in his crew who spends all day mending Adam's white swashbuckler shirts.

Every day Adam's extradeluxe silver bullet tour buses flash past us, the sun reflecting off the silver temporarily blinding us, leaving us to eat their dust. I gaze out the window of our old green Chevy and wistfully sigh and say, "I wonder if Adam is thinking about us."

We are late for sound check at the Aladdin in Las Vegas. It takes all night and most of the day to drive the 575 miles from San Francisco to Vegas.

When we pull our tiny little van onto the backstage loading dock, the stage manager shouts, "You're late! You're off the bill!"

Hearing this, chivalrous, loyal Adam refuses to perform unless we're allowed to play. We dash into a dressing room with spotlight-lined mirrors and pull our show dresses over our heads, dab on makeup, and tear onto the stage. We're on a ridiculous bill; it's New Wave Revival Night and we don't fit in with Adam and Flock of Seagulls. Thomas "Poetry in Motion" Dolby is the emcee for this affair.

For the split second we have to process what's going on, I liken us to Liza Minnelli opening for the Rat Pack. The stage is the largest yet, and extremely well lit and glitzy. The vast space between performer and audience makes me less nervous. Being outcasts on the bill makes us irreverent and we bellow "Science!" from the wings every time Thomas Dolby appears on stage in a top hat and round glasses. We rip through our set, high on adrenaline and laughter from the stage where the great Jackie Wilson sang "Lonely Teardrops" while suffering a fatal heart attack. I have no clue about the specifics.

After it's all over, in the blink of an eye, James and my bandmates are excited to explore Vegas with Co's mom, who has flown in for our show. Hit extra hard with counteradrenaline, I'm excited to explore the room service menu in our complimentary room in the Aladdin Hotel. My big night in Vegas consists of ordering a turkey club and watching *Sisters* on TV.

I hate sightseeing.

T HE venues become less opulent the farther east we travel. Adam's popularity declines in the middle markets. In Austin, Texas, a town I've wanted to play in for years, we're booked into a supper club situated in a suburban strip mall.

When we must drive from Dallas to Tampa, Adam's band invites us to ride in their bus so that we can get some proper rest. If we were to do that, James would have to drive our van by himself and meet us there. I'm all for this idea; he can ding his little bell alone to his heart's content. I am reminded that it wouldn't be fair to James to have him drive all that way by himself. I am denied my desire to stretch out in one of those fancy buses. Not that Adam himself has uttered a word to us directly.

In Tampa we play in a joint that is essentially a roadhouse

off a highway exit ramp. The waitresses all wear butt thongs and tight T-shirts. This bugs me. A woman hanging outside the club pulls me aside and confides that "Ronnie from Night Ranger is a really nice, down-to-earth guy, like a real person."

Right before Adam's stage call a storm erupts. Thunder, lightning, vertical rain, and heavy winds. Adam refuses to leave his bus until someone can muster an umbrella and will escort him from bus to stage door.

The thunderstorm evolves into a tornado that switches over into heavy snow. Snow in March; what's the big deal? The flakes are wet and gloppy as we make our way back to the Holiday Inn that we're sharing with the New York Yankees, who look very beat-up and tired up close in the hotel lounge (not that we're daisy fresh by any stretch). Outside the temperature has dropped forty degrees in a couple of hours. The snow shows no sign of letting up. Apparently this is a big deal to Floridians.

The next morning we're slated to drive to Atlanta. It's still snowing and there have been highway closings. Naturally we scoff and jump in the van. A seven-hour drive turns into fourteen as the wet and heavy snow continues to dump. Traffic is slow and some southern drivers don't see the benefit of slowing down in a blizzard. Cars careen into ditches every few minutes. It's dark when we pull in front of the Roxy, the evening's venue. The theater is also dark. The show has been canceled.

After an hour spent in a phone booth trying to find a motel room, we realize that we're in a Serious Storm. Everything is closed or put on hold. There are no vacancies in any of the motels or hotels. Examining the tour itinerary, James finds the hotel information for the Ant camp. They're sequestered in a good hotel.

Fearing the worst, a night in the van in a parking lot in the snow, James returns from the phone booth with a crooked smile. "You're not going to believe this, ladies: they reserved us a room earlier in the day."

We've become their foolhardy mascots, chasing on their heels in our rickety van with dogged loyalty. The Ant crew worries about us. We don't know how we'll ever pay for this hotel.

The entire southeastern seaboard has been paralyzed by something CNN has dubbed "Blizzard '93." By day two, the hotel bar is out of wine and beer; the hotel restaurant is down to its last box of cereal. We stare out our window from the twelfth floor and watch Georgia drivers pirouette into each other in a slow-motion ballet of bad driving. I go down to the restaurant and sit at a table to read and write letters to Paul. Adam is sitting at a table across the room, reading. He looks so alone, which he always does unless he's on stage in front of an audience. How can a person so mesmerizing on stage, so oozing with charisma, switch back and forth from stage to ordinary life? His audiences adore and appreciate him with an almost religious fervor. He's what I aspire to be, but look at him over there, he's so alone. I want to approach him, talk to him, make friends, but he hasn't spoken to us the whole time. Does being the focal point of so much adoring attention, a type of attention that has very little to do with reality, amount to nothing more than closed-off paranoia? So many rumors about him whirl around, and we're on the inside—imagine what's going on out there in the crowd.

If the kinky sex in his songs is real, he could be exhausted after a sex marathon with dominatrixes. Right now, he looks like a cute guy wearing glasses and jeans across the room, accessible. But I decide it's best to leave him alone. I assume he values his privacy. If he wanted to talk to me, he would. I wonder how it feels to have a really good new record out on the market but when you play a show, the crowd only wants to hear your old songs from ten years ago.

From Atlanta, we're supposed to play in Detroit, followed by Washington, D.C. There is no way in hell the Dream Van will allow this to happen. Again, the Ant people offer to transport us to the gig in Detroit and James could meet us in D.C. The majority of us do not think this would be fair to James. I am in the minority. When we check out of our fine accommodations in Atlanta, the desk clerk informs us that our bill has already been paid.

The venue in Washington, D.C., the 9:30 Club, is across the street from the Ford Theater. James and the girls would like to visit the site of Lincoln's assassination. I opt to sit alone in the lobby. Tourists. My head has been filled with tales depicting the monumental rat population in the 9:30 Club. I am deathly afraid of rats.

O NE night during "the Carly Simon summer," I went by myself to see a Replacements show at Irving Plaza in New York because I knew that my Vineyard friend Chris was in town visiting his dad, who lived across the street from Irving Plaza. Having two things worth seeing within a block's radius was enough of a reason for me to take a trip.

A ferry brought me from the Vineyard to Woods Hole, a bus from Woods Hole to Boston, and a train from Boston to New York. On the train I sat with a jolly group of male yuppies around my age that offered me a clear plastic glass filled with premade gin and tonics they had in an extralarge Thermos. I drank and snorted coke with these guys, making merry, wearing a black satin waitress apron "dress" from the forties that was really supposed to have a coordinating white dress underneath. Slashed down to my navel in front, I wore nothing.

"Hey," one of them slurred as we pulled into Grand Central Station, "do you know where you're going, or how to get there?"

I showed him the folded sheet of paper with Chris's father's phone number and address. My party companions hailed me a cab, told the driver where to take me, and handed him a twenty.

The night was a disaster. Chris bumped into a city friend and did some very antisocial drugs and I lost him. The Replacements sucked hard, stopping and starting, superwasted, letting some black vixen sing "Gimme Shelter" on stage, pretending they were the Stones. Paul said hello to me and offered to buy me a drink, but he was clearly distracted. I left alone and took a cab to LaGuardia's commuter terminal to wait for my flight to Boston the following morning. It was scary: the doors were open, but there was no one there but a sleeping bum and a janitor.

I put a dime in a pay phone and called my mom in Madison at three in the morning.

"Mom?" I whispered.

"My God, it's the middle of the night. What happened?"

"I'm alone in a commuter terminal in New York and there's no one here working and my flight doesn't leave till the morning and I'm scared."

"What do you want me to do?"

"Stay on the phone with me until someone shows up for work."

Which she did for over two hours. Not that she would've been able to do anything should someone had decided to accost me, but having her stay on the line with me quelled my fear. I told her about the evening and Vineyard news and she updated me on my siblings. She always let me lead my own life, and she was always there for me when I got myself in a jam.

"Mom, people are starting to come in; I'm gonna be okay."

"Please be careful."

"I will. Thanks, Mom."

Zuzu's Petals will perform at Irving Plaza with Adam Ant.

IN New York we are scheduled to visit *Spin* radio for an interview before our show. It's a slushy cold St. Patrick's Day. Walking into the large brick office building, we step onto the elevator. The seams of my Doc Martens are giving out, cold and wetness seeps into the feet of my tights, but I've adapted completely to physical discomfort.

"Hi, Dad."

My father is on this elevator. He's on a business call. What are the chances of this happening? His big bear hug is something I didn't know I needed so very badly until I'm in his embrace. I could disintegrate into powder under its crush.

He takes us across the street for a beer after our interview. I'd like to spend the day with him but he has another business call before heading to LaGuardia to fly home to Detroit.

D ON'T kick her out of school. Please," my father appealed to the panel of deans at the University of Wisconsin, "her mother and I recently divorced, and it's my fault. Let her stay in school."

I looked at him with a lump in my throat that felt like a grapefruit. It was his fault. Right? Wasn't it? The fact that I never went to class and got drunk every night was because my dad left my mother for his receptionist, thus breaking our family up and turning his, therefore my, life into a cliché. And all this time I thought I went out every night because that's what I felt like doing, and I never went to class because it was what I didn't feel like doing. Blaming my dad came as a relief.

"A parent's divorce is very difficult," admitted Dean C., my main dean, a lanky man in his thirties who I could tell was fed up with my case. He leaned forward in his creaky wooden chair. "Perhaps what Laurie needs is some time off to cope with this difficult situation? Maybe she could attend Madison Area Technical College and get her grades up and be readmitted if she's suited to the challenge of a more academically rigorous school . . ."

"She's bright enough to handle your school," my dad said, getting testy.

"Mr. Lindeen," Dean C. began, "this is the fourth time your daughter's been on academic probation. It's school policy that after four strikes, you're out."

"I'm sorry, honey," my dad said with a hug outside the administrative offices, "I tried."

"Ya, well, I'll figure something out," I said with a dark look, half-feeling sorry for myself, half-mad at him for not getting in my face and commanding me to shape up.

I hated my dad for ditching us. But he had reasons to hate me, as well:

Like the night of my eighteenth birthday when my Martha's Vineyard boyfriend flew in for the weekend and I brought him out to my parents' house for the privacy that was impossible to achieve in a dorm room—my family was out of town.

I woke up staring at the opened bedroom door and the dark shapes of my parents standing, looking at the two beautiful eighteen-year-old nude bodies passed out on their bed. I closed my eyes and reopened them. They were still there. They must've come home early.

"I think you better go back to your dorm," my mother said as I sat up, shaking Kurt's shoulder. She closed the door.

Kurt groaned, stirring. "My parents are home!" I whispered frantically.

While I fumbled around retrieving articles of clothing, Kurt dressed completely and jumped out of the ground-floor bedroom window, leaving me to face my parents alone.

Walking down the hallway, my sister Megan opened her bedroom door and whispered, "I still love you," and promptly closed it again as my mom approached.

"I know this looks really bad," I bumbled, "but it's not what you think."

"Your dad is livid, you'd better go back to your dorm. Now," my mom instructed while handing me my car keys and backpack. My dad didn't speak to me for six months. I've never been sure which part pissed him off the most.

Then there was the time I sold the family canoe to a hippie on campus so I could buy a plane ticket to Boston. And the time I deserted my car at a stoplight in downtown Madison because it stalled and wouldn't restart—and it was cold out and I didn't want to hassle with a tow truck—I really just wanted to get to the bar. Police officers rousted my parents at 2:00 A.M. at their home regarding the abandoned vehicle that was registered under my father's name.

So when my dad appears on an elevator in New York City, out of nowhere and hugs me, it's a loaded hug. He doesn't hate me. And I need more than anything not to hate him anymore.

SHOWS in Chicago and Minneapolis are canceled and Adam Ant's '93 comeback tour (titled "Persuasion" after the single on his new record that no one seems to want to hear) fizzles with no fanfare. I don't think this has put him back on the map. We've logged nearly ten-thousand miles on our Chevy van, and it's tired and ready to let go.

I HAVE a barking hack and possibly a fever. One week following the Adam Ant tour, we're back in England for eleven nights, followed by two weeks on the continent. One thing to consider: eleven nights in the UK, geographically speaking, is the equivalent of eleven nights in Iowa. We're based out of the Dalmatia Hotel again in the same summer camp room, and Mitch is our driver. I didn't know he could drive. On our first outing, our rented Euro van smashes into a lorry (a truck) on the way to a radio interview outside of London. No one is hurt, just freaked-out. I add vehicular homicide to my growing list of bad things that might happen to us.

Oh and yes, there are teenage boys who now come to our shows and sort of mope around us, pining away. And a school-boy skipped class to catch us on the way into a radio station.

But they're kids. There's no way. At least they're into us and not into anger and heroin like so many other youngsters these days. I didn't skip class until college. I realize my response is more motherly than rockerly.

I'M a psychologist and I can tell that you've attempted suicide on numerous occasions," says a tall clean-cut Brit in a corduroy jacket.

He's wrong, but I'm intrigued.

"No, actually," I inform him, "I've never tried suicide or given it much thought."

He's backstage in Derby, "backstage" being upstairs somewhere in an adjoining building that houses a disco, as well as the small club that we're to play.

"You're going to have to quit music if you want to hang on to your boyfriend," he gravely informs me, though I've made no mention of a boyfriend. What did he say he was? Psycho, psychic, or a psychologist? He touches a frazzled nerve, the only one that isn't shot.

While on stage in Derby the whole place is silent except for Linda's drums. We think we're playing, but clearly the sound system is not turned on. Or it's blown. It's hard to know because the sound engineer has left the building. We exit the stage confused. Can't put on much of a show without a sound system. Loitering around the disco waiting for an explanation, we remove a copy of Gary Numan's gold record for "Cars" from the wall. Because we are not provided with answers, we bring it back with us to the Dalmatia.

The next morning I have a hard time getting out of bed. I'm enshrouded in a black cloud, certain we're in serious danger.

"You guys, I don't feel safe," I confess, sitting up in my tiny Euro bed. "I think we should go home. Now. I want to leave."

"Why?"

"I'm sick, I'm scared; I think something bad's gonna happen to us if we stay."

"But we'll be in Europe in a week; I've heard it's much easier on the continent, that conditions are better, the food's better . . ." Linda appeals.

Unconvinced, I shake my head.

I repeat my statement to Mitch, who will pay a visit to our record label and to our booking agents. I'm sick with probably whooping cough, I've chipped a front tooth on a cough drop, and I have no idea what anxiety is. All I know is that I'm hawking up green and brown loogies that would gross out D. H. Lawrence. I'm paralyzed with panic.

My mind is set. I want to go home. Now. I don't feel safe.

"It's the boyfriend," the booking agent concludes when Mitch passes on my message. "Let me talk to her. Tell her that every show from here on in is sold out."

"The boyfriend" everyone keeps whispering about has nothing to do with this; we've spoken on the phone maybe once all week, and we're not exactly getting on at the moment. I have nothing but complaints for him, too. He's ticked off about a glib letter I've written, poking fun at his worshipers who approach me on occasion.

"It's not the fucking boyfriend; it's just me!"

I'm freaking out, okay? Plain and simple. Co and Linda don't necessarily agree with me, but they don't argue, either. They're tired, too. Maybe I'm having a premonition and I'm sparing us from looming catastrophe. Maybe I'm helping us dodge a bullet. Probably not.

A cab picks us up at the crack of dawn the following morning. We present the owner of the Dalmatia with Gary Numan's gold record as a parting gift.

Our cab breaks down. The driver abandons the vehicle, leaving us on the side of the road. When he never returns, we hail another cab from the shoulder of the road. Within a few blocks our second cab is pulled over by the police. This is a good thing because our cabbie is bombed out of his mind and subsequently arrested for drunk driving. Left to fend for ourselves, we're unclear as to whether or not the arresting officer sent for another cab. I remember aloud that Eddie Cochran was killed in an auto accident on the way to Heathrow. Co and I spot a fire station in the distance. The only KLM direct flight to Minneapolis is scheduled to depart soon. I'd like to say that we're driven to Heathrow in a fire truck with its sirens wailing, but they just called us another cab.

PART THREE

I DO WANT WHAT
I HAVEN'T GOT

15: Home Is Just Emotion
Sticking in My Throat

WHEN *No One's Looking* seems to have a life of its own. People want to talk to us. On any given day, one of us has to drop by Twintone to do a radio or press interview. Duke, our loyal college radio guy at Twintone, says, "It's really fun to work a record that people like." It's really fun to hear people say such things. There's a big map of the United States in Duke's office, a different-colored tack represents each Twintone band and Zuzu's Petals' blue tacks are all over the map in greater numbers than any of the other Twintone bands at the moment. The employees in California at Restless coordinate our interview schedules with the employees at Twintone. The employees at Twintone, once autonomous, resent being badgered by Big Brother out in California.

(*Exclaim* magazine, February 1993) Zuzu's Petals; *When No One's Looking*
Wow, three gals who don't want to rip my head off! They play happy pop music, too. No, it's not a Go-Go's reunion. Minneapolis' Zuzu's Petals are intense but don't mind being musically pretty. The songs are simple, punchy, and most of all infectious . . .

I've noticed that music-loving women who are not in bands work for record labels, music publications, radio stations, and in nightclubs. I guess that's a logical career move with your comm. arts or journalism degree and/or your love of music and the scene. On occasion we sense a minor backlash from female employees at the places we must do business. Some don't like our lack of in-your-face politics, some don't care for our music, some respond negatively to who we date or hang out with. Some got into the business to hang out with the cute boys and to get into all of the shows for free and party with the band backstage. Hell, it's fun to work around creative people with sex appeal. Why should they exert energy on us? Some act like moms to these guys, some become best friends and lovers. This anti-Petal vibe is subtle yet obvious. These overworked, underpaid women are constantly on their toes, frantically searching out herbal tea, or pot, or whatever. When we invade their turf, they glaze over with an icy reserve or they warily just tolerate us. A soundman in another city informs us that Zuzu's Petals will never get another gig in one of the clubs where he works because the female booking agent has decided she doesn't like us for one of the above reasons. On the other hand there's a pro-Petal young woman at Restless named Lindsey who is so into us that she goes out of her way to convert the nonbelievers. Lindsey is the only person who knows the words to our songs better than we do.

It's confusing; we're all supposed to be educated or enlightened feminists to some degree, yet we don't have the competition piece down—when is it healthy to compete and when is it that socialized sense of threat that we're responding to? I thought sisters were doing it for themselves, so naturally we'd all go out of our way to help one another. Not that I have a handle on how competition's supposed to work in the world or within the band. When is competition healthy? When it's the spirited thing that spurs you on to do better, which helps the whole "team" as a result? When is it a sickly pea green shade of envy?

Here's a list of everyone who hates you: Becky, Sandy, Teri, Christie, Mary, Renee, Lorna, Julie, Pam [with round curlicue signatures].

Both Co and I received these types of letters in middle school for reasons unknown to us. Co was spared a year of middle school because her family temporarily moved to Germany. I was not.

There was a day in sixth grade when I lived in fear of leaving the school building because Lorna Smith was waiting outside to kick my ass and the entire sixth grade class was waiting outside to watch my ass get kicked. I think it was because both Lorna and I had a crush on our classmate Scott and he was considered Lorna's guy. Scott, being a sixth grade boy, was probably not in the loop about any of these developments regarding his status.

Inserting a dime in the pay phone in the front hallway of school, I phoned home. "Hello, Mom? Can you pick me up in the back of school? Someone's waiting out there to beat me up."

My mom didn't ask whom or why, she just showed up. My mom was a parent caller and I had to keep information from her to prevent further ass kicking. A crowd of hateful twelve-year-olds yelled "chicken shit" as I ducked into my mom's Datsun.

On New Year's Eve when I was in seventh grade the mean girls came over to my house while my mom was at a hair appointment. Being my grade school/neighborhood crowd, the mean girls couldn't be avoided, especially during school vacations. I thought that if I switched loyalties whenever the ringleaders required it without actually being mean, I could get through middle school with my ass intact.

"Afro, go get some bottles from the liquor cabinet," Renee commanded.

They called me Afro because in adolescence the front of my hair had decided to curl and frizz while the rest of my hair was long and stringy.

An assortment of bottles gathered dust at the end of our hallway in a linen closet next to my bedroom door. Presumably

I was babysitting, but I had a group of six gathered in my bedroom wearing so many coats of Great Lash mascara that we all looked like the guy in *Clockwork Orange* while clad in ratty elephant bell-bottoms that barely covered our pubic bones.

I quietly stepped into the hallway and grabbed crème de menthe, crème de cacao, and triple sec because they all appeared to be flavored. We passed the bottles around in a circle, each of us required to take a slug.

"Get three more!"

I grabbed brandy, rum, and Martini & Rossi.

After three more snorts, some of us changed drastically; the volume increased, I felt dizzy and sweaty. The littlest girl, a gymnast named Pam, started dancing around wildly and a "binder" (universally known as a snuggy or wedgie) was ordered. Two large girls, one in back and one in front, grabbed small Pam's bikini underwear and lifted her off the ground until her panties ripped clean off her body. This symbolic rape had to hurt a lot, but Pam laughed. This incident got out of hand because presumably twelve-year-olds can't hold their liquor and *Lord of the Flies* behavior was not just for boys anymore. It made everyone uncomfortable and they all zipped up their hooded parkas to head out.

"You coming, Afro?"

"I'm babysitting."

By the time my mom came home with her complicated combination beehive-on-top long-and-curled-on-the-bottom hairdo, I had thrown up three times.

"What's the matter?" she asked.

"I think I have the flu," I moaned.

That night my folks went to a New Year's party, and I babysat in my robe and pajamas, dry heaving every twenty minutes or so. When the Burt Bacharach and Angie Dickinson commercial came on TV and they sang, "Martini and Rossi on the rocks, say yeeees!" I ran to the bathroom and heaved neon yellow bile.

Co, Linda, and I no longer hang out every day practicing and plotting our world domination. Kind of sick of one another, we retreat into separate worlds. Two months have lapsed in fast motion since ditching the post-Ant European tour (and learning that ditching a tour tarnishes your reputation and is Bad for Business, according to our record label and lawyer). It's now more lucrative to perform—yet not so much so that we can actually quit our jobs. Our Twintone contract states that we are required to play ninety out-of-town shows within six months of our record's release. During our ill-timed but necessary hiatus that absorbed sixty days that should've been spent on the road, I take a six-week round of antibiotics to treat a nasty, persistent case of bronchitis and Linda has elbow surgery to scrape off bad arthritic tissue from her sore elbows.

Paul and I ride bikes together, tooling around residential neighborhoods and lakes at the crack of dawn. At night we read aloud to each other excerpts from our library books. I'm on a Southern Gothic kick, revisiting Flannery O'Connor, Eudora Welty, and Tennessee Williams. Paul's reading A Smattering of Ignorance by Oscar Levant. Reading and bike riding are simple things that bring me pleasure, things I love to do that I'd completely forgotten about. Healthy things. I'm resettling into my skin.

Most of the time Paul and I laugh our asses off—Lord knows you need a sense of humor when your boyfriend wears a smaller jean size than you do. Sometimes we bowl with grapefruits, using empty soda cans as pins, or we'll spy on his neighbors who are entertaining on their back deck while playing the same Dean Martin record over and over, imagining that it is a cult gathering. "It's the night of a thousand Dean Martins," Paul decides, and we watch intently, waiting for the Jerry Lewis sacrifice that never happens.

"I have multiple sclerosis," I nervously sputter to Paul one evening while watching Deborah Kerr hide her crippledness in *An Affair to Remember*, "but I'm not really bothered by it or experiencing any symptoms or anything."

"I'll take care of your crumpled little body when you're in a wheelchair," he answers, nuzzling me, looking excited by the prospect.

This is perhaps the most outrageous thing anyone's ever said to me; my head swims with relief, fear, and confusion. I don't plan on being crumpled in a wheelchair ever, but the fact that Paul doesn't seem to mind facing what I can't overpowers my strong emotions at this moment. If this guy were Jim Jones, I would drink the Kool-Aid.

Spring turns to summer and Minnesota transforms from gray and brown to lush and green. Paul and I plant morning glories, cucumbers, and green beans on the side of his house. Like my mom in the seventies during our "rented plot" phase, we're grasping for something that's missing. A garden is a belief in the future. A statement saying we believe in the four months it will take for seeds to blossom, grow, and ripen. This seems un-rock. Or is it? Everyone making rock headlines these days is smacked out on heroin and looking like corpses. We're rebelling against the trend, taking an oppositional-defiant stand by rocking and doing mild things. I love playing house with this man; he calls me a "god-damned angel." I call him "hot."

I don't much feel like writing songs because I'm happy, and whoever heard of writing a song when you're happy? Paul writes songs every day, he has that thing I lack—the self-discipline to go to work every day, and the self-control to put it away every night. I don't work like that at all—I cradle a guitar like it's a teddy bear and meditate into a notebook like it's a therapist whenever life gets too angering, unjust, confusing, or sad. I can lose days and nights prostrate with a song that's trying to get born. Maybe I'm doing it wrong.

(Rolling Stone, Raves, July 1993) Zuzu's Petals, *When No One's Looking*
No riot-grrl fuss here. Just great guitar-crackle pop by three women with hooks and chutzpah.

For every bit of favorable press, it is safe to assume that there is an equally negative review out there. It's not in our record company's best interest to collect the bad press, so we rarely see it.

Somewhere along the line, we've acquired a booking agent who's based in Chicago. He gets fifteen percent of our earnings for every show that he books. On a couple of occasions Co and I have received phone calls from club managers in other cities, complaining, "Your booking agent is asking for too much money. I gave you girls a show when nobody had ever heard of you—you owe me, cut me some slack." I don't know how to respond. Personally, I'm disappointed that a booking agent from a large nationally known agency hasn't offered his or her services.

(Mankato MN, *Run, Run, Run* music column) Zuzu's Petals, *When No One's Looking*
When Zuzu's Petals appeared on the Minneapolis scene a few years ago, they were derided for using their well-oiled connections to get places. "They only get gigs," the naysayers said, "because they're friends with Paul and Dave . . . They only get gigs because they're girls. They can't play a lick."

So maybe they couldn't. Maybe they were sloppy. Who cares? They can play fine now, and *When No One's Looking* is quite an accomplished first album. Maybe the British press, who have shamelessly hyped this band for the past couple of years, were right after all . . .

Zuzu's Petals don't sound like a bunch of brainless whiners. Their songs are much more introspective, almost poetic, in a slacker kind of way. Chalk me up as a convert.

B EFORE our next tour we're scheduled to play in St. Paul on the small oddities stage for an alternative music supershow called Lollapalooza. Our allotted slot is at 10:00 A.M. When we pull in onto Harriet Island, situated on a bank of the Mississippi River, it's sunny and there are already thousands of kids with tattoos and multiple piercings gathered in a huge field. We commence playing while there's nothing going on yet except for the vegan and Greenpeace booths. The warm air is thick with curry, cumin, and patchouli, a combination of odors I associate with Madison. While cracking into our first song, a large body of people starts moving toward us en masse. I'm wearing the weirdest vintage dress I own; the fabric is yellow-and-black rayon with tiny clown heads printed all over it. Watching a herd of humans come forth is very freaky. And cool. Rocking hard in broad daylight, in the morning no less, is a challenge. And in the blink of an eye it's over.

It's high summer—traditionally my least-favorite time of year unless I'm living on an island that features cool ocean breezes. It's hot, and as you know, I hate the heat. Hot is claustrophobic. We're on tour. Not a huge tour, a regional tour for two weeks in the Midwest. High summer in Kansas, Nebraska, Missouri, Iowa, Wisconsin, and Illinois. The heartland. In August. Bites. The Great Plains are parched. Otherwise there's just corn. Corn. Corn. Your forehead is covered in sweat bumps. The van is melting hot. The clubs you play in are like saunas; it's hard to breathe.

I'm extraparanoid, on MS alert in the height of summer because prolonged exposure to heat can trigger MS symptoms. I'm one of those people, like the elderly and newborns, who are warned on the news when the heat index gets out of hand. My left hand and foot fall asleep more frequently, my energy level is below the radar, and Paul notices that my left eye droops when I'm overheated. Even before MS, I hated the heat.

My college roommate used to call me an "arctic bitch" because I always opened the windows in the winter.

I slouch in the van, sucking ice water, speaking little except to occasionally exclaim, "Ew . . . my fingernails, ankles, everything is filthy. This van is disgusting."

"Ya . . . so? What are you? A born-again priss?"

"Shut yer ass," I bellow to break the tension, to let them know I'm still tough.

M Y first job was de-tassling corn at Blaney Farms the summer before ninth grade. A yellow school bus picked up a throng of kids at the neighborhood fire station at daybreak and took us out to this endless sea of corn out in the country. If you ever wonder why Georgia O'Keeffe fixated on Western landscapes, it's because she was born on just this parcel of corn land in Sun Prairie, Wisconsin.

I did not understand what, exactly, de-tassling meant or what piece off an ear of corn I was supposed to pull while walking down row upon row, alone all day in the blistering heat. So I just faked it, pulling the silky threads hanging outside the leaves that encased the cob. I had no idea that plants could cross-pollinate or incorrectly reproduce. Our foreman was a dark, curly-haired high school girl and we kept track of her whereabouts throughout the day, listening to her sing in this powerful silvery voice. We repeated after her all day, engaged in a lily-white call and response. "Ee-eye," she'd sing, and I'd sing alone in my cornrow, "Ee-eye." Then she'd belt out "Ee-eye, ee-eye-oh" and so on until it was time for her to dispense salt tablets in the afternoon so that we wouldn't pass out from loss of electrolytes due to dehydration. Salt tablets or no salt tablets, there was at least one fallen de-tassler daily. At week's end I received a check for sixty-five dollars. I lasted about two weeks.

I USED to envy Co and Linda for being sexy brunettes. Now I covet their ability to make the most of our conditions by insisting on having fun. What's not fun about having larger, more receptive audiences than we've ever had? (Nothing.) We can play well together on autopilot. In fact, we're more functional on stage than we are the rest of the day when all of us are lost in our private thoughts. We might be about to break through to the next level on the showbiz food chain. But it's not happening big enough or fast enough; I keep comparing our progress with other femme bands like Hole, Belly, and L7; they're all on major labels while we're still schlepping away on our independent label. What if we've hit our ceiling, like this is the best it's ever going to be right here, right now? What if we have to do this for another ten years just to earn an "integrity career"? That would suck. This is a lot like being a baseball player; would I stay in AA or AAA ball at thirty just in case I got called up for "the show"? We should be staying in hotels with lobbies instead of being crammed together in the same cinder block room in a motor lodge. None of our rock star friends have to put up with this shit anymore, though they most certainly did while they were touring in support of their first album, but the industry has changed. People are hopping onto major labels faster and bigger than ever before. They're making Real Money. Why are we being passed over during the current signing frenzy? Oh, we've paid our dues. I'm a little paranoid that there's word on the street about us, that we're inept or unreliable or something—that isn't true—but something must be ruining our chances for advancement. I'm a little paranoid about everything.

And there's also the *Exile in Guyville* hysteria going on all around us. Everyone just looooves this double album. I rarely love a double album, unless it's *Exile on Main Street*. There is a lot of jealous rumor mongering about this groundbreaking record: some say that Liz Phair's producer played and arranged most of the songs and that she can't sing her way out of a paper bag. Others whisper that she can't reproduce her material live and feigns stage fright. I, of course, would rather listen to the venomous rumors because I feel threatened by her takeover while I'm on such shaky creative ground. The thing that people are noticing about Liz is her potty mouth and sexually explicit lyrics. That kind of stuff gets you noticed; everyone from Richard Pryor to Madonna has proven that. I don't buy or listen to her record and I don't need to because she's on every commercial alternative, and college radio station. Her songs show up on all the mix tapes our friends in other cities hand us after a gig. There are a couple of her songs that I wish I'd written, like "Johnny Sunshine" and "Divorce Song." I could say, "I'll be your blow job queen" if I wanted to, but I don't (for a variety of reasons). Sure, we talk like that in the van now that we've transformed into blue-collar workers, but I'm a fan of leaving things up to the imagination (as Mae West did). I'm sort of prissy and repressed. Or maybe I'm just an old-fashioned gal with manners.

No dresses," I announce, throwing myself on a bed and lighting a cigarette after returning to our motel room after sound check to prepare for the night's show. This means that I've deemed the club, the people we've just dealt with, and their level of enthusiasm subpar—therefore unworthy to receive us in dresses. This means we'll go to the show and perform wearing the same rumpled pajama tops and jeans that we traveled in.

"Ya," my mates agree, "no dresses." Ew, that will show them.

We're gathered on a foam rubber bed, staring at the long-distance commercial on TV with tears in our eyes.

After an hour in our motel, I'm cagey and my mates are content watching an erotic thriller on HBO.

"Let's get to the club," I suggest.

"It's not even eight, and we don't go on till ten or eleven," Linda notes.

I know, but I have this neurosis about getting to the venue early; I sort of need to be the first one there and have a comfortable spot staked out before everyone arrives. When we pull in right before going on stage and there's a crowd, I'm overwhelmed with nerves and feel disoriented; when I watch people gradually filter in, it's easier to keep my bearings.

"Fine," they both say, turning off the TV and gathering purses, drumsticks, lipsticks, and guitar picks out of soiled pockets.

Co has an alter ego known as Phony Co; she handles a lot of our telephone communications with the promoters, and is nice enough to (pretend to) listen to people in the audience blather on incessantly about their stupid bands.

"Oh, that's a cute rat you have tattooed on your inner thigh," I hear her say to a young lass.

"Oh yes, the [week-old] deli tray [leftover from another band] is absolutely delicious," she gushes when the promoter pops his head backstage.

Or, "Pizza again? Yummy!"

When the promoter disappears, she snaps her fingers, points her index finger at the door, and says, "Phony Co strikes again."

And then Linda chants, "Fun-ny! Fun-ny!" and I join in because we now make a very big deal about anything that might be funny.

While at home Co is considered the punk rock Martha Stewart; she's a fabulous hostess, cook, and home decorator. Seasonally she throws clothing swaps where a throng of us bring in clothing and accessories that no longer fit or that we're tired of, and we try to pawn them off on one another instead of having to cart them off to Goodwill. She knows more about hors d'oeuvres than anyone I've ever met. I don't know why "multifaceted" is such a difficult concept for me to grasp, why contradictions are so hard for me to integrate.

❧

WHEN I was born, my parents lived in a dorm for married people on the campus of the University of Illinois in Champaign. They were mere kids, twenty-one and twenty-two, and during their parties, guests had to walk through the room I slumbered in to use the bathroom. I can't imagine becoming a parent while in college, but I guess that's Just What People Did.

Because I was born in Champaign and know nothing about it, I have an acute interest in being there and playing there. Our gigs go exceptionally well when I'm engaged in our location, curious about it, wanting to make a good impression. I fail to notice how much my mood can dictate our success.

DEKALB, Illinois, twice in one summer—is that possible? The first time our opening act is a riot grrrl band from the Pacific Northwest. They are ultraserious vegans, younger than us, wearers of Buddy Holly glasses. The club has ordered pizza for our dinner requirement. The riot grrrls want their pizza without cheese. Surely they can't eat the crust, either. Why don't they just order a vat of pizza sauce and pass it around with a spoon? This makes me want to order Canadian bacon, sausage, and pepperoni on our pizza, but that would be a wasted gesture. Not even we would ruin a free meal to make a point no matter how sick we are of pizza.

The second time we play DeKalb, it's to open for L7. They're very popular at the moment and their new album (produced by Butch) has a radio hit. They're from Los Angeles or Chicago or Seattle—I've never had it straight. The women of L7 appear to be our age or older. We opened for them in Minneapolis a couple of years ago and they were very friendly and supportive. This time, however, they don't acknowledge our presence and storm around wearing shades and complaining to their crew about everything from their accommodations to their in need for a good vibrator. (They must get their own rooms.) L7 doesn't speak to us, nor do they appear to speak to one another. Hell, we're barely talking anymore and we're far from making it. What's their problem? I mean, what fun is success if you can't enjoy it with your mates after your long, hard struggles together? There's such a difference between what should be and what is, and my bubble's tired of being burst. Showbiz is a game of illusion.

Late into the tour somewhere between Champaign, Bloomington-Normal, Chicago, and DeKalb, Illinois, we have two days off in Chicago. Co's younger brother lives in Chicago. We know and love Chicago—with Co as a former resident, we know where to eat (burrito place under the el), drink (Wrigleyville Tap), and shop (Am Vets) while staying at her brother's bachelor pad in Wrigleyville. Not only that, we're booked to perform at the Cabaret Metro. Finally. It's taken us years to secure a booking at this place. Longer than any band I know, quite frankly. We've been sending the guys at the Metro demos, singles, photos, and press for years. Now we have an album. Fred and Joe are true music supporters; they personally respond to every band that seeks a gig within their coveted walls:

> Dear Laurie,
> Thanks for sending us your tape. We're always interested in hearing new material. "Cinderella Dream" [sic] is like early Bangles; nice harmonies; cool Soul Asylum feel and nice guitar solo. "Gods Cry" [sic] is Scrawl-like; way tight band. "White Trash Love" reminds me of the Bangles meets garage Sonic Youth. "Happy Birthday" starts off slow and gets more powerful; Scrawl-like. Please call us for a date. This is much improvement over your previous outings, in my opinion. Thank you for your interest in the Metro and good luck!!
> Sincerely,
> Joe and Fred

So finally, the Metro. This is like a dream come true. It also signifies a triumphant return to the spot where I was afflicted by that sudden crippling spell on the sidewalk in front of the club. It's taken about six years, but now not only will I make it through the door, I'll be on stage with my girlfriends.

And now Paul's on the road, too. I really, really miss him. Our travel schedules are not in synch. To remedy this, Paul offers to fly me home during our days off in Chicago—otherwise I'll not see him again until October. This is not enthusiastically received by my bandmates. There I go again, pulling away from the one-for-all crap, the enforced democracy that feels like the worst parts of communism as of late. The thing that makes this two-day jaunt possible is the thing that none of us has—the money to buy a last-minute plane ticket from Chicago to Minneapolis. This departure does not sit well with the troops who are left to swelter in the inner-city heat.

"Are you sure you don't mind?" I ask.

"No, just go! We're gonna have a damn blast." Maybe they're relieved to have me gone for a couple of days; I'm not as much fun as I used to be, I don't party as much, which makes me more aware of my surroundings. Sometimes I'm encouraged to smoke pot just so that I'll loosen up and be funny again. They drop me off at O'Hare to catch my flight, but I'll have to take the el back into town on the flipside.

Of course there's something unstated that says to me that they do mind. I'm stepping in and out of a lifestyle and income bracket that is not ours. I'm the bitch unhappy with where I am. I'm always pushing for more, bigger, better, farther. I take a cab from the airport to Paul's slanted cottage, a 1910 stucco that's sinking into the ground. It's also ninety-five degrees in Minneapolis and I'm tired, despondent, and happy to see Paul but unable to express it. I'm fried and I start crying, claiming to be too hot.

My boyfriend and I do not make passionate love. We sleep in separate beds and I spend the night crying. Me of few tears cannot stop crying. Paul repeats over and over that he knows exactly how I feel. I guess this is what happens when you're on the road nonstop—you're a commodity, an hour rental per night, revealing shreds of your soul under the beer lights, spending the other twenty-three hours of the day on the highway, on a lumpy motel bed, in Denny's, in a bar. It's every kid's dream, and it's a hard gritty life. I'm nothing more than a traveling saleswoman, selling the fruits of my creativity to unpredictable clients who are usually under the influence of a controlled substance or two.

"I'm sorry. I'm no fun at all. I can't stop crying."

Paul pats me on the back and says, "I understand. Completely. Is it worth it?"

"I dunno," I whimper.

"Is it financially or artistically satisfying?" he asks. "Usually, if one of those things are working for you, it's enough to keep you in the game."

I don't know because I can't think straight. Clearly it's worth it for him; he's worshiped and adored, his gift affirmed. For me? I just don't know. This is what I do; it's my dream. Business is going well for Zuzu's Petals, shouldn't I be rejoicing, enjoying it? (Yes.) Maybe this is just a rough patch or I'm too exhausted or something. But I better perk up because I need to hop a plane in the morning—Zuzu's Petals finally has a gig at the Cabaret Metro. And I couldn't be less thrilled.

I HUNG out with Syd Straw (a female vocalist in some New York–based supergroup) for the entire night," reports the house soundman at the Metro in a depressed, monotone voice after sound check. "She's really real, she's good people."

"Okay . . ." I respond listlessly, aware that I'm not going out of my way to be good people. Backstage my bandmates, who are barely acknowledging my presence, whirl in and out of our black concrete dressing room, grabbing beers from our rider and bringing them out to friends and family.

The stage at the Metro is old and wood and solid (most stages are hollow), and the big gutted theater of a room sounds fantastic, but I'm focused on the fact that there are not many people in the audience—every time I've attended a show at the Metro, the place has been packed. I perform on autopilot but Co and Linda are relieved to be playing a gig after a couple of days off because they're performing with patented exuberance. I vaguely remember that feeling.

MADISON, as a geographically logical rule of thumb, is the first or last gig of a tour. For the summer corn belt extravaganza Madison is the last show, and Zuzu's Petals is scheduled for the headlining spot at the Memorial Union on the University of Wisconsin campus. I know from experience that these free shows at the Union can be huge—and packed—I've seen everyone from the Stray Cats to Cheap Trick to the Buzzcocks at the Union. I also spent entire years of my life smoking, drinking, and plotting in the Union while posing as a college student. Coming off the Metro gig, my pre-Metro meltdown, and the large parcel of personal history I'll be revisiting, this Union gig is loaded.

The Memorial Union is dark, with heavy, stained wood, its walls are decorated with deep-shaded murals of scenes from the Black Forest, the windows covered with stained glass; it's modeled after a German beer hall (the barroom is called the Rathskellar). Inside the main gathering space it looks like the inside of a whale's rib cage. The acoustics in the room, filled with nooks and crannies and little arched niches, vibrate with sound-delayed echoes. For Co and me, this is perhaps an even more triumphant homecoming than the Metro in Chicago, and we have severe road burn; that haggard state late in a tour when nothing is funny and everything is funny and you're glued together by filth and fatigue.

When my mom, sister Megan, her toddler Casey, and cousin Brittaney pop in the Union for sound check, I'm happy to see them. Linda lets tow-headed Casey sit at her drums and pound her snare. A couple of my brother Chris's friends come up and say hi as we set up. A friend of Co's from high school pops in unexpectedly.

A crowd is beginning to gather as early as sound check, all of the tables are already filled and being reserved for later in the night. This is a good thing, but not with my family standing there discussing where I'm going to join them for dinner.

"I can't possibly go out to dinner," I snap impatiently, like, duh, don't you get it?

"Why?" my mother retorts, looking injured.

"Because!"

I'm so frustrated and pissed off that I even have to explain myself. I want to say, "Though I'm just an *ordinary* girl from Madison, Wisconsin, I'm doing something out of the ordinary tonight, and I need to be with my band and concentrate." Instead I offer a watered down, "I need to prepare and hang with the girls."

"You've got to eat; you're awfully thin," answers my mom, which is the polar opposite of her patented terms "chunky" and "heavy." She is not taking no for an answer.

"No, I can't," I say, and that's final.

My mom and Megan exchange eye-rolling looks that say, "What's *her* problem?" and "Oh no, she's in one of her *moods.*"

"Okay then," begins my mom, "but I thought we had made plans to meet for dinner . . . " That I translate as "What's this? Too cool for your own family?"

"This is kind of a big deal, I'm really nervous. I'm sorry, okay?"

They walk toward the exit arch, looking offended, and my mom adds, "Well, I'm certainly not going to sit here for three or four hours. Could you at least reserve a table for your family?"

This is an outlandish request in such an anarchic setting. "Ya, I'll see what I can do."

We take the stage to a packed room; I walk up to the mike, smile, and say, "Hi, it's nice to be back home," and tear into "God Cries," playing a song overloaded with lyrics way too fast to possibly spit out its long-winded phrases. In spite of the fact that my mom is standing on the table I asked the kids in charge to reserve snapping pictures, we manage to rock. My brother's friends dance their Dead Head dances and the women's soccer team flails and gyrates in front of the stage. This is the moment that has the most meaning, being right here, a spot where I was at my most fucked up in earlier life, commanding a hometown audience. Smoking is no longer permitted in the Union, so I light up and ruminate on mike about all the time I spent getting high and skipping class in this building. I offer some words of advice to anyone on academic probation: "Don't cry at your appeal, they'll think you're unstable." In between songs a woman I recognize as a downtown hairdresser pushes her way to the side of the stage, vying for my attention. When I lean over to get closer, she says, "Your old boyfriend Chris is here; he says hi."

"Tell him to come up and say hi himself," I suggest, then swagger up to the mike to announce, "My past has come back to haunt me," and I rip into "Happy Birthday" ("You're one year older/Got a chip on your shoulder/Cheer up, you're closer to death") because I'm feeling edgy.

It's over in a heartbeat, and my mom comes up to announce, "Chris came up and hugged me and told me that you should work with Butch."

"We've tried," Co and I say in unison.

With September looming we must be headed east again.

(*Select* magazine, February 1993) Zuzu's Petals, *When No One's Looking*
Proper female rock without the kookiness of Throwing Muses or the frothing rage of Hole. There could be a future in it.

P AUL and I would like to have our own places in close proximity so we can be together but still have our proverbial
space when we need it. While he's on the road I look for an
apartment near Lake Harriet, our favorite city lake.

While I'm inspecting an affordable studio apartment in the
back of a lakeshore apartment building, the manager says, "I
also have a lakeview apartment available, but it's considerably
more expensive."

"Can I see it?" I've always wondered what those apartments
with the picture window overlooking the lake looked like from
within. As the resident manager unlocks the door, he unlocks a
part of me that's been closed up for a long time. The apartment
has a breathtaking view; its great big picture window swallows
the entire lake. Water calms me. I am so stunned and impressed
with this apartment when I walk through that I impulsively
take it in spite of the fact that there's no way in hell I can afford this grown-up apartment with hardwood floors, a long
hallway separating the living room, dining room, and kitchen
from the bathroom and bedroom. Hey, I'm thirty, oh ya, I'm a
grown-up now. I tell Paul of my uncontrollable urge over the
phone and he offers to help with the rent. Does this make me a
partially kept woman? If so, I don't know the rules to this
game, and besides, I hate games. Taking this opulent apartment
is not a wise move in the Petal solidarity department. I'm setting myself apart. I'm aware of this.

Here's the rub: When you live in a dump, which I've been
doing since we hit the road, there's no reason to stay home.
The road is actually preferable. This new place has two walk-in
closets! And the view. When you live somewhere beautiful, you
don't much want to leave. You want to stay home.

Home. I haven't had a home, a real home, in my whole
adult life. My childhood home is long gone. I assume "home"
implies comfort, relaxation, safety, and peace. This home

thing is new for me and I like the idea of it more than anything else that's happening in my life, in spite of our first
album's favorable reception. When I wake up in the morning
and gaze at the sun rising over the lake, I'll notice that every
day looks different. Once a month the full moon will rise over
the lake and burn shadows onto my living room floor. I always thought the concept of home was overrated, but maybe
I've just been deprived.

I WAS not guaranteed recovery when I left St. Mary's Hospital
after my Thanksgiving crippling six years ago. At the time, I
thought my mom was convinced that I was not going to recover and that she would be sentenced to a life of caring for
her handicapped daughter till her dying days. She never said
anything of the sort; it was just a feeling I had (after a steady
course of paranoia-inducing IV steroids).

My youngest sister, Hillary, was discharged from St. Mary's
the same gray morning that I was. She had day surgery on her
ankle to correct a gymnastics injury; having her in and out on
the same day as my discharge was like one-stop shopping for
my mom. Hillary with her crutches and me with my cane
stared blankly up from the bottom of our steep snow-covered
driveway. At first glance, it was apparent that the shuttered,
raised ranch house of my childhood had gone to pot in the
two years without my father. The shrubs were rangy and had
grown over the windows, the driveway unshoveled. The family had pretty much broken up and ditched one another after
the divorce: Hillary was a senior in high school, an employee
of Burger King, and on the gymnastics team. She had a
boyfriend and was petite, blond, and preppie. She was rarely
home. My brother Chris was in boarding school in Indiana
playing hockey on scholarship. My other sister Megan was in
an apartment somewhere in town and dating the security
guard from Sears. My dad was in his new house with his new

family. In varying states of shock and denial, my mom and I were in survival mode.

After two stilted steps with her crutches, Hillary began crying with frustration. She, of course, was suffering from a temporary immobilization while my problems were vast, chronic, and might never cease to plague me.

"Fucking baby," I muttered while planting my cane into the icy chunks and dragging myself up the hill while narrowly resisting the urge to push her down.

Inside, the house was dim and dingy. The air was stale and forlorn with the sighs and sadness of a broken family. More cluttered with piles. Lamps with burned-out bulbs. My mom entered the full-time workforce in her forties. I didn't blame her for the condition of the house; it's just What Happened Under Those Circumstances. There's only so much you can do.

At night while my mom and sister slept, I lit fires in our orange chrome fireplace that rested in the middle of our family room. The steroids kept me vibrating and awake all night and I read books with catchy titles that spoke to me and my predicament: *Heal Your Own Damn Self, You're Only as Sick As You Think, Chronic Schmonic, The Gift of Disease,* and *Let Your Inner Child Take on Your Demons.* Many of the books ended up on the fire that I kept burning all night. It became a superstition—if the fire died, I wouldn't recover; if I kept it alive, I would thrive.

I considered spirituality for the first time since dropping out of confirmation classes at St. Dennis Catholic Church as an eighth grader. I fiddled with theories inspired by my reading; like maybe I got sick because God was trying to salvage my spoiled-brat wasted youth. Maybe MS shut me down for a reason; maybe I was supposed to search my pretty vacant insides for purpose and meaning. My prayers sounded like sales pitches: "If You allow me to get well, I will make You proud."

I tried hard to view my illness as a gift (thanks a lot, just what I always wanted), trying to utilize my incapacity as a second chance, as a chunk of time and space to find healing and clarity because there was nothing else I could do. Maybe my blind left eye was a warning that I wasn't looking at the whole picture, not seeing reality. Maybe my lame hand and foot were supposed to force me to realize that I had stunted my personal movement with my lack of specificity and goals. Maybe not. Maybe I was dealt a shitty card—that happens to people, and I somehow managed to realize that life is too short to spend it doing things you don't want to do, that there are no second chances, or that feel-good cliché "you only go around the track once."

I took on the task of healing myself because, according to some of the books, I gave myself my disease with my vile thoughts and bad habits. The three women living under our roof, my mom, Hillary, and me, didn't talk much. We communicated in meaningless snatches while stuck in our own heads doing what we needed to do to keep it together. "I'm late." "Catch you later." "Need anything from the store?" "Does my butt look big?" Adjusting to the divorce was hard enough, and now I returned home after six years of directionless gallivanting with this extremely unpleasant Health Crisis—it was all too much.

Unable to operate the clutch on my mom's car because of my gimpy leg, I was stranded on the outskirts of a college town in the upper Midwest with a harsh winter settling in. I dubbed it the winter of my discontent, and I transformed the house into Healing Central. With my first welfare check I purchased an Exercycle and placed it next to the fireplace. I needed to strengthen my crazy uncooperative leg; the muscles had completely degenerated. The skin on my left leg was slack where it was once firm and muscular. Asking my mom to drive me to my old high school twice a week for open swim, I almost drowned with the memories of high school, of being healthy and invincible, as I lopsidedly paddled down the lane. Throughout the day while my mom was at work and my sister

was in school, I slowly, methodically practiced moving my
spastic jittery arm and leg, visualizing fluid motion. I employed
the Think System for the first time while running my leaping
jittery heel up and down my good calf, trying to regain control.

To amuse myself, I pulled down the manual typewriter and
typed letters one-handed, usually to strangers:

> Dear Lorne Michaels,
> I implore you to put Joan Cusack [a college acquaintance] in
> more sketches. Hey, any female cast member for that matter.

Or:

> Dear Wendy's,
> Bad, bad idea letting your so-called founder Dave Thomas in
> your commercials. Bring back the Lillian Hellmanesque lady
> who was looking for the beef.

Or:

> Dear Walgreen's,
> What is it about you that makes me feel so good, so happy,
> so at peace when I'm within your walls? Health products,
> beauty products, candy, plus magazines equal comfort. Bravo!
> Keep up the good work.

Or:

> To Whom It May Concern,
> Fucking save me!

IN self-imposed exile—my blotchy-skin, bloated body, spastic
motions, and my face blown up ten times its normal size by
steroids—I was not fit for public consumption. Listening to my
Velvet Underground cassettes, I understood completely their
achingly vacant chanteuse Nico. My mom and sister passed in

and out of our home on their way to somewhere, anywhere. I held down the fort, an incapacitated hausfrau.

This is how I learned to walk again: an ankle weight around my weak ankle. My foot shook and flew from side to side every time I lifted it off the ground. So gross. I gripped our fake butcher-block kitchen counter and lifted my weighted foot; heel first, slowly, up and down, all day while reading or watching TV. I pulled the draggy heel up to my butt and back down to the floor. Slowly. I needed to stop its trembling and swaying. Or I'd sit down and plop the weight across my left toes and lift the top of my foot up and down, up and down. Then eventually without the weight, toes up, toes down, heel up, heel down. Square dancing with myself. It had to be done so slowly so that each jitter and spasm could be caught and extinguished.

Zuzu's Petals *When No One's Looking*
Happily skipping through a smut-stained world, these three, seemingly tireless souls paint a refreshing pop canvas for the halls of commendable female bands. Theirs is a world of little girl dreams that conjure nursery rhymes, children's song, and birthdays: caging them with psycho barflies, jackals, and dorks. The result is potently tied to strong musicianship and vocals with a pleasing touch of gifted vocal harmony. You'll feel like protecting this Minneapolis-based trio from what you already know they've been corrupted by. Perhaps the best part of Zuzu's Petals' full-length release is the strong and inspired lyrics that, at this stop of what should be a successful climb, is a reflection of innocence assaulted by the world's big bad wolves. . . .

AFTER her boyfriend, Jack, drops dead from a heart attack, my mom moves back to Peoria, Illinois, to attend graduate school at her alma mater, Bradley University. She finds a rent-free apartment by signing on as a housemother in a sorority house. I know that it's not her responsibility to provide a "home to go back to should my life fall apart"—but not having one makes me feel ungrounded, insecure, under pressure.

How would you feel if I left your father?"

I was sixteen and my mom and I were in her old Datsun driving home from East Towne Mall. How would I feel? I showed her how I'd feel by promptly bursting into inconsolable tears. In case she hadn't noticed or couldn't remember from experience, it's an emotional, hysterical roller coaster being a sixteen-year-old girl.

"Don't worry, honey—if that's your reaction, I'd never do it. Never, ever. I promise."

Three years after that exchange my dad left my mom. I will always blame myself for crying in the car that day—had she left him then, had I held back the tears, her personal finances would've been intact and she'd have been spared the humiliation of being dumped.

16: She's Come Undone

Y OU guys [meaning gals] need to strike while the iron is hot," says the president of Restless, who's calling me at my new apartment. "You need to get in the studio and crank out a new record."

They want us to record our second album immediately to ride on the crest of our small wave of popularity.

"Okay," I say, not mentioning that our once-prolific songwriting has dried up after a year on the road.

Restless moves quickly, hiring a California-based producer named Albhy.

"I want to get together with you alone before we begin recording," Albhy requests over the phone during our first conversation.

Albhy is a big name; he's worked with everyone from the Bee Gees to the Gin Blossoms. His largest successes were in the seventies while he was in Miami with the Bee Gees making the soundtrack for *Saturday Night Fever*. I'm afraid Albhy's star may be on the wane if he's willing to work with us on such a low-budget project (under fifteen thousand dollars). Maybe it's the challenge that spurs him on, or the idea of a north woods no-budget adventure. Maybe his agent is whispering in his ear, "C'mon, man, you've got to work with some of these up-and-comers. Who knows? Maybe they'll amount to something. You've got to show that you're down with the kids. . . . I mean, c'mon, Cher? Barbra Streisand?"

Naturally, those affiliations thrill me. I'm aware that these last days of 1993 are all about grunge. And I can't deliver that sound because I don't want to.

"The girls will probably feel left out or slighted if we meet without them," I offer weakly because I'd like to meet with him alone, as well. There are conflicts of vision for our next record and I want to make sure that my two cents' worth are plugged before I'm silenced by the louder, more articulate voices within the group.

WHEN Albhy arrives in Minneapolis from Santa Monica he is provided with a room in a very crappy Best Western Motel courtesy of our record company. The guy's probably a millionaire—besides his long list of successful studio excursions, he's a software inventor. There's no way in hell. The lack of refinement our people show in these matters is embarrassing. Albhy finds a more suitable hotel downtown on his own dime and I meet him there for lunch on a frozen January afternoon.

Albhy is a California New Yorker with a gray-blond ponytail and a formidable nose.

"How do things work with you chicks?" he asks. I cringe at "chicks" and know that Co will have a bird when she hears it.

"We're a democracy," I utter weakly, unconvinced of the possibility. Were the brothers Gibb a democracy?

"It never works, believe me," he injects. "Don't they know that the only reason you have a recording contract is because of your songwriting and your singing voice?"

"Um, we don't see things that way, and it causes tension when that's implied at the record label, or in the press." I feel instant guilt, though it's nice to hear him single me out and credit me for my contributions.

Albhy asks our server for balsamic vinegar for his salad. She looks stumped. I wither. I foresee a week of middle-market inferiority.

"I'd like you to get a lyric sheet to me right away," he instructs, pushing away the inedible white iceberg lettuce in front of him. It's not worth explaining to him that it's January and it's hard to get decent produce up here this time of year.

"Okay," I say with an uncertain smile. I have a hard time speaking up and saying what I really think. I get the feeling that Albhy isn't going to knock himself out working with us: If it goes well, great. If not, no big loss.

Zuzu's Petals is a band divided. I don't have a good feeling about this upcoming project. I still can't wrap my head around the fact that it's viable—the songs aren't ready. Restless insists that if we take too much time in between records, the buzz will evaporate and Zuzu's Petals will be forgotten. The door of opportunity will be slammed in our faces and Zuzu's Petals will be done; we'll have to start from scratch to rebuild if we miss out on this window of time while the proverbial iron is still plugged in. Co and Linda are dead set on this being a more live-sounding record, meaning a recording that captures all of us playing in unison, like during a live show. They don't want any of that Laurie overdubbing everything to death to make it sound slick and produced. This next record, they believe, should be a rawer-sounding punk rock record.

I believe that our musicianship is so innately rough that we are most effective when granted overdubs—separate takes, more layers upon layers of building sound—particularly on guitar and vocal tracks to smooth out the coarse edges. The more tracks we fill, and there are at least twenty-four separate tracks that can be used, the thicker our thin, simplistic sound becomes. More tracks add texture and girth. They also take more time. It's the only way, I believe, we have a fighting chance to compete in the oversaturated marketplace. The production quality is the reason our first record was so well received. We spent days layering guitars, percussion, and backup vocals.

We're going to record at Pachyderm studios in Cannon

Falls, Minnesota, for a week in January of 1994. Nirvana just finished recording *In Utero* at the same studio; it's their second major-label release and they want it to sound more live and punk rock than they did on their overproduced smash hit *Nevermind*.

Some guy calling himself Joe Mama, who's recording at Pachyderm before us, keeps calling me at my apartment. Evidently he's an L.A. musician who I've never heard of. He wants us to drive up to Cannon Falls and party with him. As if we don't have better things to do. I don't know how he got my phone number; since moving to my new apartment and changing my phone number to unlisted, not nearly as many freaks call me. I give him Linda's number. When we meet in our rehearsal space to load the van with our equipment for our week at Pachyderm, Linda complains, "Hey, who gave Joe Mama my phone number?"

I have turned the van over to Co because Paul has bought me an old used Volvo. I drive separately in my car in case we need an extra vehicle for any reason. In case I need to flee. It's well below zero outside, a sunny, frozen day for our sixty-mile jaunt to Cannon Falls. We've each packed a week's worth of wool sweaters, ski pants, and thermal socks. I'm vexed by this blindingly bright January day; why can't the sun provide warmth? Driving alone, I think about the week to come with dread. I had my whole life to write the songs for the first album. I had ten months to write the second record, and I can't write on the road. I need to be alone in a room with an acoustic guitar and a notebook, which is an unthinkable luxury on the road. I can't get used to playing guitar in my new apartment; it doesn't fit somehow.

Cannon Falls is a college town west of Minneapolis. Pachyderm consists of a large house built in the seventies, and it resembles the Brady Bunch house with its modern ranch design and glass coffee tables. There is shag carpeting throughout. The actual studio is housed in a separate building a few feet from the main house. An icy path joins the house and studio. The snowdrifts in the backyard are waist high. Albhy and his engineer Eric have master bedrooms upstairs while the kids (us) share a room in the finished basement. It is rumored that a dead former mistress of the house haunts the outside paths or sits demurely in the living room as if involved in a ghostly coffee klatch. I believe this legend and make a point to never be alone on the main floor.

I've written a song called "Do Not"; it's a fast, punky rant. It only has four chords. "Do Not" is a laundry list of the things that bother me; "Do not leave your Christmas lights out till May/Do not say hi in that fakey voice and pretend that you're glad to see me/Do not make me look at the Hoover Dam cuz I've already seen it," etc. This song is "the single" according to Albhy. It's that all-important song that might get radio attention. It's not my favorite song on the pile, but I'm not a good judge. When I listen to an entire album, I usually hate the singles, like "Sympathy for the Devil" and Steely Dan's "Reelin' in the Years." I rarely attach myself to the song selected by the powers that be for the almighty single. A single is the song that the rubes are most likely to sing along to, which is probably why I tend to dislike them.

Albhy intends to focus on getting "Do Not" sounding right and letting the rest of the material fill in. The four chords in this song need to be played really fast. Because I'm not a clean player, Eric covers two of my strings with masking tape to mute them because I keep hitting them when I should be avoiding them and it makes my guitar sound out of tune—which I kind of like. I can't come up with a smoking guitar solo because I'm not in the mood and they assign Linda guitar duty. Maybe she'll have better luck. I am so checked out.

I KNOW the guitar thing is a problem. I'm not proficient enough to hold down the band, and I'm a sloppy player, and my left hand is shaky and spastic, which means I play a lot of clams. Believe it or not, I've had many lessons. My first guitar lessons came in third grade; I was shuttled to some hippie's apartment and he taught me "Go Tell Aunt Rhody" (the G chord) and strung my guitar backwards because I'm a lefty. I found the soft-spoken dude with long hair somewhat creepy and gave up after a couple lessons and never played left handed again.

In college I took a minicourse in acoustic guitar and learned how to finger-pick the Beatles' "Blackbird." After that I invited a guy named Timmy over to my house to teach me how to play because I admired his skills. We ended up drinking ridiculous amounts of liquor and having a sloppy affair, but he didn't teach me a lick on the guitar.

When I was home recovering from MS, I scanned the papers for a legitimate guitar instructor, and my girlfriend Anita agreed to take lessons with me. On Tuesday evenings my mom shuttled two twenty-four-year-old women with electric guitars to a guy named Karl's apartment on the edge of downtown Madison. When a very straight-laced guy with round spectacles answered his door, we had to suppress the impulse to giggle.

"What do you want to learn?" Karl wondered.

"Chords, riffs, how to rock."

"I'm a jazz musician, but if you bring me a cassette with the songs you'd like to learn, it will help me figure out the best way to teach you."

Anita and I returned to her house and recorded Neil Young's "Like a Hurricane," Hüsker Dü's "Flexible Flyer," and the Rolling Stones' "Before They Make Me Run" onto a cassette. Karl transposed the chords to these tunes and wrote down a series of scales and finger exercises for us to practice. Karl was so patient and gentle-mannered that Anita and I referred to him as Mean Karl. My numb, afflicted digits felt like Twinkies, while Anita, an accomplished pianist, picked things up quickly. My mind would blank out when Karl tried to teach us pentatonic scales. This was like math, and I'd never understood math. After a handful of lessons, Anita and I discontinued our instruction.

When I moved to Minneapolis I asked a guy named John to come to my apartment and teach me guitar and he showed me a couple of Chuck Berry and Keith Richards tricks, and I asked a guy named Dave to come to my cinder block basement to show me how to play and he said, "I don't want to mess with your personal style too much."

Then I tried taking lessons from the guy who taught at the guitar store that Ang worked at and he said, "You have a record deal, you have your own style of playing, and I'd hate to interfere," so he gave me a few pages of lead charts in different keys, patted me on the head, and sent me on my way. The one thing I'd never been able to wrap my head around or mustered the desire to do was to sit around practicing guitar licks or scales. The guitar, to me, is a writing tool and performance prop. Chords and a line of melody are as far as I'd ever gotten.

THIS is what Albhy does a lot of the time: plays solitaire on his computer, talks to his wife in Aspen, plays piano, calls us "chicks." This is what I do a lot of the time: not much. Co, Linda, and Eric try to have a good time in spite of it all.

One evening while we're all sitting down to a spaghetti dinner, the doorbell in the main house rings. Curious, we all get up to see who's ringing our bell at nine in the evening in the middle of nowhere.

Two young women stand at the door and ask in broken English, "Is Soul Asylum here?"

They've traveled from Germany in hopes of tracking down their favorite band. They're two weeks early. We haven't seen Dave since he took up with the movie star and Soul Asylum became the First Daughter's favorite band. They have a hit record, *Grave Dancers Union*, and the collection of songs on this album are stunning. They deserve the limelight; they've worked and played long and hard. As sad as I am that Dave broke up with a friend of mine to date an undeniably beautiful movie star who's supposed to have a brain in her head to boot, I'm secretly relieved that said starlet is occupied with a new musician, so maybe she'll lay off my own boyfriend for a spell. I can't compete with that. Whenever I try to climb the soapbox to chastise Dave for participating in the starlet/rock star cliché, I remind myself that if a certain actor named Johnny were pursuing me with those soulful brown eyes, I'd have a very hard time shooing him away. And deep down we all want those dazzling Stars dripping off our arms, but we're midwestern and we're supposed to act like we would never. . . .

I'VE half written a blues song called "Don't Bother," this one is a three-chord rant: "Piles of laundry/Good things to come/Let me know when they get here/I could sure use some/Home is where I hang my clothes . . ." I call Paul one afternoon to ask him to come out and play harmonica on this song; it needs a boost.

He says, "You'll have to succeed or fail without me."

Thanks, fucker. Ang shows up a few times, bringing in guitars and amps and a special snare drum. Because there's nothing better to do around the time I'm supposed to record a vocal track for this song, I drink whiskey. I've been cutting way back on imbibing and, judging by my mates' reactions, sobriety does not improve my demeanor. Every song penned by me complains and questions. Aside from my old favorite "unrequited love," "homesickness" can be added to my thematic obsessions. In the song "Feel Like Going Home," I state that I "need a room of my own" and that "it seems as though the three guys I know are Scarecrow, Tinman, and Pinocchio." In "Don't Bother" I say that "my guitar sits on the couch like an unwanted guest."

"Sure beats work" is the thing that Co says every day that makes me want to strangle her. She has her least-favorite job to date, in a T-shirt warehouse, so I should cut her some slack. There aren't a lot of gratifying jobs out there that allow you to leave for months at a time to go on tour. But trying to make a record when we're not prepared feels like work to me, and it has a whole lot more riding on it than some piddly day job—if we can manage to make a decent record, just maybe we won't have to work at our jobs anymore. I'm not confident that this will happen; it occurs to me that we had two weeks (and six years) to make our first record, and only one week (and one year) to make our second. I don't think I have the authority to say, "You know what? We're not ready. I'm not ready. Making a record when we're not ready is a mistake."

T HE last time we see Albhy is when he runs back into the studio wearing his furry après ski boots because he's leaving for a European ski trip. He's running because he's excited; he thinks he's overhearing something that sounds extracool.

"Hey! That sounds great," he exclaims.

Clunk. Albhy smashes his face right onto a glass door that he thought was open. He breaks his nose badly. There's a smeary smudge mark on the glass where he hit. If I were to wipe it up with a paper towel it could be the Shroud of Albhy. I consider this accident bad karma, or a bad omen. I'm not sure which.

A week later the president of Restless calls me on the phone and says, "We'll pay for you to come to California and record another song . . . we'll pay for you to go out to New York and write one more song with a more accomplished songwriter."

I know they want me to ask Paul to cowrite a song that will have more hit potential than "Do Not." I would never ask him to do that, so I say, "No, the record is done. It is what it is."

We call the record *The Music of Your Life* and it's half-baked.

I look so snarly and pissed off in the photos for the album cover and promo it's not even funny. Co and Linda worked their butts off securing a site, crew, and props for this photo shoot.

WHEN I was a college student and new music devotee, there was nothing more magical than traipsing through blowing, falling snow at night with a wind chill of below zero to see a rock show. The empty streets sparkled with fresh snow; its whiteness brightened the dark night to almost daylight hues. Tromping into a steamy club in heavy boots, pink cheeks, and icicles hanging from our hair was an exhilarating feat. The reward for this Nordic trek was not only live music, camaraderie, and lots of beer, it was also the deep pleasure and comfort of being in an overheated building with all the other hardy souls in the know who braved the elements to gather in this room to anticipate something extraordinary about to happen. Musicians who were not afraid to tour the North Country in the dead of winter made our world a better place.

It is exactly on this kind of night that we're scheduled to play in Duluth, and I'm no longer sure that the world's a better place because Zuzu's Petals is in it like I used to believe with all my heart.

IT'S been a long tough winter, colder than usual. Extended weekends are spent on the road throughout the Midwest, our van limping and wheezing, our feet chronically cold. One night in early April, still very much winter in Minnesota, I spend the night at Paul's. The wall next to the bed on the side that I sleep is cold to the touch, though no longer covered in a thin layer of frost. Sleeping side by side in his queen-size bed off the ground, I dream that I'm awake in bed next to him. This is not an uncommon dream for me: I think I'm awake because the setting is the same, but I'm still asleep. In the dream that I believe is really happening because I think I'm awake, a corpse wrapped in a gossamer cocoon lies between us. I can almost swear that I see this corpse in a waking state, but that's impossible. The dream disturbs me into full consciousness; I'm freaked-out and feeling quite haunted. Shaking Paul's shoulder, he says, "Huh?" and "There, there" while weakly patting my shoulder, then rolls back over. Too spooked, I get out of bed and read on the couch in another room under a crocheted afghan. Analyzing the apparition, I decide that the body in my dream symbolized something or somebody trying to come between Paul and me.

The following morning shortly after returning to my apartment the phone rings. It's my friend Mia, a Minneapolis native now living in Seattle.

"Have you heard?" she asks.

"No. What?"

"Kurt Cobain committed suicide."

Shit. Why did he have to go and do a stupid thing like that? He was probably one day away from figuring out that everything was going to be okay. I know; it's an occupational hazard and a side effect of addiction. I don't think I have psychic powers of any sort, but a stomach-churning shudder moves through my body when I think about the dream I had the night before.

WE'VE been east again at least twice, and through the Midwest countless times; another summer passes while we wait for Restless to release *The Music of Your Life*. We've toured *When No One's Looking* into the ground. Linda learns that she needs another surgery on her elbow to remove more bad tissue, and we (meaning me) (gladly) cancel another European tour to accommodate her tired arms. Because of our track record as an overseas no-show, our European label, Roadrunner, decides not to press or release our new record. *The Music of Your Life* is being released nine months after its completion and we're going to have to tour all fall in support of it.

Our friend the journalist Jim is at my Lake Harriet apartment, conducting an informal Zuzu's Petals interview for a feature he's writing for the St. Paul *Pioneer Press*.

"How do you feel about the piece in today's *City Pages*?" Jim wonders.

Co and Linda flash "shut-the-fuck-up" faces at Jim. It is clear to me that my bandmates know what he's talking about and I do not. Judging by their expressions they do not want me to see it.

"Oh, you know, Jim M. trashed the record . . . nothing new there," Linda offers.

This uncomfortable moment ends the interview and we all leave my apartment and head across the street to the lake for a photo shoot. In early September it's warm enough for us to submerge ourselves in the lake in our party dresses, a Virginia Woolf moment. When everyone departs, I change out of my soaked vintage gown and storm up to the corner ice cream shop, which has a rack full of new *City Pages* next to the front door. I carry a folded copy into my apartment and sit at my breakfast table to read:

HELP WANTED by Jim M.
[A quarter page photo of Zuzu's Petals is featured; the caption under the photo reads: "Needed: Guitarist; songwriter, vocalist, and more adoring British rock crits for Zuzu's Petals"]

Zuzu's Petals: *THE MUSIC OF YOUR LIFE*
Solid drummer and steady (but rather stiff) bassist seek guitarist, songwriter, lead vocalist (in that order) to revive female trio that once seemed poised for indie-pop breakthrough (especially with ex-Bee Gees producer Albhy Galuten producing new album). First need is a real guitar player to eliminate the

thin solos that caused mass destruction on latest release. Without a rhythmically and melodically strong player, our compositional vocabulary is wearing thin, despite two willing songwriters. Lead guitarist would help immensely, but wouldn't hide the fact that recent lyrics are increasingly cloudy, loaded with lazy references, and a little too much emotional distance. Even the gossip that most of the torch songs are written about everybody's favorite Replacement's [sic] vocalist can't seem to give these tunes the full resonance they hint at. But even solving these problems might not alleviate the fact that our lead vocalist is becoming mechanically predictable. Her weak, whiny upper register sounds like nails on a chalkboard when blended with these flat, boxy tunes, and doesn't suit her honest but halting attempts at tearjerking material. Without a couple of these elements, we'll probably never regain the promise of our first album, or catch up with the hundreds of national female fronted groups who passed us by while we stood in place for three or four years. P.S. Call now! We've got two record release gigs this weekend.

Instead of "trashed our album," why didn't Linda say "Jim M. strung you up and slowly, methodically, thrashed you and you alone with the strongest weapon known to you—words"? Or, "Oh, Jim M. said that everything you do is, well, deplorable." Or, "He wrote that you suck at everything and implied that we were actively trying to or should try to replace you."

Every word I say to myself in moments of self-doubt, which are more and more frequent these days, spelled out in public for the whole metro area to see. I'm crushed. Humiliated. Ruined. Too fragile. I can't handle this. I'm an elephant with a deceptively tough-looking skin who needs a protective coating of mud to shield me from the tiny, biting flies and parasites. This hurts too much. I want out. I sit on the couch, my stomach an empty fluttering pit. My ears are ringing, my phone is ringing,

my eyes ache. I don't answer the phone. This attack is so specific and meant to inflict pain—I feel defenseless. For some reason this is worse than hearing you have an incurable
autoimmune disease, but how could that be?

Sodium pen."

You were advised by a girlfriend to request sodium pen-
tathol for your abortion sedative/painkiller. You are lying on a
cold examination table, stripped from the waist down, your
trembling feet slipping out of the metal stirrups. It is March,
still winter in Minnesota. March means ugly winter. Dirt-
encrusted snow banks frame your world. Alone and flooded
with remorse and uncertainty, you inhale the gas through a
plastic mask and become detached. In. Out. Please make this
be over, please don't hurt me, I'm sorry, I'm sorry, I'm sorry, as
tears trickle from your eyes and you're not sure if you're thinking these words in your head or saying them out loud.

You don't want this abortion.

Last week your boyfriend said with distraught sensibility,
"We can't have a baby right now."

You didn't argue, lacking the wherewithal to reason. Ever
since you peed on the stick, and it turned the color it wasn't
supposed to turn, you've been shell-shocked. You think to
yourself that if he's not into it, there's no way in hell you can
do it alone.

One bandmate said, "Do what you need to do."

The other said, "I wish I could say I was happy for you, but
I'm not."

Feeling completely alone and unsupported, you call the
clinic on the good side of town and schedule a procedure.
"Procedure" is a much milder word than "abortion." You have
Rocked for Choice on more than one occasion. You feel like
you've made the most sensible decision you could've under
the circumstances. You almost have yourself convinced it is a

responsible choice. But you are not a kid anymore; kids sometimes make big reckless mistakes playing roulette with birth
control. You gambled and lost, and you're old enough to know
better. You tell yourself, Try not to think about it, try not to
think about it . . .

"Hold my hand, sweetheart," a motherly brown-skinned
nurse urges while grabbing your cold pale hand. She allows
you to squeeze hard.

You feel a click or a pop like the opening and closing of a
garage door on the top of your head; your ears ring with angry
sleigh bells. Numb, high, you focus on the soft rock radio station being piped into the procedure room. You think it's Billy
Joel, and he's singing the saddest seafaring song you've ever
heard, something about being lost at sea and being tossed
around by crashing waves.

You are in hell with Billy Joel, of all people. The Piano Man.
Long Island's pride and joy. Sluggo marries Supermodel. Billy
Joel is partially responsible for the decline of popular music
(though you must admit you loved *The Stranger* enough in
high school to attend a live-arena performance). And here he is
again, serenading you through an abortion. At least it's an un-
characteristically poignant song instead of "Big Shot" or "We
Didn't Start the Fire."

The doctor walks in; he's the only other man in the room besides Billy Joel. He probably needs to get on with it; there was
quite a crowd in the waiting room: tearful teens with their
mothers or boyfriends, tearful and stone-faced women alone.
The doctor looks like Willy Wonka. Oh no, it's Gene Wilder.
You hope you only thought this and did not say it—you're so
out of it—and your fragile cervix is on the line. The doctor
speaks to the nurses and never to you. You assume he hates
you as much as you hate yourself at this moment.

Billy Joel sings on, his songs always too long, and the
melody rises and falls like the turbulent sea. A series of circular
metal clamps are inserted into your vagina. Intense burning.

Pressure. A clamp is locked into place; a shot of novocaine brings a sharp internal sting on that tiny pink doughnut of membrane called the cervix. You flinch, tear up; this time the pain is physical. Next a vacuum hose is stuck inside your vagina and switched on, so loud it drowns out Billy Joel. This sound track will haunt you for life. You cramp up with an unspeakable ache while squeezing the kind nurse's hand, pushing her pinky and index finger together while you squeeze. You might puke from the pressure of the suction.

Breathe in. Out. Billy Joel is still lost at sea. And it's over. Never again, you promise yourself.

One week later you are sitting in your apartment with severe cramps and you begin to gush unstoppable blood. The cramps are bend-over, stomach-on-your-thighs sharp. And the blood. Bright red, too much to be contained in a pad. You call the clinic and they instruct you to come in immediately. Sitting on a maroon towel, you drive yourself to the clinic. They examine you at once. They perform an ultrasound. The ovum is still there. They missed it. It hid. Or maybe you're taking out twins.

They must perform the procedure again. You are so tender and sore from last week's indignity. You cry hysterically, trying to place phone calls to tell someone that you have to go through it all again; you're upsetting the other women, and a nurse allows you to use the private phone in her office. Your boyfriend is working and sounds mad when you call. He doesn't offer to meet you. He just sounds mad at you. You call a bandmate and she offers to come to the office and drive you home. In a couple of months she will be on the same boat.

Enter Dr. Wilder. "How are you?" he asks.

"This is not where I expected to be today," you answer.

"This is exactly where I expected to be today," he retorts.

And the whole thing happens again. This time more painful on so many levels. This time without Billy Joel.

☙

So why am I so flattened by a cruel review? I mean, that's nothing. Maybe it's easier to overreact and fly apart about unimportant things because I've had to hold myself together so tightly under grave circumstances. It still doesn't make me feel any less traumatized. Intellectually I understand the Deal; if you're willing to put a piece of art out in the world, you need to expect and accept criticism. Art and music are subjective, and not everyone will like it. That's the chance you take when you throw it out there. While making yourself vulnerable, you must wear protective gear, an emotional suit of armor. Especially if you're leading an all-woman band in Minneapolis in 1994 that's received national and international attention. It's hubris; one should expect a midwestern backlash meant to keep us all humble. Local critics seethe when they think you suck and people elsewhere like you. Babes in Toyland got clobbered locally by their eclipse and they weathered it fine. I just feel really bad because I didn't put my all into the making of that second record, and I've been publicly outed.

Later that night at Paul's for dinner, he tries to divert my sense of defeat and grief with a series of anecdotes: "You must really have something there to make someone so hateful and jealous." Or, "The writer's got something against me and he's trying to hurt me through you." And, "Think of all the horrendous reviews the Sex Pistols got—this is good, you must really be on to something."

I don't buy any of it for a second, though I wish I could. I mean, everyone knows that Jim M.'s approval is the kiss of death within the music community. But it doesn't matter. I was fairly deflated before this scathing review; this is just the straw that crushed this woman's backbone. We have two long tours on the horizon, four weeks east and four weeks west. An acid tongue and a poison pen have burned off my skin. I'm raw; my insides are exposed.

17: Welcome to My Breakdown

ON a sunny prefall afternoon, I'm readying myself to walk around the lake after my shift at the Hi-Lo when my phone rings. It's Rob, the president of Restless.

"Good news!" he begins. "We've been circulating Zuzu's Petals posters, CDs, and bios to all of the Hollywood studios."

"Ya," I say, sitting down at my Formica breakfast table, still wearing my egg-smeared T-shirt. I could use some good news.

"Your poster is going to be on *Beverly Hills 90210!*"

"Really," I muse. "How?"

"This is great, you're gonna love this," he sputters, "they have an upcoming episode where a student working for the school radio station becomes a crystal meth addict—your poster is right behind his head while he's getting high."

"Oh, cool." I don't know what else to say.

The following day my phone rings again.

"Laurie?" It's Rob.

"Ya?"

"Have you ever acted professionally?"

"Not officially," I say, "but I can be convincing on stage sometimes. Why?"

"The people at the NBC show *Sisters* saw your photo and wondered if you were interested in a screen test to play a 'rock star in treatment' who befriends one of the sister's sons, who is also in treatment. Then—this is great—your character gets to have Thanksgiving dinner with the whole cast at the oldest sister's house."

I actually watch this show and know which sister and which son he's talking about; I knew that son was headed for trouble.

"Cool!" is all I can think of to say. "When?"

"Next week, Thursday," Rob says. "We can fly you out."

This news uplifts and excites me—what an opportunity! Then I remember that Co has acted professionally and they haven't asked her, and I feel guilty.

I call to consult her. "We're scheduled to play in Louisville that night," I'm reminded.

W E'RE on tour with a trio from Lincoln, Nebraska, called Mercy Rule. Their lead singer/bass player is a woman named Heidi who has a pixie haircut and cat-eye glasses. Her husband is the guitarist and he has the same haircut and glasses. Their drummer is a happy-go-lucky, cute guy— probably the right fit for a husband-and-wife–led band. They're very nice. Mercy Rule and Zuzu's Petals share the same booking agent and each night we take turns headlining, depending on which band is favored in which market. Mercy Rule has a record label that has enthusiastic representatives in every major city that show up to wine and dine them before the shows. Zuzu's Petals wanders the chic streets of Toronto alone. Our record company hates *The Music of Your Life* as much as Jim M. does. No one meets us in major cities.

Mercy Rule is plucky, self-sufficient, and organized; they're equipped to camp in their van if necessary, and they have friends' floors lined up throughout the country. In Toronto, Mercy Rule has a large receptive audience. We play in front of our friend Kathy from Columbus, Ohio, and her boyfriend, who happen to be vacationing in Toronto at the moment—they came across our name in a club listing. They are the only people left after Mercy Rule's audience leaves. I suggest a nice hotel in Toronto because we're downtown and I would like to sleep rather than drive to kingdom come in a foreign country trying to find something affordable.

"Someone's a little too used to living large," notes our

soundman James. Co and Linda do not disagree with this assessment or come to my defense.

James has just experienced a major personal loss, the sudden out-of-left-field death of a loved one. I do not think he should be working with such a heavy heart. He thinks that working will help him keep his mind off his grief. I am probably right in this instance.

Niagara Falls!"

"Cool."

"Wow."

"Let's get out and walk around."

I wrinkle my nose and go into the Payless Shoes we're parked in front of rather than checking out the natural wonder.

This is what "take a trip" meant to my family: a long drawn-out sing-along sometimes lasting several days. The singing began once we hit the highway and my dad warmed us up by pulling out the standards, like "I've Been Working on the Railroad." Whoever could hold the longest "oh" from the "fee-fi-fiddely-ey-oh" part was the winner. Then we might work our way into "I See the Moon," "You Are My Sunshine," and "Oh, Susannah." From there we'd explore more abstract material like "Loverly Bunch of Coconuts" and "Winchester Cathedral." In the later years, cassettes were added to our a cappella concerts and we'd sing along to *Peter, Paul, and Mommy* and *Tom T. Hall's Country Songs for Children.* John Denver was always close at hand, as was Jerry Jeff Walker. At some point the entire Rodgers and Hammerstein canon was fondled.

Our most frequent destination was to a place we co-owned with several other Madison families that was referred to as "the chalet." The chalet was a newish prefab/fake chalet down the road from a small ski resort called Powderhorn Mountain in Bessemer, Michigan. We, the car singers, were skiers. My mom, the nonsinger, was a knitter and reader of paperbacks. We went to the chalet several weekends out of the year.

The highlight of these trips occurred in the summertime when all of the ski folk were safely ensconced in Door County. Our favorite activity was taking our garbage to the dump. We'd all sing "to the dump, to the dump, to the dump, dump, dump" to the melody of the William Tell Overture (aka the Lone Ranger theme.) Once at the dump, we'd park our car and watch black bears examine discarded domestic items in a deep pit. We never tired of this nightly entertainment; in fact, we sometimes went to the dump without garbage.

And now I won't even look at Niagara Falls.

I N New York, we're scheduled to play at the New Music Seminar, and there will be people from our record label there, but I doubt they'll be as enthusiastic as the crowd from Mercy Rule's record label.

I've yet to feel as comfortable as I know I should while in New York. Like, "Oh, New York . . . I love New York." Which I do in theory, but it still feels dangerous and anxiety inducing. I wear a sequined cocktail dress for our set. A swirl of rumors that Seymour Stein, legendary founder of Sire Records (Madonna, the Ramones, the Replacements) is in the club to see his latest band the Poster Children, a husband/wife-led band from Champaign, Illinois. I just know that if he catches some of our set, he'll want to sign us. What's not to sign?

Signing. That's the big obsession with everyone these days. Including me. "Oh, they're signed to Geffen, Capitol, Atlantic . . ." "Are you signed?" "I hear they're interested in signing you." Ever since Nirvana's *Nevermind* sold millions, the recording industry is in a signing frenzy, snarfing up every band with a guitar and a van. I would like to be signed by a major label because that would entail income, perhaps a signing bonus, or an advance. Money. I would like the opportunity to reach a larger audience. Because of the massive income generated by superstars, major labels have a lot more money to spend on promoting their artists. I have absolutely no idea why no one seems to want to sign us. We've paid our dues, we have hooks, good songs, we're solid performers, we're cute. I just don't get it. I haven't seen nor heard anything about our new record that is supposedly out.

The next night in New York we're scheduled to play at the Knitting Factory sans Mercy Rule (because they're busy being wined and dined). Upon arrival we learn that Sonic Youth wants to play a surprise, unannounced show on the very same night we're to play there. What a coup! Imagine, opening for a secret Sonic Youth show in New York!

"Um, Sonic Youth doesn't wish to share the bill," we're informed. "We'll have to split the bill."

This means if you want to see Zuzu's Petals you must pay and leave, and pay again for Sonic Youth. Only a couple of relatives and acquaintances come in to see us. A large crowd waits outside until it's time for the Sonic Youth show. Why would anyone want to pay twice?

IN Washington, D.C., our friends from another band show up and say in unveiled disgust, "What happened with your second record?" I take that to mean, "Man, it really sucks hard." I don't bother to explain. What happened to tact?

After D.C., Mercy Rule branches off onto another tour, and we continue southward on our own. They probably won't miss me a lick, as I've been rather morose and dour.

IN Richmond, Virginia, an attractive man with tousled blond hair wearing a faded Ivy League suit coat sits alone at the bar drinking. He's watching us play with full absorption. I know this because I haven't taken my eyes off him. He's my chosen focal point from the stage instead of the usual exit sign. He's my type; in fact, he's possibly the most attractive man I've seen at one of our shows.

After we leave the stage, he approaches me.

"You guys [meaning gals] are great. You're going to be huge stars. You remind me of Nirvana."

Charmed, I'm sure.

"Can I buy you a drink?" he offers.

I join him at a table in the back while some other band plays. We talk. He's a filmmaker, all blue eyes and sardonic wit, and he seems smitten with me.

"God, you're so beautiful," he laments like he aches.

This type of thing never happens to me. Ever. We move beyond small talk.

"Come with me to my apartment," he begs, "it's just around the corner."

"I can't," I sigh. "I have a boyfriend." I tell him about my boyfriend.

He is neither impressed nor deterred by my boyfriend.

"Can I please, at least, kiss you?"

I say no. I love kissing. I would love to kiss him, but I don't. Here it is, my rock 'n' and roll fantasy comes true—and now that I'm close enough to taste it, I fail to respond. Maybe I don't want to blow things with my boyfriend back home with an indiscretion.

IN Virginia Beach, a porn film airs on all of the TV sets situated throughout the club while we're on stage performing. The sparse crowd alternates between watching beaver shots and blow jobs and turning their heads toward us. This worries me. Two guys in the balcony hold up a sign that says, "Playing makeup, wearing guitar." Those are lyrics to a song that Paul wrote about a girl in an alternative rock band. The song was written long before we hooked up; it's about someone else. The fact that strangers perceive me as some sort of prototype for the subjects of his songs also worries me. It's my birthday.

When we leave our motel rooms to check out in the morning, Linda is barely awake and promptly falls back asleep for the day. Co is the first driver because she's at her best in the morning. I'm on the verge of tears because I've always been an overpacker, bringing way too many outfits and shoes because I need the flexibility to be able to dress for each situation according to the day, climate, mood, and ambiance, and no one offers to help me lug my bags in and out of the motel anymore. They just impatiently wait in the van.

We now earn enough to pay ourselves twenty dollars per diem. At breakfast I tend to order an omelet, orange juice, coffee, chocolate milk, and a Coke, which pretty much uses up my daily bread before we've begun rolling.

Wow, I'm sure glad we didn't cancel that gig in Louisville so that I could have a screen test and possibly be on prime-time television. I mean, there had to be twenty people in the audience. Instead of saying, "You know what? I really would've liked to have taken that screen test," I resort to all-day silence. My emotions are so frightening to acknowledge, especially to myself, because they're so unpleasant. There's resentment, envy, sad resignation, and competition whipping into a tropical depression. I just try to keep quiet and stuff them. It's hurricane season.

Co creeps out of our lumpy bed in the middle of the night and empties a box of Kleenex in the bathroom trying to alleviate her leaky faucet of a nose; her allergies are flaring badly this season.

When she returns to bed she can see that my eyes are open.

"Are you awake?"

"Wide."

"Are you tired?"

"Dead."

I'M in the back of the van, watching Linda lovingly run her fingers through her fabulous mane.

"You just raked your hair one hundred and thirty times without a break," I tell Linda from the backseat.

"What a weird thing to keep track of," says Linda.

"Why would you point that out to someone?" asks Co.

I don't know, maybe because instead of exploding (about how bad things are going for us and wondering why we aren't assessing our situation and trying to problem solve instead of just bumping along like gluttons for punishment), it's easier to blame everything on Linda's good hair, which takes up a majority of our shared bathroom time.

It's just that Linda is so self-confident and charming, which is hard to stomach if you've been in a snit for a good year or so because you can't figure out how to speak up in a tactful respectful way about all of the things you think are going wrong with Zuzu's Petals at the moment. Guys stare at her and she just smiles at them, all direct and open, and says, "How's it going?" and they melt and follow her around like puppies (which I realize is "good for business" and should offset my snit).

Sometimes in the van when Linda is being cheeky and talking about her several thousand best friends, I'll glare at her and say, "I'm on to you, I don't buy your act for a New York moment."

And she'll laugh and say, "Minute. It's 'a New York minute.'"

And I'll stand corrected. Linda is always "on" and I envy her for that. I feel like a worker bee resentful of the queen. The next day all three of us get our periods.

☿

IN Atlanta, a darling young all-female band from Canada is the opening act. This is their first tour and they're giddy and overwhelmed. Green. Innocent. A rep from Geffen Records shows up, tells us he likes us, and says we have good songs, dynamics, all of the essential ingredients. He then goes on to say, "But I really liked the opening band, they're so young and fresh."

I buy cocaine from the house soundman and snort it in the bathroom. Shortly thereafter, in our hotel room, I need to smoke pot to come down so I can fall asleep.

Congratulations, you are now officially a rock hag. I might as well resign myself to an apartment full of cats and a revolving door of younger, semiimpressed, half-interested lovers.

When I call Paul the next day, and say, "I did something last night that I feel really bad about—"

He cuts me off: "Don't do things that make you feel bad." Duh.

IN Tallahassee, we play with a band called Clitoris Rex. In Orlando we play with a popular Sub Pop band, and their female lead singer says to me, "Ohhh, I just looove porn." What's with porn these days? I understand and am not immune to the fact that the road to immediate sexual gratification is paved by anonymous visual stimulus, but am I the only one who notices bruises, track marks, and too-young girls doing things they don't want to be doing because they need drugs or attention?

CO and I went to Daytona Beach for spring break our freshman year of college. Both eighteen, we traipsed up and down the strip, dining at Denny's and drinking foofy drinks in dark bars. Co was the beauty with a string of guys on her heels; I was her clever sidekick with the Good Sense of Humor. Co got tan; I got burned. She was naïve; I was already jaded.

This time in Florida we're both getting burned.

IN Tampa after the show some guy asks me if I know Paul and I say ya, I do know Paul. Someone in my party says ya, he's her boyfriend. The asking guy looks stunned, shocked. No way, he says. Well, actually ya. No fucking way, he insists.

Why is it so hard to believe that the guy who wrote "I Will Dare" would go out with me? Because I'm so ordinary? So beneath him on the talent Richter scale? Sheesh, I'm starting to get a complex.

I'm afraid to talk about, bring up, or link myself with Paul in front of anyone; it's so weird to feel like you're namedropping when you're talking about your own boyfriend. It feels like it needs to be a secret or else I'm inviting that degrading sea of "no way" responses.

A few other things I hate telling:

One late-summer day before ninth grade, my friend Marie and I were riding our bikes to East Towne Mall when in our wake, motoring down Leo Drive, was a maniacal eight-year-old boy pumping wildly on his too-big ten-speed, headed straight toward me and my inferior Huffy. He was playing chicken. "I'm not moving, kid!" I pronounced just as we collided front wheel to front wheel, both being tossed from our bikes by the impact. Neighbors ran from out of their houses to help the bruised and bleeding little boy. I had a contusion popping out of my elbow that was so swollen I looked like Popeye. Marie helped me walk my bike home and laughed hysterically at my idiocy, mimicking my "I'm not moving, kid" line over and over while I washed pebbles out of my forearms.

On another day when I was a senior in high school and my sister Megan was a freshman, Megan began trolling around my closet for something nice to wear to school on the day she had a basketball game; athletes were expected to dress nicely on game days. She was keenly interested in a rust-colored silky blouse with a matching vest that would look nice with a skirt and Frye boots. "Don't even think about it!" I sullenly threatened. The next day during lunch hour I spotted her sitting at a table wearing my ensemble. I promptly marched her into the girls' locker room and ordered her to remove my garments, thus forcing her to wear her smelly striped gym shirt the rest of the day.

The fact that Megan is now divorced from the security guard at Sears and has been diagnosed with MS after having a grand mal seizure in front of her two-year-old son makes it almost impossible for me to forgive myself for my high school cruelty. She says she forgives me, but really, how could I be such an ass? I just hated feeling ineffective.

THRIFT shopping in St. Augustine, Florida, Linda buys a macramé belt and a knee-length green leather *Shaft* coat. I buy second hand cruisewear. Cruisewear? This matching outfit consists of ruffly flowered rayon shorts and a matching cropped equally ruffly jacket. It's hideous. I don't want to go on a cruise, I can't think of anything more claustrophobic. But maybe I'd like the option of nixing a cruise from my leisure plans. Leisure implies extra money to spend on . . . leisure, enjoyment, folly, but then I'd have to figure out some method of earning enough money to have leisure. Sundays off from the diner would be a nice start.

As a child I was placed in the backdrop of the privileged in spite of the fact that we lived in a very ordinary middle-class neighborhood—springs in Key Biscayne, summers on Martha's Vineyard—but I was not provided with a floor plan as to how one maintains, cultivates, or keeps this lifestyle. It's sure as hell not going to drop on my lap while I'm fondling an underground zit in a filthy van.

"GET IT!!!!!" I scream hysterically, like it's life threatening whenever my bandmates display their choices outside of dressing rooms in thrift stores and shops across the country. It sounds like an order, but they always look so adorable in the dresses and slacks that they try on and because they look adorable, they must GET IT! You can't *not* buy something that looks good on you. I'm probably trying to get them to come down to my level; I'm a weighed-down-with-too-much-crap shopping addict. I never try on and I feel empty when I fail to make a purchase.

OUR soundman James is too overcome with grief and way too depressed to be working right now. He spends no more than two minutes adjusting and tweaking our sound during sound check. He eats and smokes pot incessantly. We mock the affected way he orders his eggs—"scram-buled?"—every morning. He has discontinued speaking, which is always uncomfortable—specially when I thought that I had cornered the market on that behavior. When he does vocalize, it's to yell at us. Last time I checked we were his employers, yet somehow he's become the crabby haggard dad of three bratty daughters who now hate him, which takes the pressure off of hating one another. Reunited in our hatred of James, we make off-color jokes behind his back and discuss buying him a Greyhound ticket and sending him home, but we lack the collective spine to fire him, and, besides, no one wants to do all that driving.

"Oil can," we rasp through parched lips in the backseat, too afraid to ask James to pull off so we might purchase a modest bottle of water to insure that we're hydrated enough to sing that evening.

We also toy with firing our lawyer, who acts as our manager, because he lacks the time, connections, and passion to represent us. He also wore eighties' men's elf boots in New York while hanging out with us. When we call our booking agent to complain about the mental anguish that eight gigs in Florida is causing us, he yells at us, reminding us that we should be thankful so many places want to have us, especially with a weak product on the market. When we call our record company to complain about the fact that we're on tour and our second record is nowhere to be found in any record stores, or on any college radio stations, they yell at us, "Hey, it's not our fault that no one's responding to this record."

I N New Orleans, we're booked at the Howling Wolf opening for Minneapolis avant-punk band the Cows. As usual, we have nothing in common with this band musically, but it's always nice to see familiar faces. We play a dynamite show to a group consisting of women who wear tooth extensions and practice vampirism and three couples who are new parents who used to go out all the time, but no longer do. All twelve love the show.

I'd love to hang around and chat with these well-wishers, but an interesting scene is developing across the street at the Praline Connection. Fleets of limos are pulling up. A flock of onlookers surround the club, the air is thick with star power, and I'm intoxicated by it. Old, elegant gentlemen enter the club with walking sticks and young, buff men on their arms. They float in on the sweet cloud of decadent European aristocracy.

"What's going on in there?" I ask a limo driver who's loitering outside his stretch.

"The Rolling Stones are throwing a private party," he says.

Fucking hell. I must get in there. I'm wearing a long-sleeved gold lamé skintight cocktail dress, surely there's a way. I saunter up to the doorman and casually announce myself, my voice low and throaty like Marianne Faithfull's. I'm, of course, not on the list, and he says with all sincerity "sorry" because he knows that I belong in there.

"Get me Ron Wood," I demand, impatiently flicking my cigarette.

If anyone's going to wave me in, it's "the new guy" Ron Wood. He would instantly recognize and welcome a white girl hack with a bad case of the blues. A genuine search is made and the doorman informs me that Woody hasn't arrived yet, that I should try back in a little while.

I run inside the Howling Wolf flushed with excitement. Co and Linda are sitting with the young women who have tooth extensions on their canines. But James is tired and cranky and wants to go back to the motel.

"There's no time to lose, I heard her say/Catch your dreams before they slip away." The next morning as we pull out of some godforsaken HoJo's by the New Orleans airport, the Rolling Stones are on the radio. Instead of saying, "You know what, James? If I ever get the chance to set foot inside a private party thrown by the Stones again, I'm not going to let you or anyone else's bad mood get in my way," I cry silently to the lyrics, "Lose your dreams and you will lose your mind." Not that I came remotely close to getting in.

IN between Philadelphia and Athens, Ohio, we have a night off in the Pocono Mountains. We check into a Howard Johnson's and head directly to the lounge. On the TV set above the bar, the Madonna documentary *Truth or Dare* is being aired. On the dance floor behind us is a two-piece band consisting of a husband and wife; he alternates between playing the guitar and organ, and she majestically sits at the drums. They're playing polkas and big-band dance favorites. There are approximately twenty couples between the ages of twenty-two and eighty-two dancing on the checkerboard tile floor, some in amateurish box steps, some in full-form Lindy hops. They're all smiling and laughing, having fun, in love. On the TV, Madonna is going down on a water bottle.

WITH almost one hundred miles left to drive to our next show in Columbus, Ohio, the Dream Van dies. Fortunately, I have AAA Plus, meaning we are eligible for a one-hundred-mile tow. We squish into the truck and are towed to the front door of the club. The funny, well-nourished bartender from tours past is now rail thin and jittery. He doesn't take a moment to chat or share funny stories. When a few expensive, rare pieces of equipment are missing from our arsenal, we're told to suspect our former ally, the bartender. "Ya, he's a total junkie now." The repair to the van is superexpensive, a fuel pump or an alternator or possibly the entire engine needs replacing. This is the last repair we can afford to have on this poor bandaged-together vehicle.

"I'm sleeping in the van," I say. I never sleep in the van. This is what it takes for me to stoop to a night alone in the van—a squirrel. The party house we're staying at in Bloomington, Indiana, has a mascot: a pet squirrel. An outdoor gray squirrel is tearing around the living room, leaping from lap to lap, perching on shoulders. Its glossy black eyes darting, its sharp claws going *scratchy-scratch* across the linoleum. I'm not a fan of inappropriate pets. You can bet your ass there aren't any domesticated squirrels running around John Mellencamp's little pink houses. Having a toy-dog–size rodent scampering about someone's living quarters unnerves me.

THERE'S a weird mutation occurring within our fan base; every night in the audience there's a small throng of older men who look like they could be our uncles. No one lays claim to the midlife-crisis demographic.

ONE afternoon in Madison shortly after my father had moved out, I went to what was now referred to as "my mom's house" to do laundry. Going across town to Mom's was

preferable to my downtown neighborhood Laundromat because it offered TV and a sandwich.

While I was smearing Marie's creamy Italian dressing on a
piece of bread, my dad walked through the front door, having
used the key he still possessed to the house he deserted months
before. Dropping in to collect more of his belongings while no
one was home, he was surprised to see me standing at the
counter. We hadn't spoken since he left.

"Hello, Laurie Liz, just picking up a few things that I need,"
he said, walking into another room.

There were a few things I needed—like guidance, an explanation, financial assistance, a shrink—but I had no way of knowing that, so I glazed over with outrage at his abandonment.

"You know what?" I shrieked. "This whole thing sucks! I'm
so mad at you." I followed him from room to room, sobbing,
yelling, calling him a coward.

Satisfied in securing a few items from his former closet, he
headed back toward the front door without a word. There was
no way he was going to go into the family room and start
packing up his records with me in the room. My dad had recently become enamored with the hideous songs of Huey Lewis
and Bob Seger, so we no longer had our one thing, the love of
good music, in common.

"I deserve an explanation!"

He kept walking—out the door, down the driveway, into his
car. And I followed him close on his heels, yelling and crying,
begging.

He started his engine and drove away, leaving me to the
scene I was making for the old neighborhood to see. Leaving
me in my grief and anger.

Two things I learned: My dad could not stand serious conflict; in fact, it frightened him, caused him to flee, even from his
own child. And men don't like angry women.

☿

THIS all-time low of a tour ends in Detroit in some joint called Club Hell. Club Hell is all that. Once again, porn accompanies us on the tube while we play. Our van has to be watched while we're inside because we're in a Bad Neighborhood.

We return to our hotel, which is outside Detroit in an upscale suburb, and go directly to the bar. A silver-bearded, silver-haired man who looks a lot like Kenny Rogers (pre-face-lift) is taken by my brunette companion.

He starts a conversation by telling us his story. "I used to tour in a band in the sixties," he says. "I wrote two hit songs that are staples on oldies radio." They are, though they're nothing you'd want to cover. We are mildly impressed and interested in what he has to say, though my dark-haired friend in no way finds him to be a silver fox.

"I switched into business," he continues, "more money." He draws hard on a white filtered cigarette. "My wife divorced me. Kept the kids. A real bitch, that woman."

I feel compelled to tell him that my boyfriend is a musician and the old guy looks me straight in the eye and says, "Forget about it. There's pussy everywhere. Men are different animals. I guaran-goddam-tee it that he's not turning it down because he has you sitting around at home."

I point out that it sounds like his ex-wife had every reason to be a real bitch, and that pretty much ends our conversation.

Because I believe everything that everyone says to me, I take this bad news as permission to a get really drunk. My dad drives out to the hotel and takes me out to a dinner that will hopefully sober me up; I've managed to offend everyone in our hotel room with some sort of imperious rant that I served up to an interviewer over the phone earlier in the day while loaded. Throughout dinner my dad sits and listens and is present for me, but does not offer advice or judgment. Somewhere between the bar, our room, and the restaurant, I lose my favorite pink vintage hand-knit cardigan and find that more upsetting than anything else that's transpired.

E ver hear about the time we drove through a fire?" Co and I offer weakly on the home stretch.

18: Strangled in Seattle

IN the nearly four years that we've spent on the road, we've never made it to Seattle. The thought of it gives me a rash. Grunge is the cause of my anxiety. We from Minneapolis know, of course, that grunge is nothing new, it's merely an altered state of Minneapolis/California punk rock that is now called alternative rock, only "grunge" sounds more like the hyper-masculine heavy metal from the mid-eighties. A lot of the lauded grunge singers sound like angry dads yelling at neighborhood kids. Minneapolis bands have been wearing flannel shirts and messy tresses for years. We've been writing loud, raucous pop songs for ages. Seattle is having a musical renaissance. Minneapolis is O-U-T. Totally passé.

Zuzu's Petals wore fifties housewife dresses with long johns years ago. Musically, we have more in common with Heart than Hole. I have a feeling we're not going to be Seattle's cup of espresso. We're into dressing up and laughing. Only my ears are pierced and my flesh is ink-free. Lots of those riot grrrls are from the Pacific Northwest, and it's become nothing more than a handy-dandy catch phrase to describe all-women bands of a feminine or feminist nature. Whew, that covers a massive territory. The industry and the media are nuts about keeping us all in a manageable slot so that the public knows what's going on. We are feminists with a sense of humor. We embody femininity with a sense of irony. Doesn't anyone remember subtlety?

Our usual soundman James is no longer available after the East Coast stretch; that last trip did him in. Other drivers/roadies-for-hire are previously occupied or too expensive. An eager intern from our record company, Frank, has agreed to be our driver/roadie/T-shirt salesman. Frank begins our drive with a rambling narrative about his troubled life. I don't tune him in until I hear, "I stopped taking my meds today; I didn't even bring 'em!"

We are in Iowa.

Our new van is a 1982 tan Ford van. It has an advertisement on its side for Treehouse, something we surmise is a youth charity organization because the accompanying graphic features cartoon children sitting in a tree. We speculate that it might be for poor city kids in need of nature. The only windows in this vehicle are the passenger and driver's side windows and the windshield. The rest is locked in dirty-colored tin. Not having a lot of windows to peer into along with the logo on the side for underprivileged kids are theft deterrents. I'm still in mourning over the death of the Dream Van. It was broken into twice, but oh so much more pleasing to the eye. It had charm. I hate the new van.

The badlands are all that, at least what we're seeing on I-35. You've got your Wall Drug, a gussied-up overgrown Stuckey's.

"Where should we eat?" I'm asked. According to Van Rules we had banished Hardee's, Rax, Popeye's, and Bob Evans from our culinary haunts.

"Wherever." I sigh.

Frank can't drive; he gets too close to other cars and swears, and makes impulsive lane changes. No angry, passive-aggressive drivers cut off from their meds allowed.

WHEN I was in fifth grade I wrote a book entitled *Our Trip West*. It was a school project for our "pioneer days" sequence. Our class made its books from scratch by sewing together folded sheets of paper, then binding them with gauze strips and papier-mâché. We made book covers from cardboard and wallpaper samples.

Our Trip West stole most of its material from Laura Ingalls

Wilder's *Little House* books. My book consisted of a series of diary entries recounting my fictional family's covered wagon travels from Wisconsin to Seattle. My favorite TV show in fifth grade was *Here Come the Brides,* which was about three bachelor brothers living in early Seattle, a town full of lumberjacks all vying for the affections of a hotel full of women who were there as barmaids looking for husbands. By mixing *Little House* with *Here Come the Brides* and adding in a pinch of my distorted sense of reality, I channeled mudslides, helpful Indians, five deaths including two sisters, a birth, a runaway from New York, scarlet fever, blindness, blizzards, magical waterfalls, break-ins by goodnatured drunken men, and endless fields of wildflowers. The "I" character, Candace Sutter, wrote folk songs and stayed up all night playing her fiddle (which is how she deterred the drunken marauders).

I was on fire in fifth grade; in love with learning and doing, spouting off Civil and Revolutionary War facts with fervor, and hanging out with like-minded girls who would stay up all night during sleepovers talking about how cool and interesting everything was, dreaming big dreams for our futures. That was during that glorious latent period of child development before the horror of hormones hit.

MONTANA is breathtakingly beautiful; mountains, pine trees, crisp sharp air. Natural beauty can improve one's mood. "Sure beats work," I hear from the backseat while my neck stiffens. Touring never seemed like vacation to me. I work harder on tour than I do at any day job: driving, unloading, setting up, sound check, interview or radio show if we're lucky, meal if we're lucky, find a cheap place to stay, shower if there's time, get dressed, go back to the club, wait, wait some more, play, play well to a receptive crowd if we're lucky, break down stage, load the van, get paid what was promised without any hassles if we're lucky, a bonus if we're really lucky, find somewhere still open to eat if we're lucky, or eat from vending machine fare at the motel, sleep with three others in a room, drive.

"We're gonna stop and walk around for a little while; this is amazing."

"I'll wait in the van," I say, even though I want to get out and walk around, too.

This is exactly how I used to act on family vacations: While my family gazed at Plymouth Rock—and I was the only child in the group old enough to appreciate it—I would sit in the station wagon with my dog-eared copy of *Go Ask Alice*. Oh, I know, I know, damn it; I'm doing this for the thrill, the joy, the utter release. Just think of all the wonderful people we meet. We're seeing the world. We have freedom, artistic satisfaction; we're getting paid to do this. I'm just not in the mood to acknowledge how lucky I am. I know I'm being a bitch, but I'm unable to snap out of it; an invisible vise has me locked in permanent snot mode. I used to torture my family like this, too. Now my new family, the band, has to put up with me. Why do I try to bring everyone else down with me? It never works. The cheese stands alone.

It is an insanely long drive from Minneapolis to Seattle. The reason why there are no gigs in between is because we canceled a weeklong tour of Canada that was supposed to lead up to the Seattle show—but the drives in between shows were geographically impossible to manage without a rocket ship.

Almost to Seattle the lay of the land becomes barren and ugly, which is something I've grown to realize precedes major metropolises. Women wrapped in blankets sitting at a card table hand us free coffee and cookies outside of a rest area ladies' room. I don't know why they're here, but it's awfully nice. I am disproportionately touched by their simple act of kindness, near tears, in fact. Shortly thereafter we're in Seattle, where we will stay at the apartment of transplanted Minneapolitans, Paul and Mia. They are married grown-up friends with lives. My face has completely broken out during the course of our drive.

The afternoon before our Seattle show we must drive thirty miles out of the city to a small private college because we have an interview at their radio station.

"Who?" says the guy with the stocking cap standing at the threshold, blankly staring at us.

"Um, Zuzu's Petals. We have an interview here at two o'clock to plug our show tonight at the Exit Ramp?"

Bored stares respond to this information.

"We're a BAND from MINNEAPOLIS."

"Do you know Babes in Toyland?" asks the young dude with a long hanging goatee. This handful of unimpressed future alternative-rock deejays clearly do not know who we are or why we think we have an interview.

These kids are exaggerated versions of the grunge stereotype: pierced everything. No hair. Neon hair. Filthy matted hair. Stocking caps. Tattooed everything. Doc Martens. Oddly sculpted facial hair. I'm so relieved not to be their age anymore—I can't imagine making out with a guy with a King Tut beard. To them we probably look old, haggard, and undecorated (because we are). I've taken to silently reminding myself that blues musicians do this shit till the day they die, but it isn't making me feel any better.

Co and I promptly turn on our heels, storming off to a phone booth to yell at whoever is responsible for the mess we find ourselves in—record company, manager, booking agent. We've got this part down cold as of late.

"They have no idea who we are!" we holler in unison.

"I'm sorry, but I spoke with Tanya the program director," says the new radio guy from Los Angeles who replaced the old radio guy in Minneapolis, who did an amazing job with our first record. "She said there would be someone there to interview you at two."

Come to think of it, everyone who did a great job on our first record has been fired and replaced by L.A. staff.

"Well, she's not here, they don't have any of our records,

they've never heard of us, they're totally grunge, we're in the boonies . . ."

We're shaky mad.

S OUND check is next. Silently we creep back into Seattle and locate the club, a scary dump, a bomb shelter under a highway ramp. We're no strangers to scary dumps, but this one in particular is eerie and we're not even inside yet. From the outside, the gray cinder blocks and black spray paint are uninviting.

This would be a good time to discuss heroin. Heroin is the drug of choice these days. The media about the rampant heroin use in Seattle by musicians, hipsters, poseurs, and youth is everywhere. We don't do heroin, we're too old and too chicken. We're fine with not doing it. Needles are too intense. We do plenty of other things that are not good for us, like touring in a rock band.

Walking into the Exit Ramp is like boarding a ghost ship. The shadows of people loitering about the dank, dark structure are pale, reed thin, in need of sunshine, fresh air, and a sandwich. One guy is walking around with a teaspoon sticking out of his back pocket, advertising his clichéd, overrated drug habit that is now synonymous with Seattle. Being on stage for a ten-minute sound check, running through a couple of songs, reminds us of our purpose, our connection. It feels good to bang on my guitar, to open my mouth wide and let out a big throaty sound. But days are twenty-four hours long, and these pieced-together minutes don't feel like enough to shake loose all the sedentary dust collected in the last four days.

In order to receive our obligatory meal, we retire to the adjoining room, where there is a bar and tables. A transparent beige server with bleached-blonde pigtails and a lumberjack cap tries to take our order, but she is too busy fitfully scratching her cardigan-ed forearms. She needs a fix and I need to abandon ship. I leave Co and Linda at the club with Frank, who I've been trying to ignore since Iowa.

With Paul and Mia in tow, we find an agreeable restaurant with a wine list. Mia has been a good friend of mine since my last year in Madison—she joined me on Martha's Vineyard for a couple of months and moved home to Minneapolis after college. Mia and I are not alike. She's hyperdriven, organized, and business oriented, yet she has stuck by my side in spite of our differences. She and her new husband Paul, also from Minnesota, are in Seattle for Paul's graduate program. Mia has yet to warm up to Seattle and she's working in advertising and film at the moment. I'm not sure what she sees in me, but she loves me unconditionally, which comes as a deep relief as there are not too many of those people left. For the first time, I find myself envying Mia and her decorated apartment and vegetarian cookbooks and supportive husband.

Refreshed by a good meal and good company in a relaxing environment, I return to the barroom and it is packed. A good sign. I fight my way through a sea of flannel and ennui in search of a restroom so I can change into my lucky can't-get-into-a-private-party-thrown-by-the-Stones gold lamé dress. I have a feeling I'm going to need it. Co catches my arm outside the ladies' room, the look on her face suggesting horror.

"The dinner was inedible," she begins, "and, um, my mom sent an old family friend who I haven't seen since I was a toddler. Hello? I don't know or remember him."

I peer around the corner at a pleasant-looking bespectacled gentleman in his fifties who sticks out like a sore thumb. This phenomenon is a mortifying yet regular occurrence; our proud mothers call distant relatives and long-lost friends to coerce them into attending our shows in cities throughout the country. I need to be alone and incommunicado before we play; I still have stage fright. Road managers and dressing rooms come in handy, but those luxuries appear to be things from an abbreviated past. My gold lamé dress is failing to provide that little extra boost of confidence. Coleen is an expert handler of my neuroses and jitters.

"Don't go in there," she advises with such gravity that I stop before entering the room where the opening band is performing.

"Why?"

"There's a really tough, really wasted grunge girl on stage."

I take Co's wise counsel and wait for our turn. On with the show and all that rot. During the first song of the first gig on our West Coast tour the room empties. Not a great feeling. In fact, it's a horrible feeling. I scan the empty room and see Mia bopping her head in exaggerated enthusiasm like a mom at a piano recital. Everyone that was watching the really tough, really wasted grunge girl perform has left and gone to the other room.

We're not playing so hot, which is normal on the first show of a tour. I'm aware that our songs are so, so—what's that dreaded word?—melodic. We're too sloppy to be a slick pop band, and we're too ourselves, angst-free and hopeful, to satisfy the grunge appetite. We are stuck between a rock and a soft place, a mild elixir for those thirsting for loud, machine-gun howls. It is, after all, the popular sound of the day. Here I stand in my stupid dress, my lame lamé dress, refusing to holler and scream, opting against a psycho-girl-from-hell id fest. I've outgrown all that. I just want to sing our simple songs and go back to Mia's for a glass of wine.

I spy with my desperate eye an authentic grunge stocking hat at the bottom of my mike stand. A prop! Dare I debase my beautiful dress with such an inappropriate accessory? Hell, we've already cleared the room, it can't hurt. My inner monologue is continuous on stage, like: I should've peed before we started . . . I wonder what Hungarian mushroom soup would be like if I added asparagus . . . why is Co looking at me like that . . . ?

In between songs I place the cap that has been God-knows-where upon my golden curls and offer with a grin, "Maybe now you guys will like us."

I spy with my nervous eye a very drunk grunge girl steadying herself on the lip of the stage, hurling indecipherable obscenities in my direction. I turn my back to the empty audience pit and announce to my mates that I'm about to be killed while returning to the mike to start our next melodic ditty that has—oh, they're going to hate this—vocal harmonies.

Into the second verse out of the corner of my right eye, my good eye, I see Co, bass in hand, hovering around me like a lioness protecting her young. I have no idea why, but I always like it when she likes me enough onstage to come in close. I begin the chorus, feeling icy, bloodless hands closing around my throat. Disoriented about the origins of this sensation, I plunge my maroon suede heel backward and it connects with a soft, fleshy stomach. Co closes in, wildly kicking yet not missing a note. I'm still singing. There have been so many disastrous stage incidents—broken strings, broken guitar straps, broken amp, loss of sound system, chaos, heckling. I never stop singing, as though it will make the badness go away. It's an open invitation to my denial, my still singing. At song's end I turn around to see the aforementioned really drunk grunge girl being dragged off stage and out of the building by the guy who was checking IDs at the door. I remove the hat and fling it up in the air Mary Tyler Moore style. The drama is paying off; curiosity seekers file in. Tomorrow, Tacoma!

WE pull in front of the Satyricon in Portland, Oregon, on a drizzly afternoon. Co and I get out and go inside while Linda and Frank wait in the van for parking and unloading instructions.

"Hi, I'm Coleen from Zuzu's Petals, we're playing here tonight."

A fat ugly guy barks, "We don't even want you on the fucking bill" in answer to her polite greeting.

Co and I stand side by side absorbing this verbal slap.

He adds, "Your booking agent is a real asshole."

There have been times when I might've agreed with him, but if this guy had any idea how our night in Seattle went, he might've thought twice about rudely yelling at us in our fragile state. Maybe not.

The headlining band is a group from England who's supposed to be the next big thing out of the UK, though I've never heard of them, which doesn't mean much these days as I'm behind the times. I recently discovered Joni Mitchell. We go about our business of setting up and busying ourselves where we're not wanted. A radio station is sponsoring the appearance by the English band, so there's a crowd. We play a decent show to a decent audience because we're professionals.

After our performance, a leather-clad, muscle-bound *Night Rider* look-alike approaches us and says, "You ladies are good people. You make great music. Is there anything I can do to help you?"

"You know, the folks at the club are pretty hostile. Would you mind hanging out with us until we can get paid and get out of here?"

Our guardian angel accompanies us to collect our salary and we're paid without any hassles. Then he helps us load gear and asks if he can be of further assistance.

"We're playing Eugene tomorrow, if you haven't got anything better to do."

ON our way to San Francisco we're snowed in on the top of Mt. Shasta in Weed, California. Frank takes the van in hopes of finding an open bar near our motel. Fine with us, we could use a break from his brooding. He returns a couple hours later and tells us that a girl with whom he was shooting pool gave him a hand job in our van. We, of course, could have lived without this information.

"Hey, I'm from Edina!" a teenage waif says to me at the club in San Francisco. Edina is an affluent suburb of Minneapolis.

"Oh, ya?" I answer, "what are you doing out here? Going to school?"

"No, living under a bridge with a bunch of kids I just met."

I find this information disturbing and react in my usual parental manner. "Will you please call your parents and let them know you're okay? Promise?"

IN L.A. we stay with two old college friends from Madison, one of whom has an Emmy. Our friends are television and film writers. They have a big apartment in a nice neighborhood. They were cute funny guys in college. It's difficult to be struggling with an ill-received record in front of them, but they understand the ups and downs of show business. Being bachelors, having an all-girl band crash at their pad gives them street cred. Having attended college with Co and I, Linda is the object of their attention.

When our hosts come to our show at Hell's Gate (I noticed "hell" is big these days), they stand in the crowd and do enthused white-boy new wave bops to our music. The president of Restless now has oddly sculpted facial hair and is in a hurry to get to his next, more important engagement. The soundman does a horrific job, and I'm embarrassed by the poor sound quality and our subpar performance. The second we're done, everyone is quickly ushered out of Hell's Gate by its employees because a wedding overseen by comedy-horror band Gwar is about to take place in the club.

WE intend to spend a day off in Taos, New Mexico, between our shows in Phoenix and Denver. My brother

Chris lives there. Frank wishes us to spend our day off in Phoenix so he can be with his brother. We're the bosses of him. He sulks and discontinues speaking to us. Ho hum. Being old hat at this behavior, we have no trouble ignoring him.

My brother lives in an adobe house with a friendly group of guys who are landscapers, housepainters, and bartenders. They work to support their skiing and snowboarding habits. Chris is nine years my junior. While sharing a meal, Chris's roommates start inundating me with questions.

"I hear your boyfriends used to beat up Chris when he was little."

"Um, no," I correct, "my boyfriends used to read books to him and play with him in hopes of getting him to sleep."

I stare at my brother, his face crimson, and I see the small boy he once was, injured, and I see his sadness that turned too quickly into anger.

"Is it true that Chris . . . ?"

I am barraged with questions about my brother's supposed hard-knock life. The last time I checked, our collective child-hoods were a cakewalk.

I wonder how or why he reinvented his personal history wrought with mistreatment and neglect. I guess it wasn't easy becoming the man of the house at the age of nine. My parents had money for most of my growing up years, whereas they did not for my younger siblings. I was already out of the house and flunking out of the university at the time Chris became the sole male in our house. I remember him as a little boy getting up and making sure all the doors were locked. He once ran away thinking that my parents split up because they fought about who was driving him to hockey. It must've been weird for him to go to an out-of-state prep school on a hockey scholarship surrounded by extremely wealthy kids. On his own a long time, Chris settled far away from our family. It's difficult to get to him, personally and geographically; the Rocky Mountains serve as an imposing shield, a protective womb.

Chris offers his bedroom to me, a room of my own for the night.

"Are you all right?" he asks. "You don't look so good."

"I'm shot," I sigh. "I'm so fucking sick of this."

He shakes out the down comforter that used to belong to our parents and now covers his futon.

"That's okay, I'm not picky," I say.

"I'm shaking out any scorpions that might've wandered in looking for warmth," he says matter-of-factly.

I stay awake all night on scorpion watch and think about my family. We had a sarcastic saying to describe ourselves: "When the going gets rough, take a trip." We were a family that when faced with hard times—marital strain, job stress, adolescent children, disconnection, financial woes, lack of community—sought the geographical cure, an endless form of running. A change of scenery, luxury accommodations, an ocean and sunshine can really help you put things into perspective. Vacations help your troubles melt away in a cup of sangria for a minute or two, recharge your battery to go back home and make things right if you were so inclined. And look at me now, constantly taking a trip, constantly avoiding bills that pile up at home, ignoring the years flying by—I'm trying to outrun a puzzling disease, avoid the fact that I have no solid plans or belief in the future, no long-term career goals, no clue about making or saving money. I'm a rocker, the future is now. Right? And I'm tired of running. Now I think that if I can get a handle on the "home" thing, the other adult components could follow. I need some time alone to think. Or something.

I'M nineteen and standing in my one-bedroom apartment on Martha's Vineyard. After waiting a month for phone service, the sound of its ring startles me.

"Hello?"

"Dad took all of his stuff and left." It's my sister Megan and she's frantically whispering on the phone.

"What?" I ask, unable to give her statement meaning.

"Last week Dad took all of his stuff and moved out, and Mom told us not to tell you because she didn't want to ruin your summer."

During that summer I discover cocaine and steal sixty dollars from my employer's cash register to purchase a plane ticket home. I ruin my own damn summer.

I N Denver we pull into a decent-looking club in a revitalized warehouse district that consists of a bar, restaurant, and an attached theater. The restaurant is bustling with sophisticated diners eating above-average fare. We check with the bartender about finding the promoter.

"She won't be in; there isn't a show tonight."

We saunter into the theater part of the building to find a soundman setting up; he agrees with the bartender: "There's no band on the schedule for tonight."

The bartender from the other room walks in with a sheet of paper, a copy of the club calendar. It reads: Wed. Oct. 21, Open mike night featuring Susie's Potatoes. Somewhere else along the line we were billed as Susan's Pellets, but Susie's fucking Potatoes is about as much as we can take. I could pop an artery I'm so frustrated.

A hysterical appeal is half shouted at the soundman: "We're Zuzu's Petals, a national band on tour promoting a new album." He looks suspicious but agrees to let us play before open mike night begins. Two men walk in, they're Denver engineers who liked our first record and they recently called Restless, asking them when we would be playing in the Denver area and where they might be able to find a copy of our second album. They cannot find it in any record stores. Restless was able to direct them to our show but blamed the distributor for lack of records in stores. We play our hearts out to these guys; we play, perhaps, the greatest show of our lives. They love it. Susie's Potatoes, my ass.

Afterward I order a scotch at the polished oak bar and turn to Co. "How many times do you return to a man who beats you?"

She's in no mood for a metaphor. "I know." She sighs. "I'm pretty tired of this, too."

IN Dallas as I walk off the stage after an exhilarating perform-ance at an above-average venue with above-average atten-dance, an audience member grabs my elbow and asks, "What's it like going out with God?"

I wish I were Linda Blair in *The Exorcist* spewing pea soup while my head did a three-sixty.

I think there's an old saying that there's no such thing as a perfect triangle. I already know this from being in a three-piece band and the eldest of three sisters; there's usually an odd woman out. And now, without meaning to, I'm in another awkward triangle between Paul, myself, and his adoring pub-lic. I'm not envious of him or his talent; I believe in it whole-heartedly, he deserves all of the accolades. I just think it's weird that people get so bent out of shape over another human being, especially when that person is my boyfriend. I can't help but feel like they, in some way, threaten our happiness. I don't love him on the pedestal; I love him with his feet on the ground next to mine. I'm not sure how or why, but these fan types just freak me out, make me defensive. They make me not want to be out in the crowd, they make me want to hide.

To them I'm a huge bitch because, c'mon, how do you an-swer graciously when someone asks you about dating the Lord?

SPENDING so much time at rest areas and truck stops, I'm obsessed with finding and saving missing children. In every wayside station I scan the faces and crowds for children who are pleading in their eyes for rescue, who look like they're with someone who's tormenting them. I feel the need to do Something Important.

IN Nebraska tumbleweeds fly down the highway and into our windshield like we're behind the wheel of a video game.

"I feel alive!" I proclaim because once again we're at the mercy of the elements and possibly near death.

"Chicken in the bread pan, picking out dough!" Linda sings, with Tourette'sian glee, from that awful Charlie Daniels song for no reason at all.

"At least I'm not a lap dancer at a truck stop 'gentleman's club,'" Co decides. Our new favorite driving game is At Least We're Not . . . "At least we're not blind beggars with leprosy on the streets of Calcutta." "Or crack whores." "Or single, teenage mothers in a trailer park." You get the idea.

The next day driving through Iowa after an unremarkable stop in Nebraska, Co and I are Mom and Dad while Linda and Frank sleep in the back. I've grown to fake-despise Linda because she's so easygoing and adaptable: she can sleep soundly anywhere, have a meaningful conversation with any-one, find sources of delight everywhere—and I know that's messed up. Oh ya, and that fantastic hair of hers. Still, any-thing for a laugh. Sometimes we snap, "Don't you know who I am?" at people because of course they do not, why should they?

When Co and I pass the billboard for the Toot Toot Lounge, our giggles suggest that we're thinking the same thing.

"Let's go."

"It's out of the way."

"So what?"

We all got so gastronomically ill after our steak buffet experience at the Toot Toot at the beginning of the Ant tour. The
laugh is more important than anything else going on in our
lives at the moment. Co and I snicker for thirty consecutive
minutes. We pull into the Toot Toot Lounge's gravel parking
lot and turn off the motor. Our giggles are now guffaws.

"Lunchtime!" we sing out to the nappers.

Groggy, Linda raises her head. "Huh? Didn't we already
eat?"

It's lost on her, the practical joke bombs. That's what we get
for manufacturing our own nostalgia (for group diarrhea),
hoping to recapture the magic. It never works.

Linda's been on some weird health kick where she orders
oatmeal for breakfast and jogs; fortunately, that's dissipated
over the weeks.

I REMEMBER our confused, confusing first show when a musician friend said to me, "You guys [meaning gals] have stage
presence and chemistry. Most people never get that. The rest
will come."

I believed him because it was preferable to giving up on the
spot. And he was right. Slowly and (not very) surely, the rest
did come (and go and come and go).

The actual platform, the stage, has changed shape. Initially it
was a coveted long shot, a risky attempt to conquer a foreign
land. We did all of our learning onstage, in public, in front of
others. We didn't spend a minute locked in our rooms with
Cream records (thank God). The words "serious" and "guitarist" in the same sentence gives me hives. The stage used to
be this daunting, intimidating platform where we stood higher
than everyone else in the room. Armed with microphones, loud
instruments, songs, and cool clothes, we covertly worked un-
dercover. The stage was like rock climbing on a cliff without
guide ropes. It took a couple of years to figure out how to hear

ourselves under adverse circumstances and we developed a sixth sense; the ability to play together when we couldn't hear one another while figuring out how to put on a convincing show.

Because we played anywhere and everywhere we could, whether we were welcomed or not, we developed a knowledge of the stage. Through a long trial-and-error process, our voices were located—at first screamy-yelly, then too choir girlish, finally settling on a combination of soft and strong with an occasional bellow. An "uncle fan" in southern Illinois told me as a compliment that I sounded like Grace Slick, which bums me out, makes me want to reassess.

Then the stage shifted shape and turned into a therapy couch: I once went home with a guy at bar time under the assumption that he wanted to have sex with me. Still a teen, I was too drunk and tired to protest, I lent myself out. He hitched my ankles over his shoulders and announced with great confidence, "You're gonna love this." I did not love it; in fact, I hated it. In fact, it hurt. I'm of course not divining this episode while onstage, but my body and soul blow my cover and it comes out in howls, sneers, icy stares, in dropping to my knees and strumming my guitar so hard with bare fingers that they bleed. I challenge anyone to guess that I was a cripple for six months and could be again on any given day.

Co sometimes goes into these gyrating hair-shaking trances, screaming at the top of her lungs, "Whhhhaaaat are you afraid of?" Coleen has been held up at gunpoint behind a convenience store in her neighborhood. Her apartment has been broken into and a family heirloom stolen. She used to bartend on one of the roughest blocks in Minneapolis that hosted alcoholics, frat boys, old hippies, and Somali men who brought in a set of culturally specific gender assumptions only read about in ancient histories. Co expelled all of her outrage, anger, sense of violation, and her mourning over a sadly lost innocence on the stage. Combine these heavy emotions with classic theatrical training and you have Co; articulate, ferocious, and natural, or as her fan Billy in Boston says, "The sexiest woman in show business."

Linda, the one who's supposed to be limited by debilitating rheumatoid arthritis, pounds her drums with such ferocity that her sticks break, the skin on her hands cracks, and membranes on her drum heads rupture. All the while she chews gum, smiles, works the room like a professional entertainer. And a lot of the time she's in pain. Drumming is her "fuck you" to the disease she inherited from a grandparent confined to a wheelchair in his thirties, to weekly injections of the element gold into her elbows, to the stomach-ripping eight-hundred milligrams of ibuprofen she needs to carry on. Sometimes after shows we need to help her pull her T-shirt over her head because her elbows are so stiff and she's in so much pain.

I believe what we're doing is called "acting out" in psychological circles. There is no better, more appropriate place to "act out" than on a stage, and it's preferable to being prostrate with depression, to feeling helpless and self-destructive. Onstage we can kiss off all the people who tell us to "smile" at our demeaning day jobs, to all the "you guys rock for girls" crap. We're up there reacting to constant marginalization. Rock 'n' roll in any form brings up these feelings—that's why it originated in the blues. We don't stay with our anger. We open up our mouths and put our hands to work to relieve the pressure. Then it's all over. All gone.

What in the world could three middle-class white girls need to feel fierce about? Isn't the world our oyster? Ya, I guess. We've experienced poverty and degradation. Pieces of my life have been ugly, felt ugly. Performing is purifying, a nightly sweat, a detox. We're cleansed and drained at the end of the night. I'm not a victim of anything except unrealistic dreams and believing in musicals.

THINGS that have happened onstage while opening my mouth and pulling my belly in tight to reach a high or loud note: tampon expulsion and pants pissing.

Things we've neglected to do that would probably improve our chances for fame:

1. Say really outrageous things in interviews like, "Oh, I just loooove anal sex," or "My mom used to lock me in a closet." (Neither of which is true, but they would be attention-getters.)
2. Hire another guitar player. There's a woman guitar player in Philly who is in the band the Friggs and she plays like Keith Richards. I'd love to ask her to join, but I doubt she'd want to leave Philly for Minneapolis. That means we'd have to hire a ringer (i.e., a dude)—that would spoil the vibe.
3. Have a former career in the sex industry as a stripper or worse and tell people about it often in graphic detail.
4. Say insane things onstage while breaking down crying, yelling at the audience, and getting in fistfights with band and audience members. Or have a hissy fit and leave the stage in the middle of a set.
5. Pass out drunk onstage or have very public, very serious drinking and drug habits.
6. Do provocative things like strip, dry hump our equipment, go down on a beer bottle, smash things to bits, throw glasses, spit, etc.
7. Whip tampons out of our vaginas and into the audience.

The assumption being that if you're inappropriate, high-maintenance, psycho, or depraved, you must be brilliant or you have the ability to draw attention to yourself in a way that entices the masses and could make a lot of money for other people; this assumption seems to be held more strongly for women than for men. Problem is, these behaviors are just not part of our makeup; it's neither ladylike nor polite. We're not exactly the equivalent of *Dr. Quinn, Medicine Woman: The Band* but we have our limits. Lately, the stakes seem higher, like the more outrageous and inappropriate you act, the better your chances of success. I'd probably embellish my personal history to make it more interesting like I did when I drank scotch at Liquor Lyle's, or when I was starting out in college meeting new people and regaling them with tales that made my white-trash background trashier and my few traces of blue blood bluer. The thing of it is, I have Coleen looking over my shoulder, my own personal Jiminy Cricket, who's known me since the dorms and she has no problem holding me accountable. This makes it absolutely impossible to invent some sort of personal mythology and I resent her for that. Or you could be so undeniably talented that your eventual success was inevitable.

John Lennon once said in a *Playboy* interview that in order to make it in the music industry, you have to be willing to be a complete asshole, a total jerk, a cold ruthless bastard. I think I'm getting close to achieving all of those requirements without the stardom. Maybe he meant you need to be able to pay other people well enough to be assholes for you so that you still seem nice to the general public.

A FTER the solid year on the road followed by album followed by road, the stage has changed shape again and become a platform of boredom. We are so tired of playing the same songs every night, so disgusted with our patented moves: During "Psycho Tavern," Linda and I jam together with my back to the audience while Co sings. I turn around to slap my strings with the palm of my hand to produce a harmonic clang, then kneel in front of my amp and pretend to be rocking out ferociously while thinking about the day's shopping adventure. We look at one another between songs and check imaginary watches and speculate off-mike how much time must lapse until we can go back to our room. You are not supposed to be bored when you're putting on a rock show. Maybe being paid handsomely inspires one to put on a good show. Maybe a deeply engaged crowd helps. Maybe I'm supposed to be providing that and the crowd feeds off it. Without an abundance of new material, I feel stale.

What is the audience's role in a performance? They pay to enter the club in which you are that evening's appointed entertainment. Many people are there, presumably, to see you. Or discover you by chance because they felt like going out that night. Or they saw your picture in the paper and they were curious. Or the cute guy from your existential film class is going and you want to hook up with him. Or you're a new music fan feeling disenfranchised, and you're looking for representation. Or your friend in St. Louis told you to check us out. Or you like that song on the college radio station about unrequited love. Whatever the reason, what do we owe one another?

Some people go out and watch a band because the people onstage are not well. They're sicker than you'll ever be. There are some people onstage who are more depressed, drunk, more drugged, angrier, more daring, and more talented than you'll ever be. Some performers are so shy and anxious that the only way they can have social intercourse is from the stage—from the stage they can control the interaction. And somehow this is exhilarating for audiences, it provides some sense of relief: Did you see her fall over wasted last night? Did you see him smash a really expensive guitar to bits in a fit of rage? Did you hear her rip her heart out just for you? This is thrilling for the audience, and then they go home and study, or eat, or by accident fuck a stranger. But that's about it. Rock bands live the life for you, so that you don't have to. You can just listen and watch and be entertained, which is the whole point. That transfers into you thinking they've got it all: sex, drugs, adoration. Ha.

I guess going to a rock show is akin to ancient peoples going to a Greek tragedy; you watch someone else act out your most unspeakable and sometimes vile impulses—like Oedipus stab-

bing his eyeballs out—and then you, the audience, are relieved
and absolved, freed from those bad feelings because someone
else has expressed them for you. And if that's the case, I'm not
really doing a very good job.

I've been watching, noticing the performer/audience relationship for a long time, from both sides. I spend a lot of time
trying to figure it out. I think I made a mistake when I forgot
to create a persona to wear onstage to cover up and protect the
real me. One time a British journalist pointed out that it was
like indecent exposure to watch someone without an "act."
What does that make you? A voyeur? What does that make
me? Naked? An exhibitionist? A big baby?

I T'S the end of October, my favorite time of the year: cold
nights, falling leaves, the smell of fires from chimneys. Paul's
on tour and I'm ironing clothes in my lakeshore apartment and
watching MTV's *120 Minutes*. A singer/songwriter from California, Victoria Williams, is the featured guest artist and she's
plugging a record called *Sweet Relief*. A myriad of musicians
donated tracks to this record, playing cover versions of songs
penned by Ms. Williams. This record was conceived to help
Victoria raise money for her medical bills after being diagnosed
with MS. It's her hope that other musicians lacking medical insurance can benefit from this fund. Her husband accompanies
her on the show and plays in her band; it's Mark, my old grillmate from the Global café and member of the Jayhawks. She
plays a duet with one of my idols, Lou Reed, a musician featured on the record. I watch with a mixture of sadness, anger,
and envy: I've been hiding MS for years, and now we have an
MS poster girl because she's brave enough to be forthcoming
and ask her community for support.

19: The Beginning of a New Age

ON an early morning in the Hi-Lo Diner, I carry a white oval plate filled with scrambled eggs from the back room up to the front grill so the cook can add hash browns and toast to the plate. The problem is that at the end of my journey down the alley is a cat-size gray rat on its hind legs staggering toward me like a man. I place the plate on the counter, turn around, grab my coat and keys, and walk out the back door. No one in the restaurant sees this dreadful monstrosity except for the grill cook and myself. I am cajoled back several minutes later after the rat has been quietly stomped to death in the back room. But I'm scared. I no longer feel safe in the Hi-Lo because red eyes are watching me from behind every potato sack.

I have a desperate fear of rats, complete rodentaphobia. When I see one, my insides freeze and white terror consumes my body. I don't know why or how I ended up with this particular fear, but it's acute. Fight or flight? I flee. Always. Seeing a rat for me is the equivalent of being chased by a psychopath with a machete. Spiders and insects: no problem. It's just rats and to a smaller degree mice. Those cruel, hairless tails. Their ability to survive and thrive in the rudest of circumstances. Their size. They're just so fucking gross.

I'm starting to see rats regularly on the road—inside a club in Philadelphia, on the sidewalk in New York, in the back alley in Washington, D.C. It's undoing me.

WHEN I'm not on tour, I spend one afternoon a week at the home of a composer named Randall who's a regular at the diner; I've asked him to teach me music theory. This is done primarily at his piano, and he asks me to transpose the melodies to my best songs using one finger. Randall explains the keys and the intervals and I glaze over and check out—just like all the guitar lessons, my mind cannot or will not comprehend.

He says, "You have an amazing ear, why do you think you need to learn this stuff?"

"Because I feel like an idiot in the studio working with producers and around other musicians, I don't know anything about any of this."

"Did you know that Irving Berlin couldn't read music and he wrote all of his songs with one finger?"

"No, I didn't."

"How many copies did you sell of your first record?" he wonders.

"I dunno, something like twenty-eight thousand."

Randall looks astounded; his jaw is dropped and he runs his fingers through his unruly dark hair and pushes his glasses back up on the bridge of his nose.

"Are you aware that ninety-five percent of all recordings sell less than ten-thousand copies? Are you aware that selling ten-thousand copies of a classical record puts you on the best-sellers list? You are on the top-five percentile amongst musicians!"

I remind him that twenty-eight thousand is small beans in pop and rock numbers.

"You must be making a handsome profit from your publishing company. Who tracks your publishing?"

"I think our lawyer signed us up with ASCAP and our record company tracks something too, I think . . ." I mumble because I've never understood publishing. "I've never gotten a penny."

"Then there's something very wrong with your approach," he points out, still exasperated. "I'll teach you this stuff if you think it's going to help you, but I think your problem has to do with self-confidence. Don't you realize how great you're doing?"

Where does self-confidence come from? Are you born with it?

I T'S so weird to have complete strangers know my name; it makes me feel at a complete disadvantage.

"Excuse me, Miss Lindeen?"

"Yes." I smile, wondering where I might know this person, feeling alarmed about the state of my memory; have we met? I can't very well say, "Like, do I know you?"

Sometimes I whisper to Co, "Do we know them? From where?" My eyes have looked at so many faces, my mouth has spoken to so many strangers, and my memory fails to store any short-term data (pot).

We now hang out in our hotel room until minutes before showtime. We breeze in, perform, and promptly return to our room, where we watch movies on HBO while hoping we don't burst from the erotic content. Our performance time is starting to interrupt a fine meal or a good movie.

Some guys fantasize about our life on the road; they picture us lazily lounging about motel rooms in slips and slinky underwear, having wild girl-love orgies. This is not happening. Our only alone time is in the bathroom with others waiting to get in. Sometimes one of us shrieks, "I'm so horny!" But that's about it.

O NE morning at home, I decide to take a yoga class in my neighborhood because I've heard that it's A Good Thing to Do.

My body is very flexible from all the torture it endured in gymnastics, and yoga sounds like a logical outlet for my predisposition. Taking a hit of pot in my apartment, I breeze out the door and up the block to the little storefront that has been en-couraging me to Try Yoga Today!

"Welcome!" says a shiny-faced woman who seems to be glowing, but maybe it's the pot. She guides me and six other women and one man through a series of moves that require balance and poise. Never go to a yoga class stoned; I feel like I'm having a heart attack.

At the end she has us lie on our mats and whispers in sooth-ing tones to relax every joint in our bodies. Enya is melodically chanting through a cassette deck, and I drift off to sleep, wak-ing when everyone else is sitting on their mats with their hands in prayer.

"Namaste," the jolly instructor says to me, bowing her head while I scramble to a seated position.

"Whatever," I say, crinkling my nose, mimicking her bow.

She explodes in the laughter of the superiorly enlightened and I feel like an ass.

M Y illustrious career has been on a downslide for a while. If I'm so unhappy, why am I doing it? I know it's frus-trating to listen to me blather on. But I hate giving up. This is my kooky dream: If I become a famous singer, all of my prob-lems will be solved. All creative types have highs and lows, brights and darks, times of popularity and times of obscurity. We have no control over that. One bad record shouldn't spoil my whole career.

But there's more going on. I no longer know why I'm react-ing when I muster the energy to protest our current state of af-fairs. More often than not, I shut down and fall mute. I'm often overwhelmed with a grief that goes much deeper than missing a boyfriend. I am underwhelmed by our career trajec-tory. If we were traveling by air, first class, staying in hotels with star ratings that had lobbies, elevators, and room serv-ice—would I be happy? Probably not. Rooms of our own and a soundman/driver/equipment tech would relieve some of the pressure. If our record was selling, if we had a nationally recognized manager and booking agent with clout and connections, if we were signed—*then* would I be happy? It might help, but probably not.

This might be some sort of deferred mourning over having MS, over my parents' divorce, over ten years of running, figuratively and literally. All the things that happened in my early adulthood, all the things I've been so deft at sweeping under the rug or drinking away—abortion, promiscuity, all the times I've failed to speak up for myself out of fear of rejection or abandonment, all the power I've handed to others on a platter—it's all catching up with me. I'm legally blind in my left eye, and now it's like all the darkness I've managed to stuff all these years is seeping through the cracks, oozing out of my pores. All the ugliness refuses to stay inside, my demeanor's wearing thin. I'm a fucking basket case and I can't keep the lid on.

I always thought a life devoid of normalcy and stability was preferable to being average, a rube, a lamb following the flock. But. Maybe "normal" and "healthy" are two different things. I don't want my grip on reality to loosen any further. I don't want to be more isolated than I already am. I don't think I want the people of the night to be my only community. I want to try to be healthier and I don't know where to start.

IN the van, not only do I write long laborious letters to Paul, I dabble in the higher arts of poetry and philosophy:

J. CREW HAIKU

J. Crew couple walks on the beach
looks like she's having a
relaxed fit

✢

"SOMEONE wants me to write something for a book written by musicians," Paul complains one evening at home while we eat dinner.

People are always asking him to do things other than write terrific songs.

"I'll do it," I offer.

Paul gives me a name and phone number and I ask the editor if I could please submit something. He says fine, but he'll need it in a couple of days. I return to my apartment and set up my Brother typewriter and begin to type:

The Many Faces of Zuzu's Petals, or Sybil Does Dallas

Road stories, yawn, everybody has them. Traveling musicians try to one-up their peers with tales of arrests, breakdowns (vehicular and nervous), stolen gear, practical jokes, sexual exploits, scummy promoters, abuse (substance and equipment), illegal trysts, and blown-up sound systems. Gender-specific experiences, snore, we've got thousands. Yes, our cycles synch up. Yes, we've been patronized and discriminated against. And yes, we initially received a curious amount of attention by virtue of our voluptuous birth rite. It's not as if our naturally still-perky breasts have been menacing the coveted pages of *Rolling Stone* or anything. To hell with road stories and gender, they leave me catatonic with boredom.

To me the real meat lies in the drama of self-preservation while being subjected to less-than-ideal conditions (straddling no-budget touring while wallowing in indie rock hell, for example). Your quality of life hinges on the cleanliness of public restrooms. You are in the real external world, cold and harsh, without a safety net or a calling card. You struggle with the elements daily. Be it severe thunderstorm, blizzard, hurricane, earthquake, or tornado, your livelihood depends on your ability to get to the next gig. The van becomes a person with a name, and you coo and cajole its dysfunctional innards, gently caressing the dashboard and cheering it on. You are at your van's mercy, and like most things born in 1979 (like the Knack), it needs a lot of love.

You see, smell, hear, feel, and unfortunately taste Detroit, Des Moines, Albany, and Tampa. Their inhabitants wear their towns on their faces, hands, but mostly in their eyes. Meanwhile you are performing every night, giving away pieces of your soul for next to nothing, and you are vulnerable. You are not immune to the sixteen-year-old pregnant waitress with the kind, tired eyes, nor to the down-and-out alcoholic slumped over the bar as you breeze in for sound check. You are a soldier at an imaginary war created in your mind; you conquer one city, only to find yourself hobbling and defeated from the next. It's boot camp, baby, and no amount of daydreaming about the officer's club can filter out the ugliness.

Numbing yourself with vices and denial generally results in lost years, problems at home, and psychiatric problems you cannot afford to remedy. Zuzu's Petals has learned to cope thanks to the development of nice healthy multiple personality disorders. Some personae are useful in day-to-day survival, some are amusing, some save our career, and some get us into a lot of trouble. As with all multiple personality disorders, we have no control over who is going to emerge, no clue as to the when, how, and why of these mysterious women.

The hard-boiled wisecrackin' good-time girl is the one who got us into this mess to begin with. She was our dominant personality during the early years. She's bawdy, a hair dumb, and in touch with her masculine side. She's been known to slap a random ass and mutter, "Give Mama some sugar." She bellied up to the bar and stumbled onto the stage. She'll talk to anyone especially if they're buying. She strikes ballads from our set list in favor of New York Dolls covers and wears cutoff shorts, ancient rock T-shirts, and cowboy boots. She has a filthy mind, a

guttural mouth, orders bacon for breakfast, and loves Aerosmith. She's a Marlboro-smokin' gum cracker and we don't see
too much of her anymore. I miss her spirit, though not her
hangovers. She lives on in our sarcastic sneers, raspy voices, and
low, hardy chuckles.

I get up and walk around my apartment for a minute, stopping at the picture window to watch the snow drop onto the
lake in fat glops. I am so lucky. Glancing at the clock, I'm surprised that two hours have passed. I go back to the typewriter
and review what I've written. The "good-time girl" that I so affectionately refer to is dead. Gone. I used to be her.

I return to the typewriter and chronicle our various person-
alities: the phony, the snot, the crab, the unapproachable, PMS-
addled skag, the midwestern hick, the "I feel alive!" idiot, the
health nut, Tallulah Bankhead, and the lady. An entire day has
passed, and I've spent it happily, feeling more affection for
Zuzu's Petals than I have in ages.

But I gotta go now, it's a snowy late-December morning in
Minnesota and there are soaps-on-ropes to be purchased and
eggnogs to be sipped. On days like this there are no showbiz
tramps haunting me, I'm just relishing the pure delight of being
home.

I MAIL off my essay and the editor enthusiastically approves it.
I haven't had so much fun creating in years.

I N the Minneapolis *Star Tribune* for the Best of '94 rundown,
Jim M. proclaims that *The Music of Your Life* by Zuzu's
Petals is one of the year's best local releases. In *Melody
Maker*'s list of all things grunge, entitled "Grunge A–Z,"
Zuzu's Petals are given the letter Z. I thought we were out of

favor in England because we weren't a proper grunge band. I
don't get it.

A T a show in Fargo, North Dakota, a college student sum-
mons me to the lip of the stage and asks, "Is Paul here?"
    No, he's not here, he's never here, you jerk. I don't say this, I
only think it.
    I turn my back on the throng of students gathered in front of
the stage and whisper our long-standing joke into Co's ear: "I
hate the kids."
    I have officially reached the state of "job insensitivity." I've
been working at an unrewarding job long enough to not care
anymore. It doesn't occur to me that I'm the one responsible
for making it rewarding.

I N Chicago I look on as an A&R person from a major label
offers our opening band a recording contract. This has been
happening a lot; we're the headliner that all the labels have
passed on and I'm convinced there's some backstabbing background chatter within the industry that is *untrue* being spread
about us. While we're onstage, an audience member hollers at
me, "The Hi-Lo Diner!" This has also happened to me in
Boston. I have become better known for my role at my day job.

W E'RE driving somewhere and Dylan's "Like a Rolling
Stone" is on the radio and we're tuned in to the song
with weary all-knowingness. The part where he says, "When
you got nothin', you've got nothing to lose . . ." it's dead quiet in
the van. My face is drenched in my own tears and I dare not look
around to see if anyone else feels like I do right now. The answer
to Bob's question "oh how does it feel" is that it feels like shit,
and definitely unlike any Rolling Stone I've ever watched.

M Y great-uncle Harrison died suddenly of an aneurism when I was in third grade. Having grown up without a father, Uncle Harrison was my mom's father figure. My family drove from our new home in Madison to Peoria for the funeral. My mom had just buried her own mother, my other Gogi, less than a year before; she died of breast cancer in her early fifties. At the age of twenty-eight, my mom was a mother of three, living in a new larger city where she knew no one, and suddenly an orphan, but fortunately my Gogi made sure that her daughters were financially secure. Regardless, it's safe to say my mom was stretched thin.

"When you're weary, feeling small . . ." Art Garfunkel whispered through the radio while we drove in silence in the rain to Uncle Harrison's funeral. By the time "Bridge Over Troubled Water" had concluded, my mother had dissolved. She never quite fully rematerialized.

I N St. Louis I call Paul on a Saturday night to check in. "Bob's dead," he says quietly, his voice cracking. The founding member of the Replacements was discovered dead in his apartment of an apparent drug overdose. That's too dangerous. And really sad.

Bob Stinson used to practice in another boxcar farther down the tracks from Sven's with his band at the time, Castles of Depression. Bob, like Sven, looked right at home passing around the Wild Irish Rose bottle with the hoboes. I never talked much to Bob; he kind of scared me and seemed too far gone with his ragged flannel shirts, difficult-to-understand stutter, and chronic state of drunkenness. Bob, however, took a keen interest in Zuzu's Petals, and more specifically in my lack of guitar finesse, trying to encourage me to play through a different amp that would better match my style of play. I went so far as to purchase the amp he recommended, only to find it too confusing, and reselling it. After Zuzu's Petals signed with Twintone, we'd see Bob regularly stumble into the office with a pissed-off scowl, demanding his share of money from the early Replacements records, making a scene, inevitably being gently sent on his way. That's how we treat our heroes.

One afternoon while I waited in the Twintone office for a phone interview, Bob tromped in, noticed me, and said, "I like your record."

"Thanks," I replied, meaning it.

"Who played the guitar?" he wondered.

"I did," I answered, because I did, every note.

"How about that one solo?" he challenged.

I knew what solo he was referring to, the solo that Paul rewrote for "Cinderella's Daydream." "I played it," I said defensively.

Bob rubbed one index finger over the other in a "shame on you" gesture and walked out. He could recognize Paul's touch anywhere.

I NEED a home, a family, and a community; I don't see how to make that happen from the road. I'm not willing to admit that we do need another guitar player to take the pressure off me, as I'm more of a singer than a guitarist. It's true when Co says that I'm not interested in the songs that my bandmates are writing; I want them to accept me as the primary songwriter. And I hate how much hatred there is among us, how each of us has someone on the outside whispering in our ears about how underappreciated we are by our bandmates. I especially hate what's happened between Co and me; our friendship is more like a bad marriage piled to the ceiling with bad feelings. I don't want to lose my friend.

When three little boys play together, if there is a conflict over the rules of the game, they argue about it, enjoy the dispute, and keep playing. When three little girls play together and there is a conflict, one girl is left out, and she will grab her toys and go home. Like Phyll. Like Vicki. Like me. End of game.

Like George Bailey, I really do have a wonderful life but I have no problem-solving/people skills at the moment. Unlike F. Scott Fitzgerald, I do believe there are second and even third acts in American life as long as you don't kill yourself drinking. If this band thing isn't working, I'll just do something else. I don't know if the urge to rock and write songs ever goes away, but I do know that it needs to change shape. No problem. I'm sure I can come up with a new impossible dream, I always do. I mean, look at my life right now. It's the ultimate musical; leading man and understudy fall in love . . .

I've been "taking a trip" for years now and it's failing to re-capture the magic it held for my family. For the Lindeens, tak-ing a trip was where we felt safest and most comfortable together, but the unresolved problems at home never went away by constantly running away. Every time we returned home, the sad marriage and bad memories were still there. In my convoluted way of thinking, I equated "taking a trip" with being a happy, contented adult. But every time I come home the unpaid bills, unsatisfying job, and unfulfilled dreams are still there. It turns out the things that made me happy as a child—reading and riding my bike—just might be the keys to my happy adulthood. My parents did the best they could, half of all marriages end in divorce, and most American kids have experienced the dissolution and reconfiguration of their fami-lies. My parents did a lot of good things like valuing education and manners and friendship, and making us feel at home in the world. Neither of them ever stayed stuck in their own lives. The largest problem I seem to be having is trusting in the process that gets you to commit to making a family. It begins with home and whatever that's going to mean to me. And it can't mean anything to me if I keep avoiding it.

❧

ON our last drive home from Wisconsin on 94 West after our last out-of-town gig, Co and I say nothing as we pass the burned-out patch where there was once birch and pine trees, the remains from the forest fire we once had the courage and stupidity to drive through.

IT'S June 1995 and Paul and I are on Martha's Vineyard with my entire family for my sister Hillary's wedding. Hillary, the youngest sister, the beauty under the radar, is marrying an upwardly mobile preppie with a kind face.

I'm excited to be sharing the island with Paul. He seems pleased enough with his surroundings, but he's clearly not grasping my pathological enchantment with this parcel of land.

The Harborview Hotel overlooks Edgartown Harbor, and the crowd gathered for Hillary's wedding must walk across the street and out to the beach where an old white lighthouse stands. The last time I visited this lighthouse I was drunk after happy hour at the Colonial Inn and off walking by myself when a fat gray rat scrambled toward me. I swiftly turned on my heels and headed back toward civilization. Even Martha's Vineyard is not immune to rats. Remembering this, I begin to weep.

My heels sink into the sand and I scowl when the hired photographer discloses to me that she "loves my 'look.'" Paul grasps my hand and I'm crying before we even get to the lighthouse. It probably looks like I'm crying because I'm happy that my baby sister is getting married, or bitter because I'm the oldest daughter and still an unwed old maid. The reason for my tears is pettier; I'm pissed off because I am the only member of my family to have actually lived and worked on Martha's Vineyard. I consider it My Place, not hers. She's robbed me of my perfect wedding spot should I ever wed. I guess that's payback for being "the meanest babysitter in the world." I guess that's Hillary's right to be married in the place where my family was at its happiest. And I'm crying because I remembered the rat, and that makes me think about the band I dismantled four months before.

When my parents walk Hillary down the aisle, they do it as two adults who have moved on with their lives, who will forever be bound by the four children, now all adults, that they brought into the world. And it's time for me to move on, too.

Epilogue

P AUL and I are married. We became parents to an amazing son in 1998.

Coleen is a happily married yoga instructor.

Linda is a kick-ass drummer residing in New York. She still runs into some of the characters in this book while on the road.

Acknowledgments

I'D like to thank my tireless, kind agent Jeff Kleinman for his help and friendship, for constantly correcting the passive voice, and always getting back to me in a timely manner (it's true, he's one of the Good Guys). Thanks to the Faulkner Society's Words & Music literary conference for hooking me up with lifelong friends. Thank you to my insanely amazing (and handsome) editor Peter Borland who believed in and brilliantly guided the manuscript, and to Judith Curr, Gary Urda, Kathleen Schmidt, and Sarah Wright at Atria. Thanks to Nick Simonds, Peter's assistant, for all of his help and encouragement with the specifics. Thank you to Carly Sommerstein for awe-inspiring copy editing. Thanks to Graybill & English literary agency (especially Ellen Pepus) and Folio Literary Management. Thanks to Lauren Marino and Mary Ann Naples for reading, encouragement, and guidance. Yo thanks to Mark Rotella who's always there when I have a question or need a pep talk or red pencil.

This book would've never come to fruition without the years spent within the University of Minnesota's MFA program (don't fear the MFA if you're already a writer); special thanks to Patricia Hampl, Madelon Sprengnether, and Julie Panebianco for thoughtful reading and drawing out, and to Gretchen Scherer, Jill Christman, and Kathleen Glasgow for helping me hide my techno-handicap and letting me rest in their office. Thanks to all of the early, supportive, helpful readers Kate Hopper, Terri Sutton, and inspiring, talented MFA literary nonfiction students during my extended stay. (How often do nonfiction specialists get thanks and praise? Not often enough, my fellow asses of the literary world!) To Ashley Holman and Dawn Anderson for loving, attentive child care while I was in school. To the families and staff at Morningside nursery school, Carondolet Catholic school, and in the 'hood for community, support, friendship, meals, and play dates. Thanks to Ronna's Tuesday morning yoga group for all of the overflowing wisdom, strength, and generosity. Thank you to my friends, especially Abbie Kane and Melanie Miller who always encouraged (hey ladies!) and my suburban posse, and neighbors for years of interest and support—I'm so dang lucky. Thanks Peep for all that I have (mostly) and to all you other fuckers who rock.